COLLINS REAL-WORLD TECHNOLOGY

Series editors: Colin Chapman and Mike Finney

ELECTRONIC
PRODUCTS
DESIGN • SYSTEMS • CONTROL

Barry Payne

Senior Lecturer in Design & Technology,
University of Brighton

David Rampley

Head of Design & Technology,
Heathfield Community College, E. Sussex

Collins Educational

An imprint of HarperCollinsPublishers

Contents

5 · Amplification

6 · Timers and timing

7 · Decisions, counting and memory

8 · Output Devices

The Collins Real-World Technology *series is approved by the Technology Enhancement Programme.*

Full details of the TEP can be obtained from:
TEP 5 Old Mitre Court, London EC4A 1YY
Tel: 0171 583 0900, Fax: 0171 583 0909

MIDLAND EXAMINING GROUP

The Collins Real-World Technology series is approved by the Midland Examining Group to support the teaching of their GCSE Design and Technology syllabuses.

MIDLAND EXAMINING GROUP
SYNDICATE BUILDINGS
1 Hills Road, Cambridge CB1 2EU
Tel: 01223 553311
Fax: 01223 460278

The Authors

Barry Payne has considerable experience in Design & Technology education as a teacher, adviser, consultant and lecturer. He was previously Chief Examiner for Lincolnshire's CDT: Technology (MEG), he is now a member of the EdExcel development group for A-level Design & Technology. **David Rampley** has taught Design & Technology, and Electronics at GCSE and A level for 17 years.

1·Designing electronic products

HISTORICAL BACKGROUND

The technology that is today at the heart of many electronic products has been developing rapidly since the invention of the transistor in 1948. The transistor replaced the thermionic valve (Figure 1.1) for nearly all applications because it was much smaller and needed much less power.

In the 1960s the quest to make circuits smaller and smaller was made possible by the advent of the integrated circuit (IC). ICs increasingly allowed engineers the opportunity to pack more components into very compact products.

Fig. 1.1 *The thermionic valve, invented in 1904*

Fig. 1.2 *A transistor*

Fig. 1.3 *An integrated circuit*

The technological advances we enjoy today have developed from a variety of situations: the will to fund ambitious research projects in order to make advances in warfare technology during the 'Cold War' the race to put a human on the moon; and the commercial gains to be made in selling new consumer goods.

The results of such technology allow designers today great freedom in the way that they style and package electronic products (Figure 1.4). Compare the size, appearance and cost of products available today with those available ten or twenty years ago .

Valve wireless

Mobile phone

Transistor radio

Portable 'discman'

Fig. 1.4 *Developments in electronic products*

ADVANCES IN ELECTRONIC PRODUCTS

The timeline in Figure 1.5 shows some of the advances in the development of electronic products from 1904 to the present.

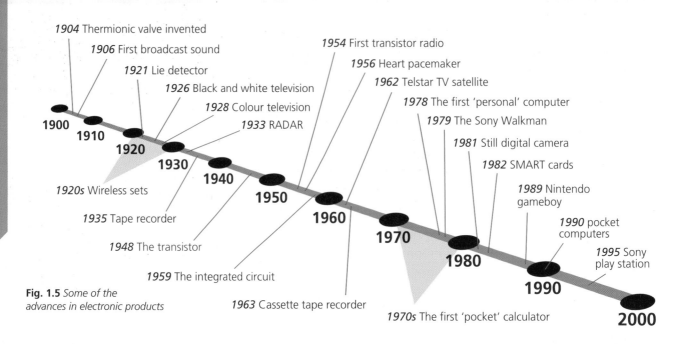

1904 Thermionic valve invented

1906 First broadcast sound

1921 Lie detector

1926 Black and white television

1928 Colour television

1933 RADAR

1954 First transistor radio

1956 Heart pacemaker

1962 Telstar TV satellite

1978 The first 'personal' computer

1979 The Sony Walkman

1981 Still digital camera

1982 SMART cards

1989 Nintendo gameboy

1990 pocket computers

1995 Sony play station

1900 1910 1920 1930 1940 1950 1960 1970 1980 1990 2000

1920s Wireless sets

1935 Tape recorder

1948 The transistor

1959 The integrated circuit

1963 Cassette tape recorder

1970s The first 'pocket' calculator

Fig. 1.5 *Some of the advances in electronic products*

DEFINING A NEED

In order to make certain that a product will be a commercial success manufacturers must first decide what product needs to be designed. One difficulty faced by designers of electronic products is that the most adventurous designs rely on foreseeing what consumers will want to use in the future.

Market pull

Many electronic products are improved versions of existing products. Improvements may be as a result of better technology, critical evaluation by the designers, or the result of careful market research. Some examples of improved products which are a result of what is known as 'market pull' or 'demand pull' are lighter headsets for personal stereos, smaller mobile phones and VCRs that make timed recordings easier (Figure 1.6).

Technology push

The other extreme to market pull is a factor known as 'technology push'. This term is used when products have been developed for which, initially, there is a very small perceived need. Such products use the latest technology and are very expensive. They do not have the advantage of being made in large quantities and are frequently bought by a small minority of specialist users. Products that have started in this way include the personal computer which had a very limited initial consumer demand (Figure 1.7). High technology products that begin life in this way are often the result of 'radical design' (adventurous design leaps). This is the opposite of 'incremental design' (designing in small manageable steps) that characterises 'market pull' influenced products.

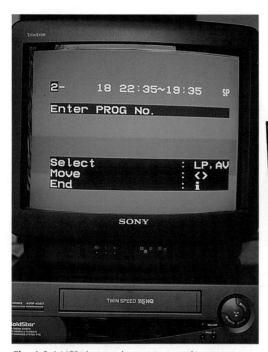

Fig. 1.6 *A VCR that can be programmed on-screen – designed to ease the problem of timed recordings*

Fig. 1.7 *The Sinclair Spectrum – an early home computer*

PROBLEM ANALYSIS AND 'TOP DOWN' DESIGN

When tackling complicated design tasks it is necessary to consider the factors that will influence a product's design. Once these have been considered it is then possible to formulate a product design specification (PDS). This sort of approach to designing is sometimes called 'top down design'. There are some factors that are common to many design areas:

- **Environment**. Will the product be subject to extremes of temperature, humidity?
- **Weight**. Will the product need to be portable?
- **Size**. Does the product, for example, have to fit into a pocket?

- **Power requirements**. How long will the product need to be switched on? Will battery operation be necessary?
- **Interface**. Will the design need to link to other electronic or mechanical units?
- **Ergonomics**. Who will have to use the unit, how long will they use it for, and under what conditions?
- **Performance**. Are there upper and lower performance limits?
- **Conformity to relevant standards or legislation**. What safety parameters will need to be observed? A commercial design will need to conform to EMC rules (these govern the electro-magnetic interference that may interfere with other nearby electronic equipment).

Fig. 1.8 *Some operating environments*

SYSTEM DESIGN

The choice of components available to a designer of electronic products is becoming increasingly large. Any method, therefore, of reducing the number of components that need to be used is a definite bonus. The method used by designers is to use building blocks of units known variously as sub-systems, modules or system elements. Individual sub-systems can consist of one component or many hundreds. For instance, the parts of a home audio system can be readily identified as separate elements packaged individually. However, in most applications the sub-systems are not so neatly divided.

Fig. 1.9 *An audio 'system'*

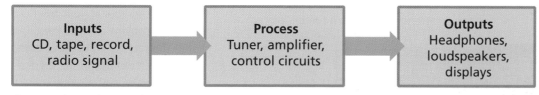

Inputs CD, tape, record, radio signal	→	Process Tuner, amplifier, control circuits	→	Outputs Headphones, loudspeakers, displays

Fig. 1.10 *Diagram for an audio 'system'*

Electronics as part of a solution

Electronics is often a key part of an overall system that uses a range of systems. For example, industrial robots need electro-mechanical devices that incorporate pneumatic or hydraulic systems. These offer immediate linear (straight line) motion that is more difficult to achieve using electric motors. Electronics enables computer-based systems to be used that offer programmable routines to control the robot's movement. These routines can either be programmed using a processor or the robot maybe 'taught' by having its effector (hand or tool) guided manually by a technician.

User interface

Electronic circuits are usually unseen but they still need to be packaged and presented in a way that allows them to be protected and used effectively. The design appearance and ease of use are of utmost importance in presenting a well designed solution.

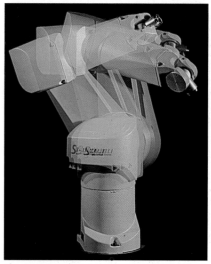

Fig. 1.11 *An electro-mechanical robot*

PROJECT MANAGEMENT

In commercial terms the time spent designing a product and developing a prototype must be very carefully planned. Design teams will often be working on several projects at the same time and it is important that each team member is able to contribute at the appropriate and most effective time. The project manager has to co-ordinate all aspects of the work from research through to costing and sourcing components.

Starting points for design

The way that different companies manage the development of a new product varies greatly. However, most will follow a similar pattern starting with an initiative that might start from a client, the design team, the marketing department, or as the result of some technical break through. A project proposal will usually have to be approved before designing can start.

The initial design phase will seek to clarify what is needed and define a list of design criteria by which the designs will be judged.

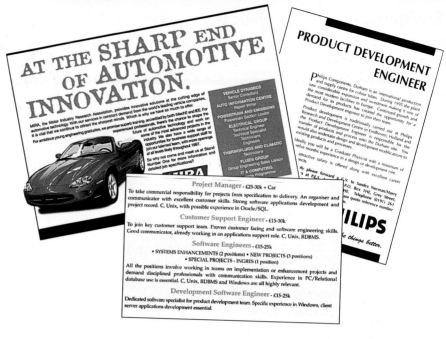

Fig. 1.12 *Product designers work as part of a team*

Technical research

In addition to appropriate market research, design teams must familiarise themselves with the latest technology. They will need to be aware of any patents that may cover similar products. It is quite common for small specialist companies to contribute to large projects managed by one design team. Contact may have to be made with component manufacturers to arrange for custom made devices.

School-based technical research

Your work will often consist of a period of technical research. Some appropriate sources might be magazines, text books, data sheets and manufacturers' component suppliers' catalogues (Fig. 1.13).

- **Magazines** – use libraries. Search the index issues first. Beware of attempting projects that you don't fully understand. Model the circuits first and adapt as necessary to suit your own design problem. Always check that the final design is your own, not that in the magazine, and acknowledge any designs you have used in the process that are not your own.
- **Textbooks** – again, model a circuit first if it looks promising. Check for availability of all components — don't settle for the first one with an appropriate title!
- **Datasheets** – these describe, often in much more detail than you need, how a device works. The most useful information is often in the form of examples of the device being used for typical applications.
- **Suppliers' catalogues** – these give brief technical descriptions of components, circuit modules and kits as well as prices.

CD-Roms

Catalogues

Textbooks

Fig. 1.13 *Research sources*

Budgeting

In commercial ventures it is very important to stay within a fixed budget, and it is important to take into account that the raw materials are only one aspect of the cost of the finished product. The time taken to develop prototypes, the production of tooling (for processes such as injection moulding), for example, all need to be costed. Budgets are divided into fixed and variable costs. Fixed costs are those that stay the same no matter how many products are produced (e.g. rent and leasing of machines). Variable costs are those that increase with the number of products produced (e.g. raw materials and labour).

It is equally as important for you to predict and model potential costs and to accurately cost a final solution for your electronic product. (Mass-produced goods have the advantage of lower unit costs due to bulk buying of components and the use of automated assembly techniques.)

An extremely useful computer modelling tool for costing a project is the spreadsheet, which allows you to easily calculate and revise costings.

Surface Mount Test Clips

| S.S.M. = 1 | | price each | | |
type	stock no.	1-4	5-9	10+
5764	400-078	£270·00	£210·00	£189·00
5765	400-084	£345·00	£265·00	£240·00
5829	400-090	£452·00	£350·00	£315·00
5751	400-107	£166·00	£129·00	£106·00
5643	400-113	£206·00	£160·00	£144·00
5769	400-129	£206·00	£160·00	£144·00
5644	400-135	£243·00	£188·00	£170·00
5772	400-141	£260·00	£202·00	£182·00
5773	400-157	£480·00	£375·00	£335·00
5645	400-163	£480·00	£375·00	£335·00
5774	400-179	£347·00	£270·00	£242·00
5771	400-185	£403·00	£313·00	£281·00
5770	400-191	£540·00	£420·00	£377·00
5746	400-214	£11·80	£9·20	£8·30
5413	400-236	£10·50	£8·20	£7·40
5515A	400-208	£255·00	£198·00	£179·00
5514	400-220	£72·00	£57·00	£51·00

Fig. 1.14 *Buying in bulk can save money - examples of suppliers' quantity discounts*

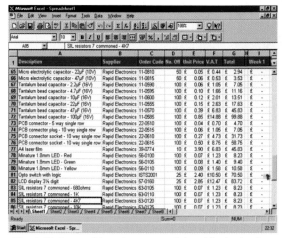

Fig. 1.15 *A spreadsheet is a very useful tool for budgeting*

Gant charts

Planning charts known as Gant charts are widely used in industry to allot time to different stages of a project. This enables multi-disciplinary teams to co-ordinate their efforts to produce a solution on time and within budget.

The charts have time on one axis and a list of design/production stages on the other. Blocks of time are then allocated graphically to each task. As time progresses the chart can be updated and resources allocated to take account of unexpected delays or early finishes.

Aerotech are a company that design and manufacture wind tunnel balance and instrumentation (Figure 1.16). Successful project management is an important factor in their success. An example of one of their Gant charts can be seen in Figure 1.17.

Fig. 1.16 *A wind tunnel*

Fig. 1.17 *An Aerotech Gant chart*

COMMUNICATING IDEAS

When exploring different design ideas it is important to be able to use a quick but informative method to communicate them clearly and quickly to others. Quick design sketches and calculations are all valuable in setting out all your ideas before you forget them (even ideas that you scrap later). Keep all your rough work to show how your ideas develop — this is important when presenting your work for assessment.

The illustrations on this page show various methods and stages of communicating your design ideas.

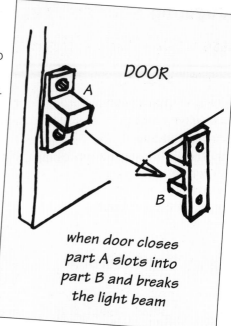

Fig. **1.18** Use quick sketches to help you record existing devices or systems

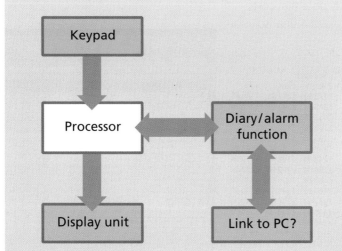

Fig. **1.19** Use block diagrams to record possible systems

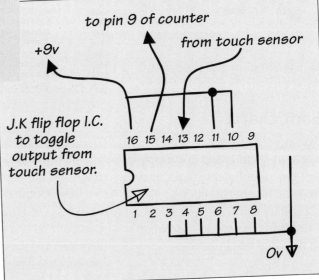

Fig. **1.20** Use quick sketches for circuit ideas

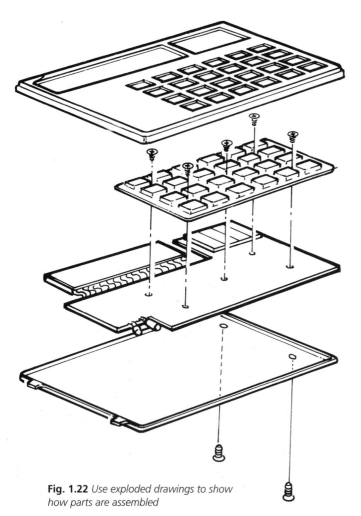

Fig. **1.22** Use exploded drawings to show how parts are assembled

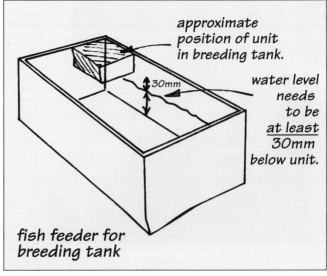

Fig. **1.21** Use pictorial sketches to show general arrangements

DEVELOPING AN ELECTRONIC PRODUCT

Case study – the design process of the Thermapen

Identifying an opportunity

The Worthing company ETI (Electronic Temperature Instuments) specialise in the design and manufacture of temperature instruments. The company anticipated a demand for a new product after concern about food safety resulted in new regulations. The concern centred around the temperature at which food was stored whilst being processed, distributed, cooked and displayed. Bacteria can multiply very quickly if food is stored at too high a temperature, or if it is cooked for insufficient time. ETI, therefore, recognised a need for a robust easy-to-use instrument that would meet the monitoring demands of the new food handling regulations.

The Thermapen design brief

ETI conceived the idea of the 'Thermapen' in reaction to the design brief which evolved from their market research. You can see the design brief in Figure 1.23.

Specification

In order to proceed from the brief, ETI needed to agree on a specification so that the different members of the design team could work towards the same objectives (Figure 1.24).

Timetable

Once the specification had been agreed the next step was to agree a timetable to keep a check on the progress of the project. This is shown in Figure 1.25. You will see that the work has been divided into 'mechanical' and 'electronic', with a dashed line showing the work that is carried out by other companies.

It is not unusual to use other companies to help initiate work such as this. They will very often include component suppliers, tool makers, injection moulders, specialist PCB manufacturers and model makers.

Thermapen design brief

To design and manufacture an easy-to-use pocket size device that can be used by anyone concerned about the safe handling of food.

Fig. 1.23

Thermapen product design specification

1. The unit must be easy to use and truly 'pocketable'.
2. It must have an accuracy of +/- 0.3° C.
3. The LCD display should have '3 1/2' digits.
4. The display should have a range of -30 to +80 °C.
5. The probe should be 100 to 150 mm long and be made of stainless steel (to allow for thorough cleansing).
6. The probe should either retract or fold alongside the case.
7. The device should turn itself on when the probe is brought into use.
8. The unit should turn itself off if left unused.
9. The unit needs to be powered by an MN21 12v alkaline battery (lighter size).
10. The unit needs to be easily manufactured despite its small size (easy to assemble and access to PCB etc.).
11. The device must give a 'low battery' warning on the display.
12. The 'Thermapen' must sell for around £30.

Fig. 1.24

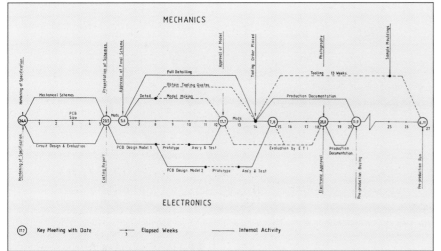

Fig. 1.25 *Project time plan for the Thermapen*

Evaluation of existing products

The design of electronic products like the 'Thermapen' seldom happens from scratch. Often, as in the case of ETI, the company concerned will have developed an in-depth understanding of the technology involved and may already be producing similar devices. As the available technology improves so a product can, be developed further. Features that were previously too expensive, too large or difficult to manufacture can be incorporated into the product.

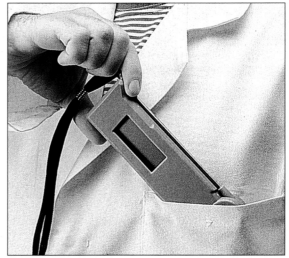

Fig. 1.26 *One of the specifications that the 'Thermapen' had to meet was that it should be truly 'pocketable'*

DEVELOPING THE THERMAPEN

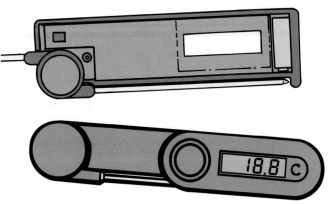
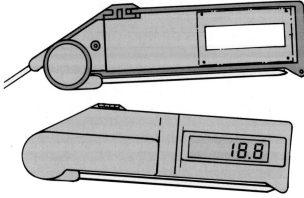

Fig. 1.27 *Some of the early designs for the 'Thermapen'*

Researching the technical specification

The design of the casing for any electronic product has to take account of the internal components as well as the way in which the product is going to be used. A useful first step is to measure all the items that need to be contained within the casing. The 'Thermapen', for instance, requires a battery of a specified size (see specification on page 11). The circuit board size could be varied but needs to be decided on quite early (see the time plan in Figure 1.25).

The data that the designers collected at this stage was very important to the final design of the 'Thermapen'. The PCB could not be much less than 35mm wide without causing problems with the width of the copper tracks. The display took up a large area as did the main integrated circuit (IC). Therefore, to reduce the product's size it was decided to mount the display over the top of the IC, like a bridge (Fig. 1.33).

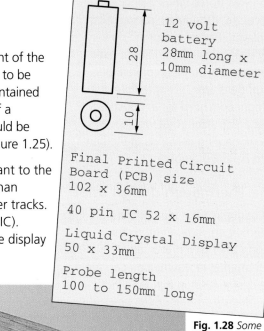

Battery size

12 volt battery
28mm long x
10mm diameter

28

10

Final Printed Circuit Board (PCB) size
102 x 36mm

40 pin IC 52 x 16mm

Liquid Crystal Display
50 x 33mm

Probe length
100 to 150mm long

Fig. 1.28 *Some critical sizes*

Modelling ideas

Once some promising design ideas had been developed detailed drawings and models could be made. Wood was used for modelling the 'Thermapen', but other materials can be used such as Styrofoam or modelling clay (Fig. 1.29). This stage of the design process is very important as it communicates elements that are otherwise difficult to evaluate, such as comfort and ease of use.

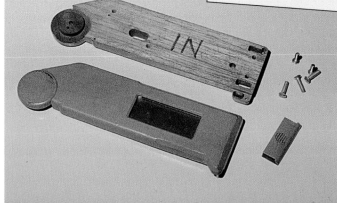

Fig. 1.29 *An early model of the 'Thermapen' case*

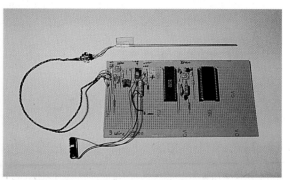

Fig. 1.30 *A stripboard model for the 'Thermapen' circuit*

Bench-top prototype

At this stage the electronics needed to be modelled too. In the case of the 'Thermapen' stripboard was used to quickly assemble a circuit to evaluate the electronics (Fig. 1.30). Other methods can be used (see Chapter 2).

Design tip

When considering the physical sizes of components draw each one out on a separate piece of card and arrange them on a flat surface, or use a computer drawing package to draw each one and rearrange them.

Working drawings

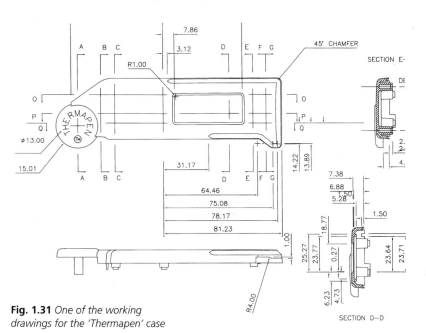

Fig. 1.31 *One of the working drawings for the 'Thermapen' case*

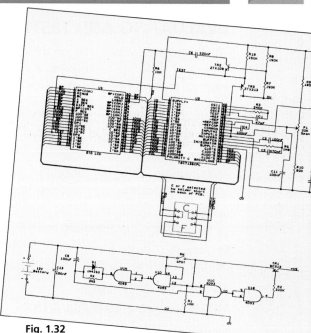

Fig. 1.32
Part of the final circuit diagram

To avoid costly mistakes great care needs to be taken when producing the working drawings of a final design (Fig. 1.31). It is from these drawings that the people making the product will get their information. For instance, toolmakers made the die for the injection moulded case for the 'Thermapen' from the working drawings the designers produced. ABS (Acrylonitrile Butadiene Styrene – a thermoplastic) was chosen as the material for making the case because of its high-impact strength and ability to give a good surface finish.

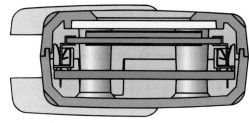

Fig. 1.33 *This sectional view of the assembled unit shows how important it was to use every bit of space. The display is shown in red and the circuit board in green*

The working drawings for the 'Thermapen' case were produced using CAD (Computer Aided Design) software. Similarly, CAD was used to produce most of the circuit drawings (Figure 1.32). This meant that the drawings could be readily updated.

Parts list

Each new product that is produced needs to have an accurate component list to ensure that the new production line can be supplied and the product accurately costed. ETI ensure that supplies are never interrupted by using at least two suppliers for each critical part.

Description	Qty	Cost
Custom made LCD	1	1.40
Thermapen PCB	1	1.02
ZTX 109 (NPN)	1	0.09
20 pin SIL socket	2	0.12
Probe	1	2.58
Screw No. $4x\frac{1}{2}$ (countersunk Pozi)	5	0.02

Fig. 1.34 *Part of the 'Thermapen' parts list*

Pre-production prototype

Before production could start a final check needed to be made. A pre-production prototype of both the PCB and the mouldings needed to be made to highlight any unforeseen difficulties. Many minor modifications are usually necessary on a complex project such as the 'Thermapen'. For this reason careful testing and documentation is necessary to make sure that nothing is overlooked.

It was only after much hard work that the 'Thermapen' could be launched. The name 'Thermapen' is registered as a trademark to prevent it being used by other companies.

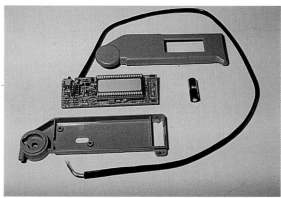

Fig. 1.35 *Pre-production PCB and case*

Fig. 1.36 *The 'Thermapen' in use*

EVALUATING AND TESTING

The importance of evaluating in the process of designing and making is essential in the production of quality products. It forms part of a quality assurance programme, which includes quality of design, quality of performance and quality of manufacture. Within this process you must consider:

- What to evaluate
- When to evaluate
- How to evaluate

What to evaluate

The 'Thermapen' specification is concerned both with ergonomics (the relationship between products and the people that use them) and the electronic requirements. A specification of this type can be useful but the complete evaluation process will often involve more. For example, the retraction or folding alongside of the probe is concerned with function, as is the display, but the designer will also be concerned with styling.

In order to achieve quality assurance evaluation must take place throughout the designing and making process. Evaluating existing products is a useful starting point. Design ideas need evaluating as to their viability. Development of the design proposal will need evaluating carefully against the design specification (Figure 1.37). During manufacture evaluating methods, function and finishes will be important.

These evaluation processes need to be carefully considered and recorded. You may find it helpful to list the evaluation procedures to be considered and describe how you intend to carry out the process (Figure 1.38).

Thermapen product design specification

1. The unit must be easy to use and truly 'pocketable'.
2. It must have an accuracy of +/- 0.3° C.
3. The LCD display should have '3 1/2' digits.
4. The display should have a range of -30 to +80 °C.
5. The probe should be 100 to 150 mm long and be made of stainless steel (to allow for thorough cleansing).
6. The probe should either retract or fold alongside the case.
7. The device should turn itself on when the probe is brought into use.
8. The unit should turn itself off if left unused.
9. The unit needs to be powered by an MN21 12v alkaline battery (lighter size).
10. The unit needs to be easily manufactured despite its small size (easy to assemble and access to PCB etc.).
11. The device must give a 'low battery' warning on the display.
12. The 'Thermapen' must sell for around £30.

Fig. 1.37
Using the specification for evaluation

When to evaluate

Evaluation is often considered as a procedure to be carried out at the end of the making process. It can be seen under 'What to evaluate' that this is not true.

The evaluation of existing products is likely to be carried out fairly early on in a project. The methods and results from this need to be carefully recorded as the designer may wish them to be repeated on the new product.

Fig. 1.39 *Testing the product in use*

Extensive evaluation will, of course, be made once a prototype has been completed. At this stage the product can be tested in use but the function of the circuit will have to be tested and evaluated thoroughly at the modelling stage too.

How to evaluate

When the designer has determined what to evaluate, and when, the next consideration is how to evaluate. There are three basic methods that can be adopted:

- research methods
- laboratory test methods
- the product in use

Research methods can include evaluating against known facts or information (e.g. knowledge from books or information from questionnaires). Laboratory test methods will involve testing against known parameters (e.g. testing the circuit under different voltage conditions). The product in use will demonstrate how the product actually functions in use (Figure 1.39). All results need to be carefully recorded and considered.

Compromises in design often have to be made, but with good evaluation techniques the final design will be based on sound evidence and help provide a quality product.

Evaluation Sheet – Thermapen

Evaluation topic	Evaluation method/procedure	Evaluation results
Electronic function +/- 0.3% accuracy	Laboratory testing using ??-calibrated thermocouple	

Fig. 1.38 *Planning for evaluation*

2. Modelling

INTRODUCTION

When designing and making electronic products it is important to use modelling to test the circuit which has been designed. This should be done before producing a final printed circuit board (see Chapter 10), even when those circuits to be used are from books or magazines. However, modelling should not be considered simply as a means of testing a final circuit design, but as part of the process in reaching the final design. Modelling will provide the opportunity to try out ideas quickly without the long and expensive process of producing numerous circuit boards. Parts of the whole circuit can be tried out and measurements and calculations made. Modifications can be easily made ensuring that the circuit matches the specification and works efficiently. Not to model a circuit before production can result in expensive loss of components and costly delays.

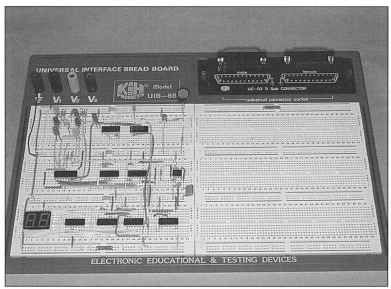

Fig. 2.1 *Prototyping board*

METHODS OF MODELLING

There are many options available. The chosen method of modelling will depend on many factors, including the availability of equipment and the complexity of the circuit. The options include the use of specialist prototype boards (Figure 2.1) wood block and screws (Figure 2.2), purpose-made system boards (see page 16) and computer software (Figure 2.3). Some methods are more 'permanent' than others and can provide the option of testing the circuit in the housing of the product, checking for reliability in use.

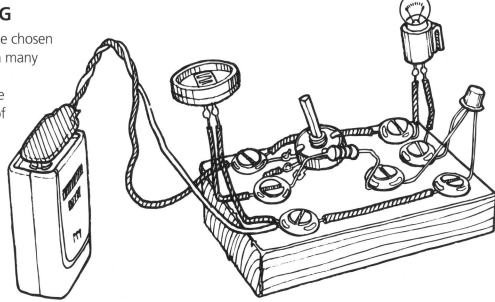

Fig. 2.2 *Modelling a circuit using a wood block and screws*

Fig. 2.3 *Computer modelling*

Design issues – modelling

1. What method of modelling is suitable for the circuit design?
2. What tests will be required once the circuit has been modelled?
3. At what stage/s should the circuit be modelled?
4. How can the circuit be modelled safely?
5. Can the circuit be modelled in parts so that checks can be made in stages rather than modelling the whole circuit in one go?

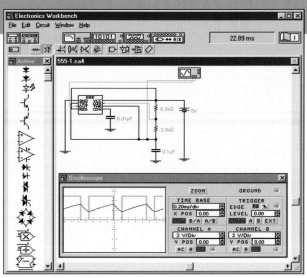

Robinson Marshall (Europe) plc are a company based in Coventry that distribute a computer modelling package for designing and testing electronic circuits. The program 'Electronics Workshop' is a comprehensive modelling package which is used in industry as well as in schools. It is sold in 33 countries, in 11 different languages. In industry it is used within training programmes as well as to help design some of the electronic circuits used in equipment and products.

The Test Engineering Manager from Marconi Radar and Defence Systems Ltd. explained that part of the benefits of modelling tools such as this is being able to try out circuit designs without the need to purchase components or incur costly mistakes when by using real components they would be damaged due to faults in the design. The illustration above shows a screen that is modelling a 555 timer, and testing it using the oscilloscope window.

Systems board modelling

As this modelling option is based on a systems approach it can provide a very useful method of developing circuits during the early stages of design. Components come on assembled circuit boards and are fastened together using clips or plugs (Figure 2.4).

DARLINGTON PAIR	ASTABLE FLIP-FLOP	BUFFER	BUZZER	RELAY
TRANSISTOR SWITCH	ASTABLE	LATCH	LIGHT SENSOR	LED INDICATO
DIFFERENTIAL AMPLIFIER	DARLINGTON PAIR	MOTOR	SCHMITT TRIGGER	DARLINGTO PAIR
COMPARATOR	MONOSTABLE	TEMPERATURE SENSOR	PRESSURE SENSOR	DARLINGTO PAIR

Fig. 2.5 *Identified systems*

Each circuit board is usually an independent system which will have been identified in the early stages of design (Figure 2.5).

Using the available systems (boards) a working block diagram can be designed (Figure 2.6). The modelling boards are selected to match the systems and assembled to see if the circuit works as designed (Figure 2.7). Because the availability of systems boards may limit ideas, substitutions may sometimes be made, e.g. an LED output may be used as an indicator simply to show that the output signal is working.

Fig. 2.7 *Modelling boards are assembled to check that the system works*

If the system works and meets the design specifications then the circuit, using discrete components, can be designed. The circuit diagram will be drawn and the circuit modelled to check it works to the specification. As components may have changed or additional components used from the circuit first modelled, using the system boards, it is important to model the circuit again so that checks and tests can be made.

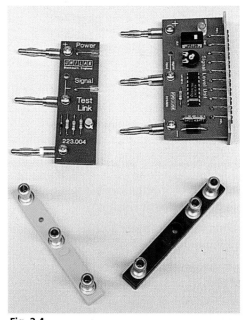

Fig. 2.4

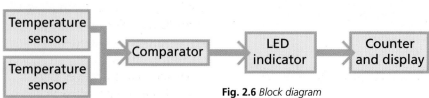

Fig. 2.6 *Block diagram*

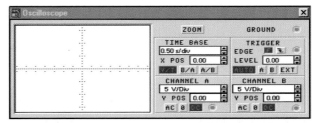
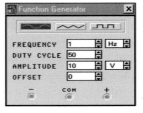

Another important advantage of modelling tools like this is the inclusion of expensive test equipment. On this page you can see a few of these as they appear in Electronics Workbench – a multimeter, function generator, oscilloscope, and a word generator. Modelling systems like this are becoming increasingly popular and used by a range of people for home use right through to industrial applications.

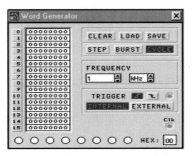

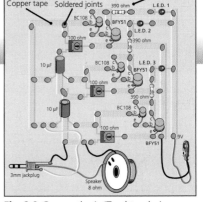

Fig. 2.9 *Commotion's 'Tracktronics'*

Discrete component modelling

There are a number of methods by which modelling using discrete components can be carried out. As with the 'systems board modelling' method it is worthwhile designing the circuit as a number of smaller systems. Not only does this have the advantage of simplifying the circuit into smaller blocks but it also provides a means by which elements of the circuit can be built and tested. When you have modelled a system block test it.

> Do not model the whole circuit before testing – build sufficient parts so that tests can be made to show that each part works.

Components carriers

This method can provide a quick means of modelling circuits. Each individual component is held on its own carrier. These carriers are clipped onto a moulded plastic board with metal posts (Figure 2.8). The metal posts have holes in the top so that 4 mm plugs can be inserted either for connections to other parts of the circuit or for testing. This method has the advantage that the model closely represents the circuit diagram. It is less suited for integrated circuit modelling as the large number of pins does not lend itself to the limited number of connections available between the metal posts, although some 8-pin devices are available.

Copper tape

The copper tape method of modelling provides a quick and semi-permanent method of circuit construction (Figure 2.9). Like the component carrier method, it has the advantage that the layout of the model can be based on the original circuit diagram. Circuits can either be drawn by hand onto paper (taking account of the component sizes) or photocopied master circuits can be used building up a circuit from a set of system blocks.

Self-adhesive copper tape is used for all the tracks. The components are soldered into place simply by placing the leg directly onto the surface of the copper track (a very simple form of surface mounting). Special connecting pads are available so that components such as 8-pin dual in line ICs can be used in the modelled circuits. However, this method is not particularly well suited for circuits with components that have a large number of connections.

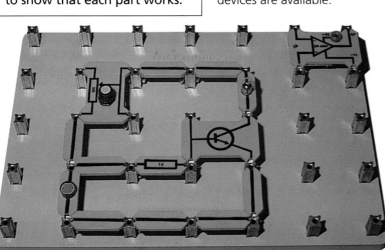

Fig. 2.8 *Locktronics modelling system*

Prototype boards

Prototype boards (Figure 2.10) provide a very effective method of modelling circuits, from the simple to complex. If ICs are to be used, this will often be a preferred method. Prototype boards have rows of holes which are connected together by copper strips to form the circuit tracks (Figure 2.11). It is important that you know which holes are connected together and this may differ if using different makes of board. Components should be used, where possible, to link between the connections otherwise wire links are used (Figure 2.12). Try to avoid a 'rats nest' (lots of wires going in all directions) by keeping the wires neat. This will make it easier to trace connections and find any errors that may occur when making connections between components.

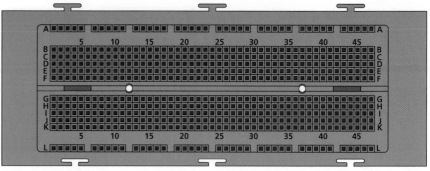

Fig. 2.10 *Prototype board*

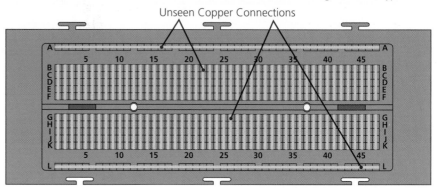

Unseen Copper Connections

Fig. 2.11 *Prototype board connections*

Computer modelling

The computer modelling package shown in Figure 2.13 is used both in schools and industry and provides the electronics designer with a method of modelling circuits quickly and cheaply. It has the advantage that the designer does not need to purchase components in order to try out all the design ideas. Also the component values are always ideal, i.e. a 10 K resistor will be exactly 10,000 ohms. This may not be true when using real components. Simulated equipment, such as oscilloscopes, function generators, multimeters etc. that may not normally be available in schools, can be used enabling the circuit to be tested and values checked. Components do not have to be purchased in order to try out ideas. Errors in circuit design can result in expensive components being damaged as can incorrect use of test instruments. To have a tool that can offer 'what if' situations in complete safety has many advantages. Computer modelling does not replace modelling with real components but can provide opportunities that would not otherwise exist.

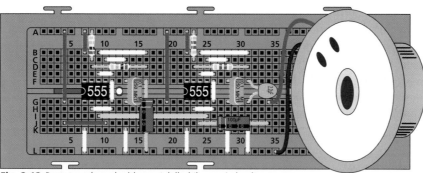

Fig. 2.12 *Prototype board with a modelled 'buzzer' circuit*

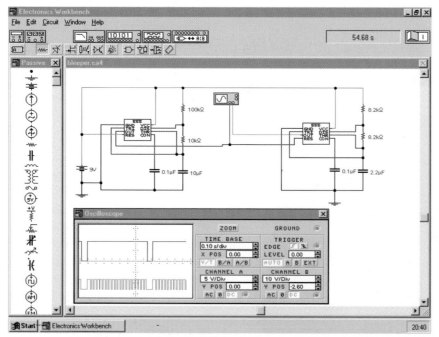

Fig. 2.13 *Computer model of 'buzzer' circuit*

3·Power sources

CHOICE OF POWER SOURCE

Without a power source no electronic device will work, so the choice of power source is important. There is a large choice, although the power source for most of your projects will be a battery. However, other sources should not be discounted. If the device does not have to be portable and is likely to use fairly high levels of energy then a 'power supply' which runs from mains power source may be a preferred option. As with other design decisions it is important to make an informed choice.

Fig. 3.1 *Batteries – likely to be your first choice but why?*

Batteries

The batteries shown in Figure 3.1 represent just a sample of those that are available. Some batteries can only be used once and then have to be thrown away; others can be recharged. There are different types of 'disposable' batteries, some of which are better suited for particular tasks and therefore it is not always necessary to purchase the most expensive. Rechargeable batteries are popular and in the long term can save money. The initial cost of these batteries can be expensive and they require a special charging unit. The batteries shown in Figure 3.1 are relatively large and are not suited for very small devices. Special button batteries such as those that fit into a wristwatch may be the answer in some situations. Clearly you will need to make decisions about size, voltage and type (see pages 20–21).

External power supplies

Mains power supplies can be purchased that will provide a wide range of voltages. The type shown in Figure 3.2 plugs directly into the mains socket and is quite common in many commercial electronic products. As no power source is needed within the housing of the electronic product if a mains supply is used, this can have the advantage of reducing the amount of space required. Mains power supplies can be expensive especially if your electronic product needs a current source which is greater than 200–300 mA. Two sorts of power supply are available – unregulated and regulated (see pages 24–25) with the regulated being more expensive. Some products will need a regulated power supply.

Fig. 3.2 *Mains power supply*

Internal power supplies

Not all electronic products are suited to external power supplies. Some require a power source which fits directly into the housing. Many products have internal power supplies, e.g. computers, hi-fi systems and television sets. Although there are parts of these systems, such as the monitor or tube of a television set that need high voltages, much of the circuitry will be working at a very low voltage, typically 5 V. Making your own power supply is possible but great care is needed and any work must be checked by a qualified person before any connections are made to the mains supply.

> ### Design issues – power sources
> 1. What voltage is needed?
> 2. How much current will be needed by the circuit?
> 3. Does the device need to be portable?
> 4. Will the power source be internal (inside the housing) or external?
> 5. If the power source is to be internal, how much room is available inside the housing?
> 6. If a battery is to be used, how will it be replaced?

19

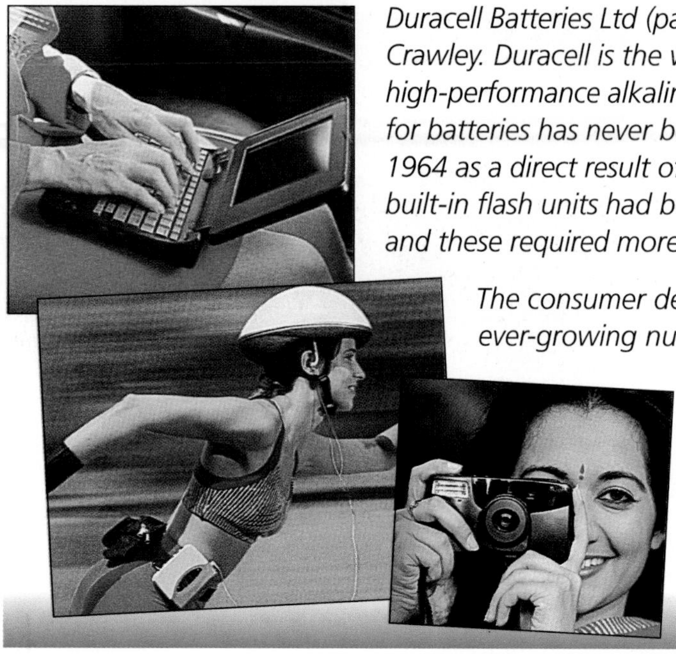

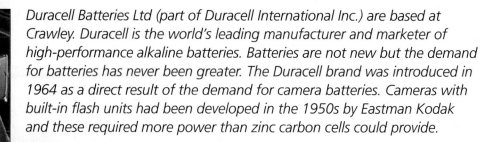

Duracell Batteries Ltd (part of Duracell International Inc.) are based at Crawley. Duracell is the world's leading manufacturer and marketer of high-performance alkaline batteries. Batteries are not new but the demand for batteries has never been greater. The Duracell brand was introduced in 1964 as a direct result of the demand for camera batteries. Cameras with built-in flash units had been developed in the 1950s by Eastman Kodak and these required more power than zinc carbon cells could provide.

The consumer demand for a mobile lifestyle in which we enjoy an ever-growing number of devices that formerly required 'plug in' power has ensured that the technological development of batteries continues. Flashlights, personal CD players, portable sound systems, video cameras, laptop computers and cellular

BATTERIES

Batteries provide a very safe source of electrical energy and are the most likely power source to be used in your electronic products. They come in various dimensions (sizes) and have different voltage levels and properties which are best suited for particular uses.

Battery sizes

For most of the electronic products you design the choice of battery will be from those shown in Figure 3.3. Figure 3.4 shows the actual dimensions of these batteries and their common coding and shape. How these are to fit into the housing and connections made to the circuit is an important consideration in the design of your product.

Fig. 3.3 Battery sizes in common usage

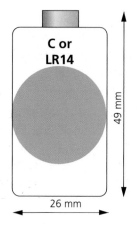

Fig. 3.5 PP3 battery connector

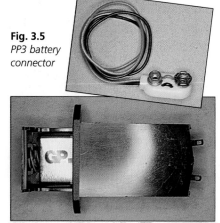

Fig. 3.6 Panel mounting battery holder

Battery connections

The PP3 battery is a popular choice because a simple battery connector can be used (Figure 3.5) and the making of a holder is a relatively simple task. Other types of connectors can be fixed to the housing. Internal battery holders that mount directly onto a printed circuit board are an option or external (panel mounting) holders that allow changing of the battery without the need to open the housing (Figure 3.6).

Fig. 3.4

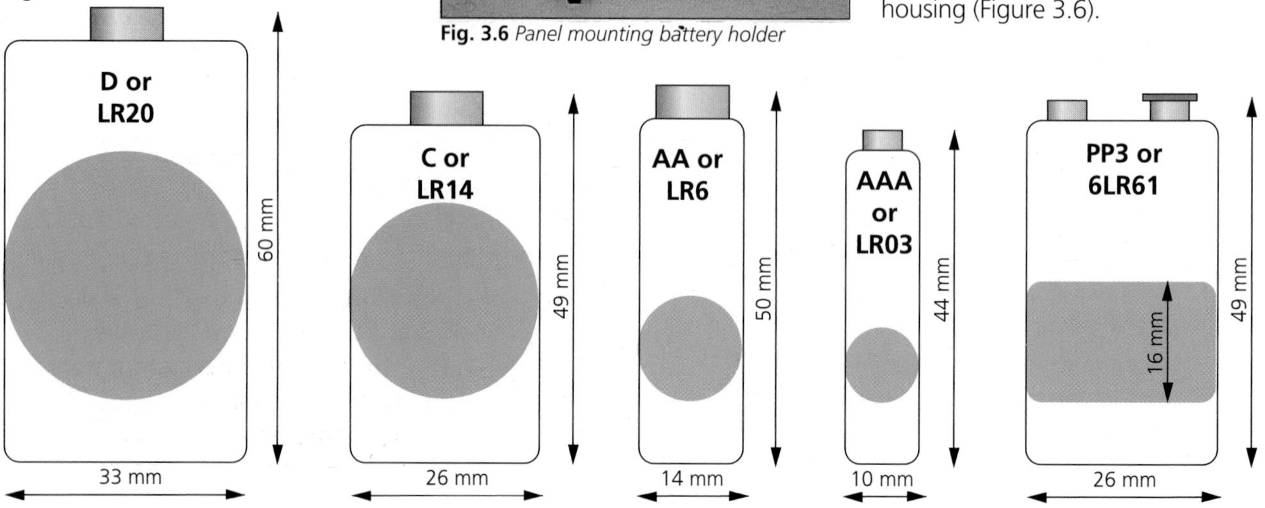

D or LR20
60 mm
33 mm

C or LR14
49 mm
26 mm

AA or LR6
50 mm
14 mm

AAA or LR03
44 mm
10 mm

PP3 or 6LR61
16 mm
49 mm
26 mm

telephones are just a few of the electronic products that require high power in the form of batteries. More than 20 billion batteries are sold annually in the five most common sizes (AAA, AA, C, D and 9-volt) and the demand by consumers for the more powerful alkaline battery is increasing this sector of the market. Increased demand for battery power is also growing because of changes in semiconductor technology with lower power requirements. Developments, such as better display technology and motor technology, mean that devices that previously needed 'plug in' power are now able to be powered by battery. Literature produced by Duracell, such as that shown in the photograph, provides useful information about the technology of batteries and can help in decision making when designing and making electronic products.

Battery voltages and current

The voltage required by some circuits will be critical. Some integrated circuits will need a supply of exactly 5 V (see pages 24–25). Other circuits can operate in a wide voltage range. The type of battery used will partly depend on the voltage output required (see Figure 3.7) but the capacity of the battery should also be taken into account. The capacity of the battery will provide helpful information on how long the battery will last. This is given in ampere hours (Ah). For example, if the battery has a capacity of 5.0 Ah it will sustain a current of 0.5 amps for a period of 10 hours. With some batteries however the voltage during this period will drop. Therefore, batteries which maintain their voltage level should be chosen.

Battery Type	Size	Voltage	Capacity (Ah)	Properties
Zinc Chloride 'high power' (non-rechargeable)	D	1.5	7.90	Cheaper alternative to the alkaline battery. Suitable for products that do not need high outputs other than for short periods of time. Voltage level drops considerably during use in comparison with alkaline batteries.
	C	1.5	3.30	
	AA	1.5	1.20	
	AAA	1.5	0.60	
	PP3	9.0	0.40	
Alkaline (non-rechargeable)	D	1.5	18.00	More expensive than zinc chloride but have a much higher capacity (more amp. hours). Alkaline batteries also have the advantage that the voltage level does not drop off so quickly, therefore, more suited to voltage dependent circuits.
	C	1.5	7.75	
	AA	1.5	2.70	
	AAA	1.5	1.18	
	PP3	9.0	0.55	
Silver oxide – Button Cells (non-rechargeable)	11.6 × 5.4	1.55	0.14	These batteries provide an almost constant voltage until dis-charged. They are small and therefore, useful in small products – used extensively in watches, calculators etc.
	11.6 × 2.1	1.55	0.04	
	9.5 × 3.6	1.55	0.06	
	7.9 × 5.4	1.55	0.07	
Lithuim (non-rechargeable)	AA	1.5	2.50	These tend to be expensive but offer a very good constant voltage level and capacity.
	PP3	9.0	1.20	
Nickel Cadmium (rechargeable)	D	1.25	4.00	Nickel Cadmium rechargeable batteries retain their voltage levels well while charged. Their capacity is much lower than alkaline batteries but can be recharged many times so can make a cost effective solution.
	C	1.25	2.20	
	AA	1.25	0.60	
	AAA	1.25	0.22	
	PP3	8.8	0.11	

Fig. 3.7 *Batteries data*

Fig. 3.8 *Batteries in series*

Connecting the batteries together in series will increase the voltage. For example, if you connect two 1.5 V batteries in series then the voltage output will be 3 V (Figure 3.8). If the same batteries were connected together in parallel the voltage output would remain at 1.5 V but they would be capable of producing a higher current or maintaining the power for a longer period of time.

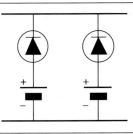

⚠ Warning: it is not safe to connect some types of battery (e.g. Nicad and lithium) in parallel without special circuit protection.

ALTERNATING CURRENT

> ⚠ Mains electricity can kill and any work which requires direct use of mains must be carried out by a suitably qualified person. Reading this chapter will not qualify you to carry out work of this nature.

The mains supply comes into your home via the wall sockets as an alternating current (a.c.) source. This is different from the batteries discussed on the previous pages which provide a direct current (d.c.) source. Figure 3.9 shows a graph of the mains voltage plotted against time. It can be seen from the graph that the voltage changes in one complete cycle (known as the period) from a peak voltage of +340 V to –340 V. This happens 50 times per second (50 Hz). As the voltage of the a.c. supply is constantly changing the problem arises as to what the voltage value should be. The average voltage is 0 V over the complete cycle. The peak voltage of 340 V could be used. To provide a useful voltage level a value is given that would produce the same heating effect when using direct current. This is the root mean square (r.m.s.) and is given by the formula:

$$r.m.s. = \frac{peak\ value}{\sqrt{2}}$$

Using this formula gives a mains supply voltage of 240 V.

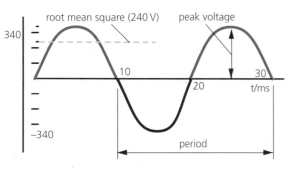

Fig. 3.9 Graph of a.c. waveform

D.C. POWER SUPPLIES

For the electronic products you are likely to make you will need no more than 30 V and for most 9 V will be sufficient. For some products a power source with a constant (stabilised or regulated) current will also be needed. The output voltage from batteries and unregulated power supplies decreases as more current is drawn, due to their internal resistance. Figure 3.10 shows the block diagram of a stabilized power supply which will overcome these disadvantages.

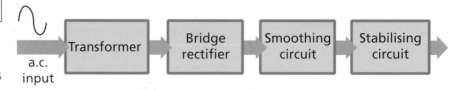

Fig. 3.10 Block diagram of a regulated power supply

TRANSFORMERS

The 240 volts a.c. from the mains supply needs to be reduced to a smaller voltage for use. In order to make this change a device called a transformer (Figure 3.11) is used.

Fig. 3.11 Transformer

Transformers work by electromagnetic induction and are made up of two coils of copper wire, called the primary and the secondary coils. These coils are insulated from each other and wound around a core, usually made from thin soft iron sheets, and laminated together.

Passing an a.c. current through the primary coil creates a magnetic field in the core. As the voltage changes so does the magnetic field. This changing magnetic field creates a changing a.c voltage in the secondary coil.

The ratio of the voltages between the primary and secondary coils is related to the number of turns in each. The output voltage can be calculated by the formula shown in Figure 3.12.

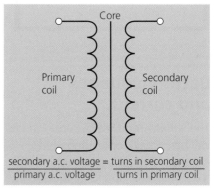

$$\frac{secondary\ a.c.\ voltage}{primary\ a.c.\ voltage} = \frac{turns\ in\ secondary\ coil}{turns\ in\ primary\ coil}$$

Fig. 3.12 Transformer symbol

When choosing a transformer it is important to ensure that it is capable of producing the required current. Generally the more current a transformer can produce the bigger its dimensions. Good transformers are able to change the voltage between the primary and secondary coils without too much wasted energy being given off in the form of heat. If too much current is drawn from the secondary coil the insulation will melt causing the transformer to fail. To help protect against excessive currents a suitable fuse should be placed in series with the primary coil (Figure 3.13). The iron core should also be earthed.

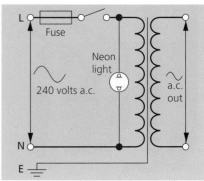

Fig. 3.13 Transformer circuit

RECTIFIERS

Although the transformer reduces the voltage the current is still alternating. A rectifier carries out one of the stages required to convert AC to DC Rectifiers (Figure 3.14), which usually come as integrated circuits, are made from diodes (Figure 3.15) which only allow current to pass in one direction.

Fig. 3.14 *A bridge rectifier*

Fig. 3.15 *Diodes*

The input and output waveforms from a regulated power supply are shown in Figure 3.16. The 240 V DC input is a sine wave while the output is a straight line showing a constant DC positive voltage.

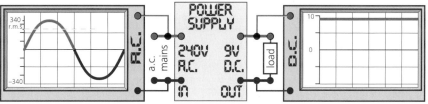

Fig. 3.16 *Input and output requirements of a power supply*

Half wave rectifier

Placing a diode into the circuit, as shown in Figure 3.17, will change the waveform so that the negative half is blocked. A diode will only let the current pass in one direction so when the AC current changes to the negative half of the wave the oscilloscope shows that no current is flowing and the voltage is zero.

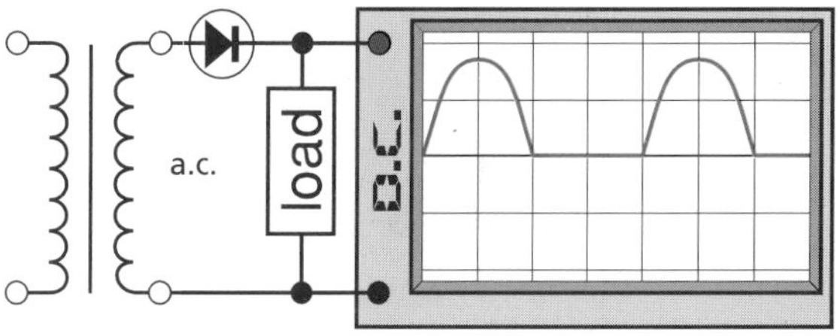

Fig. 3.17 *Half wave rectifier with output waveform*

Full wave rectifier

The disadvantage of half wave rectifier is that only half of the power is available. Full wave rectification can be achieved by using a bridge rectifier. This consists of four diodes arranged as shown in Figure 3.18. The output wave form shows that there is no negative voltage. Figures 3.19 and 3.20 illustrate how this is achieved. The red lines show which part of the circuit is positive and the black negative. The yellow lines show the blocking action of the diodes in each phase.

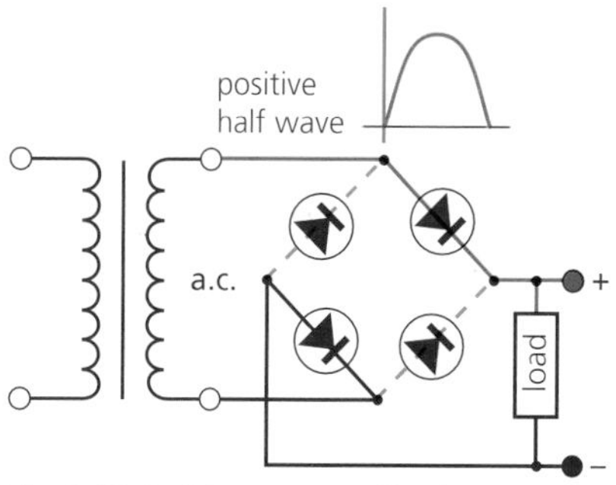

positive half wave

Fig. 3.19 *Positive wave rectification*

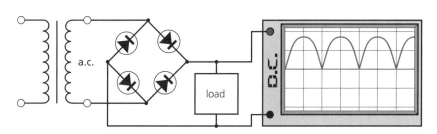

Fig. 3.18 *Full wave rectifier with output waveform*

negative half wave

Fig. 3.20 *Negative wave rectification*

Smoothing circuit

Although there is no negative voltage at the output of the bridge rectifier it is far from the steady voltage shown in Figure 3.16. To smooth the output a capacitor is used. It is placed at the output of the bridge rectifier (Figure 3.21). The capacitor stores electrical charge and is a bit like a rechargeable battery (see Chapter 6 for more information on capacitors). The capacitor is quickly charged up to the peak voltage. When the voltage begins to drop the capacitor begins

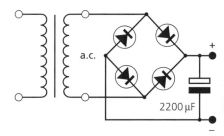

2200 μF

Fig. 3.21 *Smoothing circuit*

to discharge holding up the voltage. It recharges as soon as the output voltage from the bridge rectifier matches that of the capacitor (Figure 3.22).

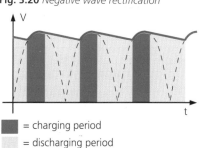

■ = charging period
□ = discharging period

Fig. 3.22 *Smoothed output*

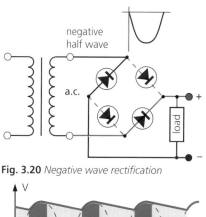

Opus Technology have been producing PC computers for over 15 years and are now one of the UK's leading computer manufacturers. They produce a wide variety of desktop computers used in industry, health authorities, universities and schools. In their sales literature Opus, like most other manufacturers, describe in some detail the specification of their computer systems. However, what you will not see in this information is details about the power supply, without which the system would not work. Computers use a wide range of power supplies including batteries, plug in mains power supplies like that shown in Figure 3.2, and dedicated internal power supplies to meet the specific needs of the desktop computer. Opus have to ensure that these internal power supplies meet the demanding specifications required by modern computer systems. These demands are increasing because of the additional components that users are able to connect to their systems.

REGULATED POWER SUPPLIES

The internal resistance of an unregulated power supply or battery results in the voltage decreasing as more current is drawn from it. For some circuits this is unacceptable, e.g. circuits that use TTL (transistor transistor logic – see Chapter 7). An ideal regulated supply would give a constant voltage regardless of the current being drawn.

Zener diodes

Figure 3.23 shows two zener diodes and their circuit symbol. The zener diode works slightly differently to the diodes used in the bridge rectifier. When forward biased (the current travelling in the same direction as the arrow) the zener diode behaves as a normal diode. However, if the zener diode is reversed biased (the current running in the opposite direction to the arrow) with a voltage greater than its breakdown voltage then the

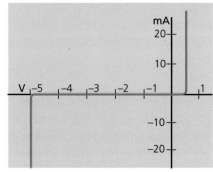

Fig. 3.24 *Zener diode characteristics*

current will rise very rapidly. In the example shown in Figure 3.24 the zener diode has a breakdown voltage of 5.1.

Zener diode and power transistor

The circuit shown in Figure 3.25 can be further improved to give greater stability and power by using a power transistor (Figure 3.26). The output voltage will be 0.6 V below the zener diode voltage.

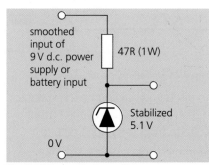

Voltage regulators

Voltage regulators (Figure 3.27) are integrated circuits with complex circuitry to provide a compact solution to many of the problems of regulation. They come in a range of packages and many are designed for specialist applications. For example, providing 5 V supplies for TTL circuits or ±15 V for operational amplifiers.

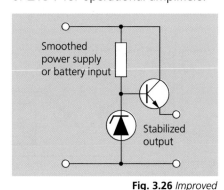

Fig. 3.26 *Improved zener diode regulator*

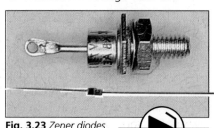

Fig. 3.23 *Zener diodes*

Fig. 3.25 *Zener diode regulator*

Fig. 3.27 *Voltage regulators*

The photograph on the right shows the inside construction of one of the Opus range of computers. The power supply is the large box with the label on top, towards the front of the photo. This particular power supply is mains powered (230V) and has four output voltages (+5V, +12V, −5V and −12V) each of which will be regulated to ensure that they remain constant. Each of the output voltages has a specified current rating (20A, 8A, 0.3A and 0.3A respectively) which will be well above the normal requirements of the equipment. The main computer logic circuits will operate at 5 volts, while devices such as disc drives and CD ROM players require 12 volts to drive the motors. These power supplies work on the same principles as the circuits shown in this chapter although additional electronic systems are used to ensure stability and prevent electrical interference.

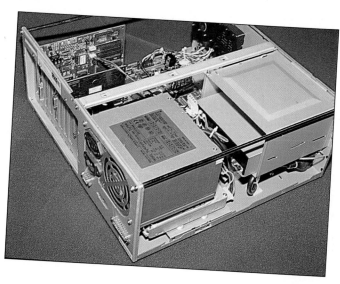

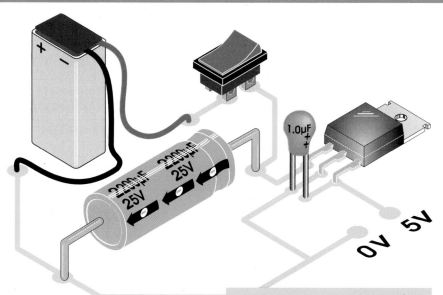

Fig. 3.28 *IC regulator circuit*

Fig. 3.29 *A heatsink*

Solar cells

Having unlimited power without the use of batteries or mains would have many advantages. You may have a calculator which does not need any batteries but gets its power from light (Figure 3.30). Calculators of this type are powered by photovoltaic cells or solar cells. The current required to run these calculators is very small. For devices which require larger amounts of current the solar cells would be very expensive and the space required by them would be large. Solar cell technology is developing and, although relatively expensive, it is possible for you to design and build electronic products powered by solar cells.

Figure 3.28 shows a circuit for a 5 V supply using a battery source. The 7805 can provide an output current of 1 A. The 78L05 is a smaller voltage regulator that will provide an output current of 100 mA. It is important that when you are designing circuits and intend using a voltage regulator, you are able to calculate what current the circuit will consume so that you can choose the correct type of voltage regulator. If using the 7805 a heatsink may be required to protect the voltage regulator (Figure 3.29).

The regulator circuit shown in Figure 3.28 would also be suitable for the type of power supply described on pages 22 and 23 or for an unregulated external power supply, as shown in Figure 3.2. The range of voltage regulators is increasing and some provide options for variable outputs making it possible to have a regulated voltage supply for any circuit you are likely to design.

Fig. 3.30 *Solar powered calculator*

Wiring of a mains plug

All new electronic products which require mains electricity will be purchased with a suitable plug already fitted and this will normally be of a moulded type which cannot be rewired. However, it may be necessary to change the fuse and the correct value should always be used. Many products will give a power rating in watts. To calculate the value of the fuse required use the formula:

$$\text{I (amps)} = \text{Power (watts)} \div \text{V (volts)}$$

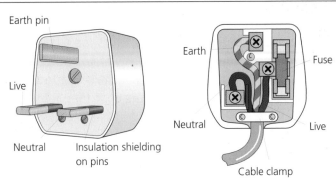

Fig. 3.31 *Wiring of a mains plug*

Putting it into practice

1. Identify three electronic products, other than those mentioned in this chapter, where a battery is more suitable than a mains power supply. Give reasons for your choice.

2. Draw a table similar to that shown below. Using three examples of electronic products from this chapter describe one advantage of using batteries and one advantage of using a mains power supply in each case.

Electronic product	Battery advantage	Mains advantage

3. Find the cost of four 'D' size zinc chloride batteries, four 'D' size alkaline batteries and four 'D' size rechargeable nickel cadmium batteries. A torch uses a high intensity 6.5 V bulb which draws a current of 490 mA. Using the table on page 21 and ignoring the cost of recharging calculate which of the above batteries would be the most cost effective over:
a) 15 hours; **b)** 100 hours.

4. Explain with the aid of a graph of voltage against time why alkaline or lithium batteries are better suited to circuits which are dependent on stable voltages.

5. Draw the circuit symbol for a rectifier diode and using diagrams explain how it operates.

6. Draw the symbol for a zener diode and explain how it differs from a rectifier diode.

7. The block diagram shown in Fig. 3.32 is of a stabilised power supply. Explain briefly the function of each part and the output waveform at each stage.

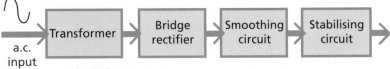

Fig. 3.32

8. Using the block diagram in Fig. 3.32 draw a circuit diagram of a stabilised power supply using a mains transformer that would supply a +5 V supply. Show all relevant calculations and component values.

9. The a.c. waveform shown in Fig. 3.33 is of a mains supply with an r.m.s. voltage of 240 V. Other countries use a 120 V supply. What is the peak voltage value for this supply?

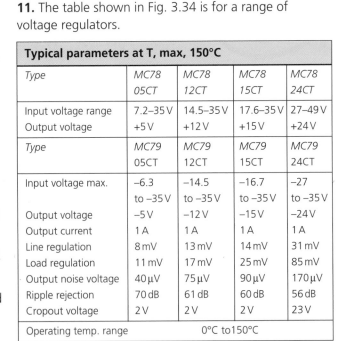

Fig. 3.33

10. The frequency of the supply shown in Fig. 3.33 is 50 Hz. A frequency of 60 Hz is used in some other countries. What is the period time in milliseconds for a 60 Hz supply?

11. The table shown in Fig. 3.34 is for a range of voltage regulators.

Typical parameters at T, max, 150°C				
Type	MC78 05CT	MC78 12CT	MC78 15CT	MC78 24CT
Input voltage range	7.2–35 V	14.5–35 V	17.6–35 V	27–49 V
Output voltage	+5 V	+12 V	+15 V	+24 V
Type	MC79 05CT	MC79 12CT	MC79 15CT	MC79 24CT
Input voltage max.	−6.3 to −35 V	−14.5 to −35 V	−16.7 to −35 V	−27 to −35 V
Output voltage	−5 V	−12 V	−15 V	−24 V
Output current	1 A	1 A	1 A	1 A
Line regulation	8 mV	13 mV	14 mV	31 mV
Load regulation	11 mV	17 mV	25 mV	85 mV
Output noise voltage	40 µV	75 µV	90 µV	170 µV
Ripple rejection	70 dB	61 dB	60 dB	56 dB
Cropout voltage	2 V	2 V	2 V	23 V
Operating temp. range	0°C to150°C			

Fig. 3.34

a) Which of the types shown in the table would you use for a +15 V and a −15 V power supply?
b) What is the minimum input voltage for the +15 V regulator and what would be the maximum input voltage for the −15 V supply?
c) What is the maximum amount of current that should be drawn from the regulated power supply using these regulators?

12. Why do some regulators need a heatsink?

4 · Sensors and switching

SENSORS

Light, heat, moisture, radiation, touch. How can a system know about these sorts of conditions?

If you need to design a system with inputs that measure or detect physical changes, then you are going to need sensors.

An example of a sensor in a system is shown in Figure 4.2. A bimetallic strip (Figure 4.3) forms the sensor in a thermostat for a central heating system.

Two metals, which expand at different rates when heated, are bonded together. Changes in temperature cause the strip to bend. When the strip is heated the degree of bending will depend on the temperature change.

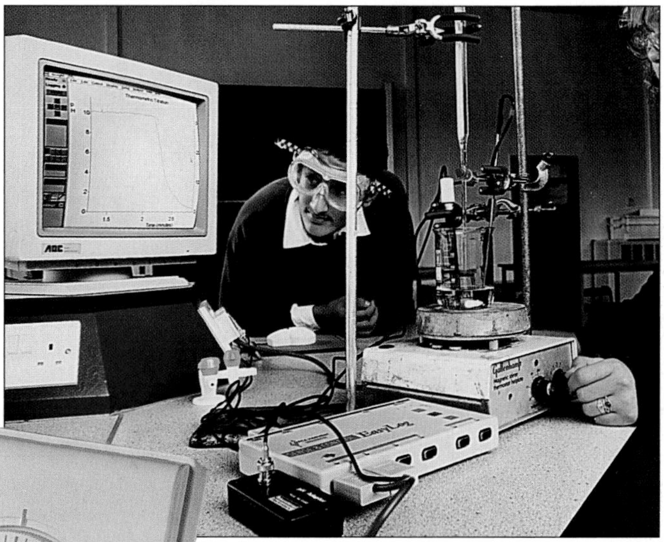

Fig. 4.1 *Using sensors to detect change in pH values*

Fig. 4.2 *A thermostat for a central heating system*

Cool

Invar

brass or steel

Hot

Invar

brass or steel

If you listen carefully you can hear bimetallic strips click as they change shape. Listen to an automatic kettle as the water comes to the boil and as it cools down. The first click of the strip turns off the heating element and the second click is the strip returning to its previous shape.

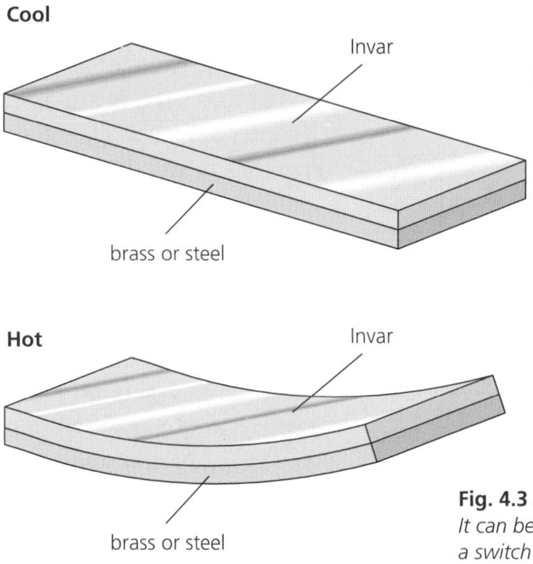

Fig. 4.3 *A bimetallic strip bends when heated. It can be used both as a temperature sensor and a switch that turns a heating element off and on.*

WHY ARE SENSORS USEFUL?

Electronic systems rely on receiving some sort of information (input), and processing it ready to give an output of some description. This is often summarised as ...

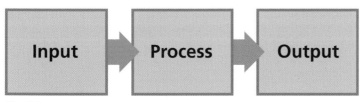

Fig. 4.4

Inputs will often come from sensors and can give the system information about the physical world. This information might be about temperature, radiation, humidity, air pressure, movement or the presence of a particular gas. The list is endless. It is not hard to see that sensors play a very important part in electronics.

> ### Design issues – sensors
> 1. What will you need the sensor to detect?
> 2. How accurate will you need the sensor to be? If for example it is to be a temperature sensor, will plus or minus one degree Celsius be accurate enough?
> 3. What range will the sensor need to operate within? If for example it is to sense heat, what will be the maximum and minimum temperatures required?
> 4. Once you have chosen a sensor, how will it be connected to the rest of your system?

SWITCHES AS DIGITAL SENSORS

Switches that can either be on or off can only provide two signals as inputs to a circuit. For example, the courtesy light switch on a car door can only indicate whether the door is open or closed. This makes it a digital sensor. (A more sophisticated sensor might be able to show how far the door is open and would be an analogue sensor.)

Push button switches

A door bell switch is an example of a simple switch (Figure 4.5). When pressed two connections are joined together and complete a circuit. Push buttons of this type are known as 'push to make' switches. The opposite type of switch is the 'push to break' switch, which is far less common but has uses, for example in the courtesy door light circuit of a car and refrigerator compartment lights. The symbols for push to make and push to break switches are shown in Figure 4.6. Figure 4.7 shows some examples of simple series circuits with the two types of push button switches.

Reed switches

A reed switch (Figure 4.8) is an enclosed switch which reacts to the presence of a magnet. It has a delicate metal conductor that bends when a magnet comes close. As shown in Figure 4.9, it can be used in a door frame with the magnet attached to the door as a sensor for a burglar alarm.

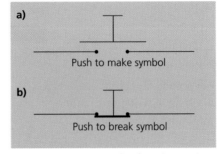

a) Push to make symbol

b) Push to break symbol

Fig. 4.6 Circuit symbols for **a)** push to make and **b)** push to break switches

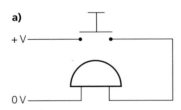

a)

+V

0V

Fig. 4.7 a) Door bell switch

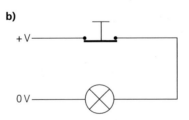

b)

+V

0V

b) Refrigerator door switch

Fig. 4.5 A simple switch

Digital signals in a system

To send a digital (definitely ON or OFF) signal to another part of a system a switch has to do a slightly different job. Instead of just making or breaking a circuit it must provide a logic level. This is explained in Chapter 7. Essentially the switch now has to switch the signal between a high and a low voltage.

This means that the output is never left disconnected; it always has a clear route to either 0V or + V, as shown in Figure 4.10. In the system shown in this diagram the push to break switch causes the output to be high when the switch is pressed and low when the switch is released.

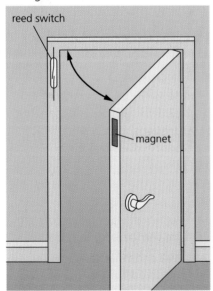

reed switch

magnet

Fig. 4.9 A reed switch can be used as a sensor for a burglar alarm

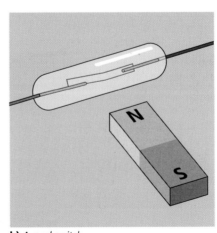

b) A reed switch

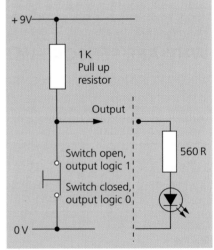

+9V

1K
Pull up resistor

Output

Switch open,
output logic 1

Switch closed,
output logic 0

560 R

0V

Fig. 4.10 A switch circuit to send digital signals

Try this:

Using a push to make switch, what happens to an LED connected between the output and 0V? Swap the 1 K resistor and switch over. What happens now?

Tilt switches

Tilt switches (Figure 4.11) sense when they are being held at an angle. The most common include a bead of mercury which can, when tilted, bridge a pair of contacts. It is possible to make up a tilt switch using a ball bearing to touch a pair of contacts. It is also possible to devise a tilt switch that uses a pendulum.

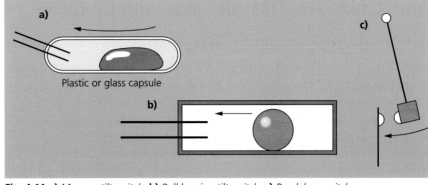

Fig. 4.11 a) *Mercury tilt switch* **b)** *Ball bearing tilt switch* **c)** *Pendulum switch*

Water level switch

A water level switch (Figure 4.12) uses a reed switch and a magnet within a float combined into one unit.

Keyboard switches

Keyboards and calculators (Figure 4.13) have switches that are either mechanical push buttons or membrane switches. Membrane switches are useful in hostile environments where dirt or moisture might otherwise get into the device.

If you make up a membrane switch, then it is important to test the size and thickness of the 'window' before deciding on the overall switch layout. The top layer can be a thin vacuum-formed cover that may include a relief of the 'button' shape. Figure 4.14 shows how a membrane switch is assembled.

Fig. 4.13

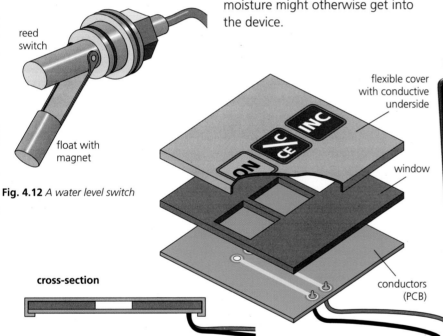

Fig. 4.12 *A water level switch*

Fig. 4.14 *Assembling a membrane switch*

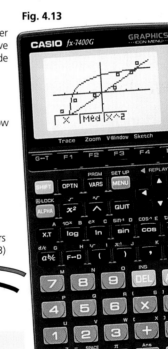

Try this:

Switch-type sensors for alarms

1. A student is investigating ways of setting an alarm on a briefcase when it is left unattended. She is considering using a vibration sensor. Sketch a simple vibration sensor using a spring, a small weight and a copper tube. To assist her, can you suggest some of the disadvantages of a system that relies on vibration to trigger it?

2. Small shop windows often have a self-adhesive metal strip running across them which if broken will trigger an alarm. Figure 4.15 shows a shop display window strip as part of a circuit diagram. Complete the diagram to show how the alarm circuit could receive an 'on' signal if the foil strip is broken by someone breaking the window.

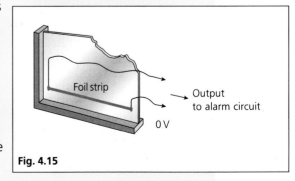

Fig. 4.15

ANALOGUE SENSORS AND VOLTAGE DIVIDERS

Analogue sensors and resistance

In contrast to switch sensors, analogue sensors allow 'in between' states to be recognised rather than simply 'on' or 'off'. It is possible for example to have a sensor that can not only tell the difference between light and dark but can detect the level of light too. Sensors that work in this way can give this kind of signal because their electrical properties change. For many sensors, as the conditions change so does their resistance. The changing resistance can be made more useful by making the sensor part of a voltage divider (see below). Using a voltage divider with a sensor can produce a changing voltage as a signal.

An example of a sensor that works in this way (Figure 4.16) is the light dependent resistor (LDR). As more light falls on an LDR so its resistance decreases.

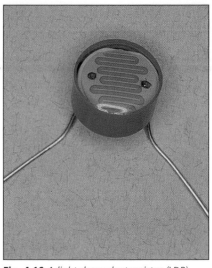

Fig. 4.16 *A light dependent resistor (LDR)*

Variable resistors as movement sensors

By using the spindle of a variable resistor you can convert angular motion into an electrical signal. Joysticks often use two variable resistors (Figure 4.17) at 90° to each other to convert the motion of the 'stick' into signals that indicate the change in the x and y coordinates.

Voltage dividers

A voltage divider may consist of two or more fixed resistors that stretch between the +V and 0V rails of the supply that is to be divided (Figure 4.18). It may also be made using a variable resistor (Figure 4.19).

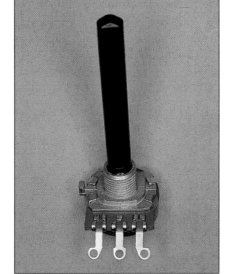

Fig. 4.17 *Variable resistors (also known as potentiometers) can be used as sensors to detect changes in position*

When two fixed resistors of equal value are used, the output voltage is half the supply voltage (from a battery or power supply). Any required voltage can be obtained by adjusting the values of the resistors. The method of calculating the values of the resistors is quite simple. The formula is given on the next page where V_s is the supply voltage and V_o the output voltage. Look at the examples in Figure 4.20 first to see how some simple fractions of the supply voltage can be obtained.

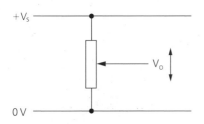

Fig. 4.18 *Voltage divider using two fixed resistors*

Fig. 4.19 *Voltage divider using a variable resistor*

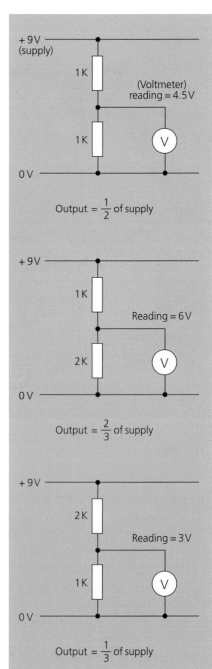

Output = $\frac{1}{2}$ of supply

Output = $\frac{2}{3}$ of supply

Output = $\frac{1}{3}$ of supply

Fig. 4.20 *Examples of circuits using voltage dividers*

The voltage divider formula

By using a voltage divider, a fraction of a supply voltage can be obtained. The fraction will depend on the values of the pair of resistors used in the voltage divider. Don't forget to check in the reference section when choosing your resistor values to see which ones are available (from the range of 'preferred values'). Notice from the previous page that two resistors of equal value halve the supply voltage. This is true whatever their value, as long as they are the same resistance. This formula helps us to predict other outcomes when the resistors are unequal:

$$V_o \text{ (output voltage)} = \frac{R_2}{R_1 + R_2} \times V_s \text{ (supply voltage)}$$

An example is shown in Figure 4.21.

What will happen if one of the resistors is replaced by a sensor whose resistance varies? Instead of remaining constant the output voltage varies with the physical property that the sensor is detecting. In the example shown in Figure 4.22 a light dependent resistor (LDR) can create a voltage signal which varies according to the amount of light falling on the LDR.

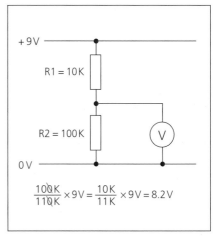

$$\frac{100\,K}{110\,K} \times 9V = \frac{10\,K}{11\,K} \times 9V = 8.2V$$

Fig. 4.21 *Voltage divider calculations*

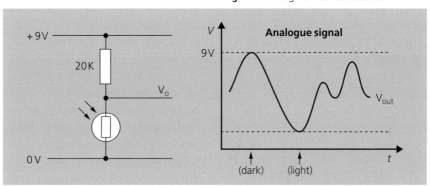

Fig. 4.22 *Varying voltage output*

LIGHT, HEAT AND MOISTURE SENSORS

Analogue sensors and symbols

A low resistance indicates the presence of light.

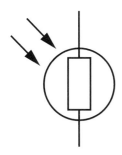

Fig. 4.23 *Light dependent resistor (LDR)*

A low resistance indicates a high temperature.

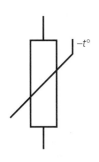

Fig. 4.24 *Thermistor (heat sensor)*

A low resistance indicates moisture.

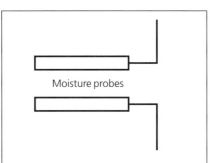

Moisture probes

Fig. 4.25 *Moisture probe*

Light, heat and moisture voltage dividers

The circuits shown in Figure 4.26 each produce a varying voltage. The signal obtained can then be used as information for a variety of subsequent stages, for example as an input to a computer for a weather station. To achieve the required output voltage (V_o), you may need to use resistors of different values.

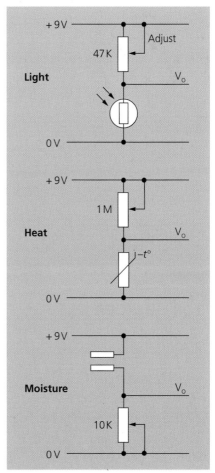

Fig. 4.26 *Examples of light, heat and moisture voltage dividers*

SENSOR CHOICES

Sensors and output signal conditions

If you understand the way a voltage divider works (pages 30–31), you will be able to use a variety of sensors. To match the type of sensor and the voltage divider to your design you will need to decide when the output will need to be at a high voltage and when it will need to be low. For example, if an outdoor light needs to work only when it is dark, this means that the output from the potential divider should be 'high' when it is dark. A selection of sensor and voltage divider combinations are shown below. These should help you when you are designing systems.

Light

A light dependent resistor (LDR) is very good for sensing light levels but may need to be placed in a tube (Figure 4.27) if you need to sense light from a narrow field. (See also phototransistors and infra-red sensors on page 34).

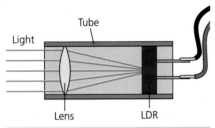

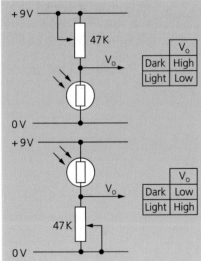

Fig. 4.27

LDR data (ORP 12)

Illuminated – low resistance; in darkness – high resistance.

Typically approximately 1 M ohm in darkness and 1 K ohm when fully lit.

LDRs rely on cadmium sulphide which reacts to light but becomes less effective with age.

Heat

Thermistors (Figure 4.28) are available for a variety of temperature ranges and you will need to consult the manufacturer's data sheets if an accurate result is required. If very high temperatures need to be sensed then some research into thermocouples will be needed. Other alternatives to the thermistor include temperature transducers which produce very accurate current or voltage signals that relate precisely to the temperature (typically 1 micro Amp or 10 mV per degree Kelvin).

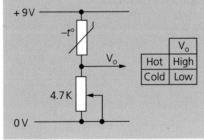

Fig. 4.28

NTC thermistor data

NTC = negative temperature coefficient.

High temperature – low resistance.

Typically these range from 1 K ohms at 25°C to 70 ohms at 100°C.

Check the thermistor type carefully to match your intended temperature range and resistance.

Moisture

Although very simple, this arrangement (Figure 4.29) works very well so long as the contacts are kept clean and the distance between the probes remains constant.

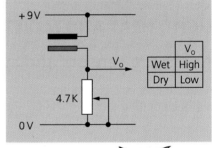

Fig. 4.29

Moisture sensor probes

When dry, high to infinite resistance. When wet, low resistance.

The resistance depends on moisture, the distance between the probes and the nature of the medium between the probes. Always check the resistance of your probes in situ before designing your circuit.

SENSING SIGNAL LEVELS

Sound

Microphones are the obvious sensors to use to pick up sound. Microphones work by detecting sound energy, but the way that they convert this to an electrical signal varies according to the type. Any sensor that converts one form of energy into another in this way is called a transducer.

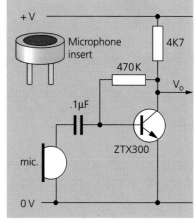

Microphones can be expensive to buy and for this reason they are not commonly used for prototype school projects. However, it is possible to use microphone inserts or piezo transducers which are much cheaper. The circuit shown in Figure 4.30 will convert the signal from a microphone insert to a signal that can be fed directly to an earpiece. If a better quality output is required then this needs to be followed by an amplifier, which could be a simple Darlington pair (see below) or a dedicated integrated circuit (IC).

Microphone types

The main types of microphone are:

■ carbon

■ moving coil

■ moving iron

■ piezo-electric. These are the ones most commonly used in schools. These microphones generate a very small voltage when vibrated by sound waves.

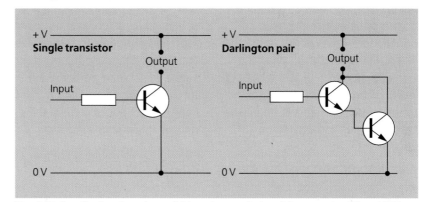

Fig. 4.30

Using transistors to detect voltage level

Figures 4.31 and 4.32 show how transistors can be used to detect a voltage level from a sensor voltage divider. A single transistor can detect a voltage that is greater than 0.6 V. By putting two transistors together (a combination called a Darlington pair) twice this voltage, i.e. 1.2 V, can be detected. A voltage above the critical level (0.6 V for a single transistor, 1.2 V for a Darlington pair) will cause the transistor(s) to 'turn on'. For a more precise explanation, see Chapter 5.

Fig. 4.32 *By adjusting the voltage divider values or choice of detector, the ON and OFF response can be varied*

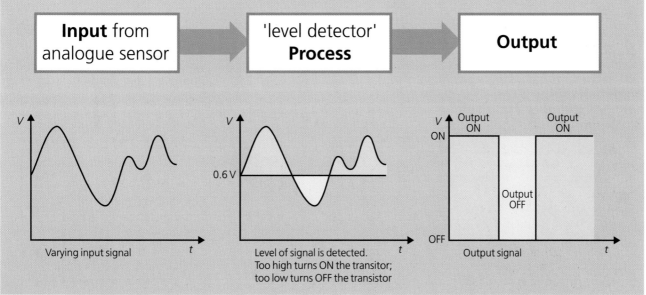

Fig. 4.31

Servomex plc design and make a large range of gas analysers. These analysers are used in areas where the exact composition of gases needs to be monitored, such as emission control, agriculture and medical applications.

One of the techniques Servomex use to analyse gases is infra-red photometry. The infra-red spectrum is made up of numerous wavelengths of infra-red radiation, in the same way as visible light is made up of a number of colours. With some gases, when just the right wavelength of infra-red radiation hits a molecule it is absorbed. If an instrument records that one particular wavelength of infra-red is absorbed, this can be used to measure the concentration of a particular gas. This of course will be true only if that gas is unique in absorbing infra-red at that wavelength.

PHOTO TRANSISTORS

All transistors are sensitive to light but they are normally shielded with a metal or plastic case. Photo transistors (Figure 4.33) have a transparent end and only two connections (unlike the three connections on a normal transistor). The light received through the transparent end acts as the base (the missing connection). Therefore, when light is present the transistor conducts and is 'switched on' (Figure 4.34).

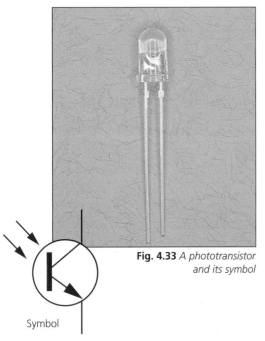

Fig. 4.33 *A phototransistor and its symbol*

Symbol

Infra-red

Infra-red light sensors are used in preference to visible light sensors where room lighting might interfere with a normal light beam signal. TV and video remote controls use a stream of infra-red light pulses to send coded signals to the receiver. Imagine trying to do this with a visible light beam (rather like a torch). The signal would be confused (or corrupted) by the natural daylight in the room.

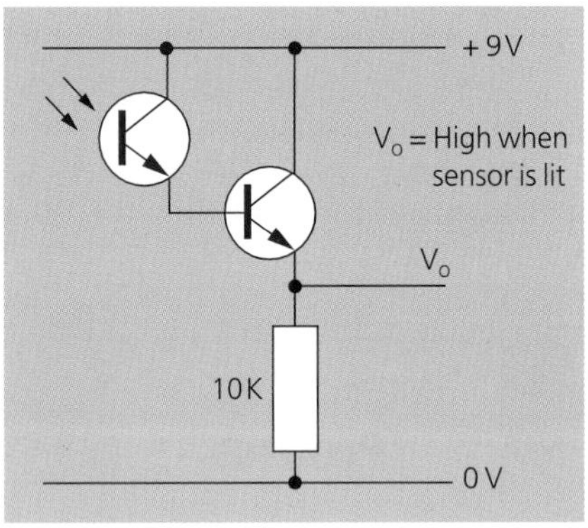

V_o = High when sensor is lit

$+9V$

V_o

10K

0 V

Fig. 4.34

Infra-red light sources (Figure 4.35) look like clear light emitting diodes (LEDs) but the light they emit cannot usually be seen with the naked eye. (There are however visible red sources too, which makes testing much easier as you can see when the source is on!)

Infra-red sensors are often covered by a black or dark red translucent casing. The casing acts as a filter to reduce interference from other light sources. However, infra-red is of limited use outside as the interference from sunlight is often too great.

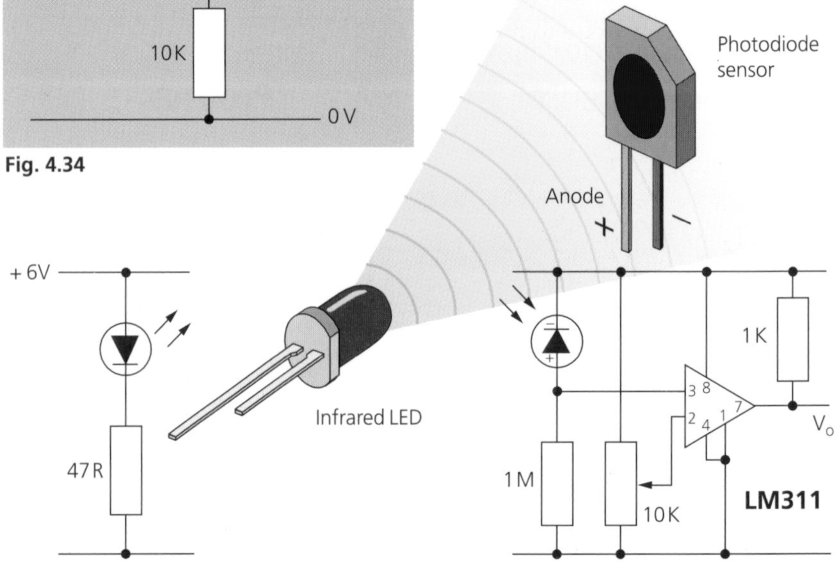

Photodiode sensor

Anode

$+6V$

Infrared LED

47 R

1 K

V_o

1 M

10K

LM311

Fig. 4.35

Gases that absorb infrared include carbon dioxide, methane, carbon monoxide and some rarer gases such as freons and solvents.

Infra-red sensors are used in medical applications to measure the carbon dioxide concentration in the air breathed out by a patient. These analysers must be small in size and capable of responding within milliseconds to rapid changes in concentration. Carbon dioxide analysers are used by anaesthetists during surgical operations.

Sports scientists also use this type of analyser to assess the performance of the body during exercise.

Key design requirements for this type of equipment are accuracy, reliability and compactness.

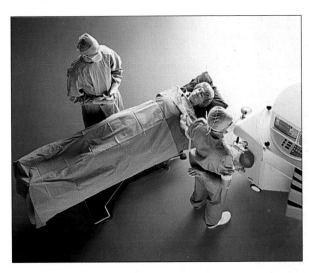

Combined sources and sensors

Components that combine an infra-red light source and sensor in one package make alignment of the beam unnecessary. Two readily available components that do this are the reflective opto sensor and the slotted opto sensor.

Slotted opto

The slotted opto registers obstructions to a beam of infra-red across a slot. Slotted optos can, for example, be used to register whether a door is shut, or the position of a shaft, using a slotted disc. If the number of turns of the shaft can be counted then it is possible to work out how far a DC motor has moved a load (Figures 4.36 and 4.37).

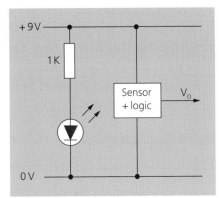

Fig. 4.37 *Slotted opto circuit*

Reflective opto

In the reflective opto the beam is bounced off a close surface. If the surface is a light colour (reflective) then the beam is reflected back on to the receiver. In this way it is possible to register black and white coded message patterns (Figures 4.38 and 4.39).

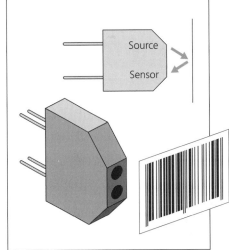

Fig. 4.38 *Reflective opto*

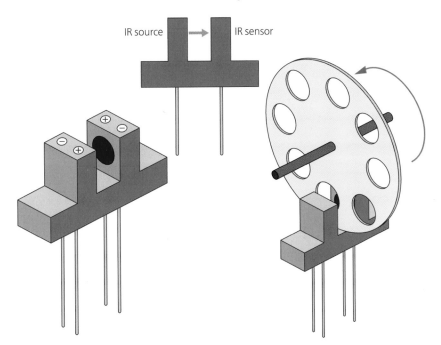

Fig. 4.36 *Slotted opto*

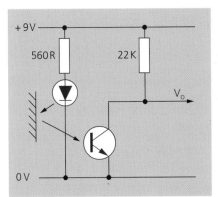

Fig. 4.39 *Reflective opto circuit*

SWITCHES

Rather like the points in a railway track, switches can direct the current around the circuit by re-routing or breaking the connections that make up the circuit.

Switch vocabulary

Make or break. When two conductors of a switch touch it is described as making a connection. This is often abbreviated to 'make' so a 'push to make' switch is a push button switch that connects when pressed. 'Break' is the opposite of make so a 'push to break' switch breaks the circuit it is connected to. Figure 4.40 shows a push to make switch in both make and break positions.

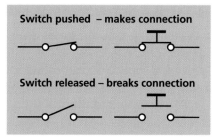

Fig. 4.40 *Make and break switch positions*

Poles and throws. The moving parts of a switch are referred to as the 'poles'. The symbols (Figure 4.41) are drawn to look like the old fashioned knife switches (these are a familiar part of Frankenstein films!). The places where the poles rest and make a connection are the 'throws'.

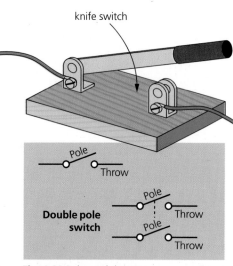

Fig. 4.41 *Poles and throws*

Common. The common is the connection of a switch which is used regardless of the position of the switch poles (Figure 4.42).

Normally open (NO) and Normally closed (NC). If a pole normally rests at one particular throw until operated then this is called a normally closed (NC) connection. The reverse of this is a normally open connection. The difference is shown in Figure 4.42.

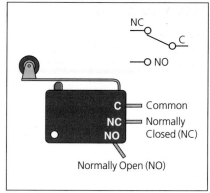

Fig. 4.42 *Normally open and normally closed conditions*

Types of switch

Single pole single throw (SPST)

This type of switch (Figure 4.43) can only make or break a circuit.

Fig. 4.43 *Single pole single throw*

Single pole double throw (SPDT)

This type of switch (Figure 4.44) can offer a choice of two directions for the current to take depending on the position of the pole.

Fig. 4.44 *Single pole double throw*

Double pole double throw (DPDT)

This consists of two SPDT switches together in one package. They operate simultaneously. The dotted line on the symbol (Figure 4.45) indicates that the two poles move at the same time but are connected by an insulator.

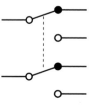

Fig. 4.45 *Double pole double throw*

Key switch

This is a simple switch (Figure 4.46) that can only be changed with a key. Larger versions are commonly found in school workshops to prevent unauthorised use of equipment.

Fig. 4.46 *Key switch*

Rotary switches

These can be single or multi-pole switches (Figure 4.47) that allow a selection of many throws depending on the type. Some can even offer a series of binary coded connections.

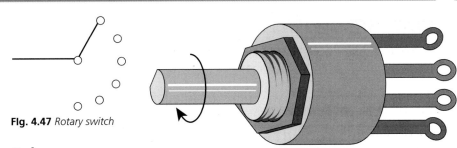

Fig. 4.47 *Rotary switch*

Dual in line (DIL) switches

These are commonly found with connections that need to be changed very infrequently. One example might be the setting up arrangement in an alarm system or a computer printer. This type of switch is shown in Figure 4.48.

Fig. 4.48 *Dual in line switch*

Relays

Relays provide a way of switching using an electric current rather than a finger for operation. It is then possible for a circuit to pass a signal ('relay' a message) to another circuit.

A relay (Figure 4.49) consists of a coil of wire that acts as an electromagnet when current flows through it. When the coil is turned on the switch part of the relay works. The poles then move just as in a normal switch.

The precaution of using a diode in parallel with the coil helps to protect the rest of the circuit from back EMF (electromotive force – which can destroy transistors) when the coil is turned off.

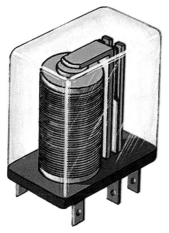

Fig. 4.49 *A relay*

A REVERSING CIRCUIT FOR A DC MOTOR

It is possible to reverse the way a motor turns using a DPDT switch. The motor terminals are connected to the switch poles, which allows the polarity of the motor connections to be exchanged when the switch is used.

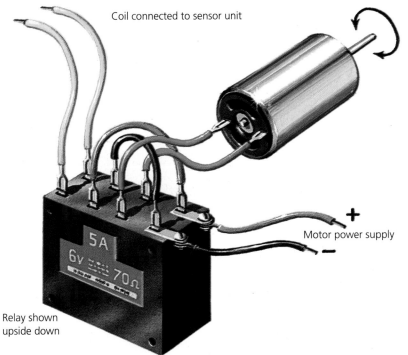

Coil connected to sensor unit

Motor power supply

Relay shown upside down

Fig. 4.51 *A relay reversing circuit*

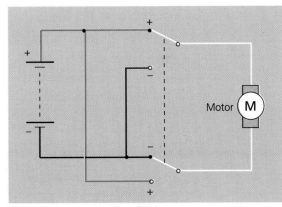

Fig. 4.50 *A motor reversing circuit*

Using a relay, two circuits can operate at different voltages or currents. For example a battery operated circuit could turn on a mains operated circuit. At school it is not normally permitted to use mains electricity for student projects.

A common example of a relay reversing circuit is shown in Figure 4.51 where a sensor circuit has to operate a motor to reverse its direction.

MONITORING TEMPERATURE CHANGE

The use of electronic devices to monitor the well being of patients is perhaps most obvious in special care baby wards.

It is important for the survival of premature babies that the temperature of their environment is carefully controlled. Very small babies (below 1 kg) need to be kept at approximately 37 °C and those who are slightly bigger at the slightly lower temperature of 36.3 °C.

It is for this reason that the ward temperature is kept uncomfortably high for adults. However, extra heating is still required in the immediate area of the infants.

To monitor the skin temperature a thermistor can be lightly attached to the baby's skin. This provides feedback to the heater positioned above the baby. The heater can then be turned on only when the temperature falls too low.

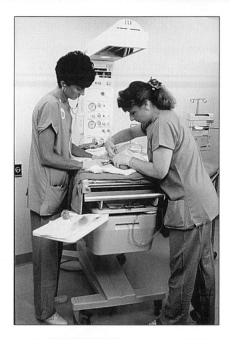

MONITORING TEMPERATURE RANGES

When sensing many physical quantities it is useful to be able to set a maximum and a minimum level and to allow for alternative outputs according to which limit has been reached.

For example, you could monitor the exact temperature of a greenhouse. If the temperature rose too high then a fan vent could be operated. If the temperature became too low then a heater could be switched on.

The system would be continuously switching the two outputs on and off. One of the outputs would always be on.

A better system would set an acceptable range of temperatures. When the temperature exceeds the upper limit or falls below the lower limit, then the appropriate output is switched on.

A circuit that uses 'op amps' (operational amplifiers) is shown in Figure 4.52 and this can be adapted for many sensor types.

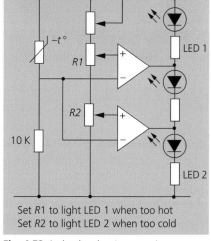

Set *R1* to light LED 1 when too hot
Set *R2* to light LED 2 when too cold

Fig. 4.52 *A circuit using 'op amps'*

PASSIVE INFRA-RED (PIR) SENSORS

Passive infra red (PIR) sensors are a common feature of many security alarms and lighting systems. They use pyroelectric devices to detect changes in infra-red radiation in the area being surveyed. The infra red given off by warm objects is received by the sensor and this information is split into a number of zones. By comparing the zones and reacting to changes over time it is possible to react to intruders.

This is in contrast to active infra-red sensors that react to the light received from an infra-red light source (as with a slotted opto, see page 35).

The associated electronics and optics of these systems at the moment means that for school projects it is necessary to purchase them as ready-made units. The output of the unit is usually made via a small reed relay.

P.I.R zones
Side view

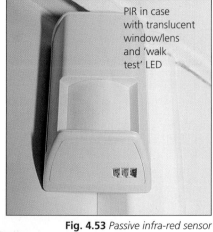

PIR in case with translucent window/lens and 'walk test' LED

Fig. 4.53 *Passive infra-red sensor and side view of PIR zones*

Vickers Medical are one company that make equipment that, amongst other functions, warms new born babies. This equipment is of two types: the radiant heater, which allows easy access to the baby but which leaves the baby exposed to possible cooling effects of draughts, and the incubator, which restricts access to the baby.

The radiant heaters need very powerful heat sources to keep the temperature at the right level. It is therefore essential that the sensors are reliable as any failure could result in the baby becoming too hot or cold and becoming distressed.

In practice the temperature of any controlled environment will never stays exactly constant but will vary between an upper and lower limit.

Watch how an electric oven or iron tries to maintain the temperature between set limits. You can see this by looking at the temperature indicator light (this shows when the heater is on).

SENSING SMALL CHANGES

Strain gauges (sensing forces)

To sense changes in the length of the components in a structure, and hence the strain that is being exerted on them, strain gauges can be attached to the part to be tested. These gauges are very thin wires that move with the structure. When these wires are stretched their resistance changes. To see this change in resistance a resistor arrangement called a Wheatstone bridge is used.

In the circuit (Figure 4.54) a dummy gauge (a second gauge) is used to compensate for any temperature changes that might affect the active gauge that is being measured. The output from the Wheatstone bridge is balanced with VR1 (to get all four resistors exactly equal). VR2 adjusts the amplification of the 741 IC and VR3 allows the needle of the ammeter to be set at the centre of the dial before the test starts.

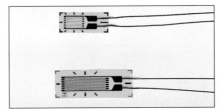

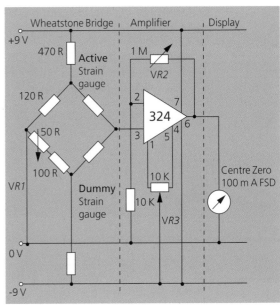

Fig. 4.54 *Strain gauge and Wheatstone bridge circuit*

SENSING SMALL LIGHT SIGNALS

Fibre optics

When sending a message over a long distance it is possible for the signal to be corrupted (confused). This is often due to interference from other electrical equipment or by electrical storms.

By replacing wires with a glass fibre it is possible to send coded light pulses. This is known as fibre optics. The light signals cannot be corrupted and have the advantage of being able to carry more data than a conventional wired link. Figure 4.55 shows a fibre optic source and sensor.

Fig. 4.55 *Fibre optic source and sensor*

39

SENSORS – EXTENSION MATERIAL

Touch sensors

These work by allowing a small flow of electricity through your body. The change in resistance between the two contacts in the circuit (Figure 4.56) allows the circuit to sense that a touch has been made. The circuit may only need one contact to be 'earthed'. This effectively joins the contact to 0 V. (Notice that it is an SR latch – see Chapter 7.)

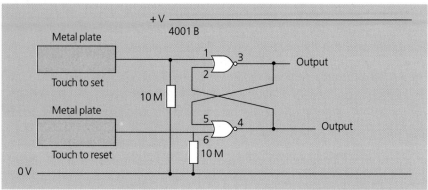

Fig. 4.56 *Touch sensor circuit*

Magnetism – a quick response

A Hall effect switch (Figure 4.57) is quicker than a reed switch, has no switch bounce and is often used to sense rotating shafts. It is commonly found on cycle trip computers. In dirty conditions it is better than an optical device like a reflective opto switch where the sensor could become obscured.

When the South pole of a magnet is near the output is low, and it becomes high when the magnet is removed.

Using a thyristor

A thyristor may be used as a latch to remember an input from a sensor (Figures 4.58 and 4.59).

A thyristor senses a signal in a similar way to a transistor but once turned on it cannot then turn off again unless the power is turned off or it is shorted out by a switch. For more information on how a thyristor works turn to Chapter 8.

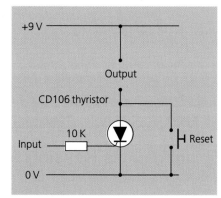

Fig. 4.59 *Thyristor circuit*

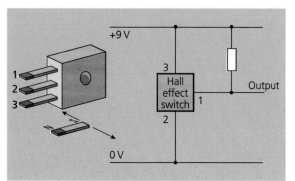

Fig. 4.57 *Hall effect switch circuit*

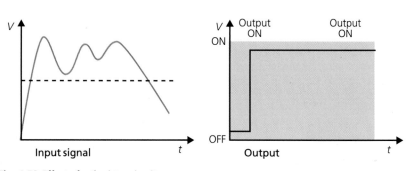

Fig. 4.58 *Effect of a thyristor circuit*

Schmitt triggers

'Cleaning up' a fluctuating signal

Sometimes a signal that is constantly changing by small amounts can confuse the rest of a system. This is particularly true when a logic circuit follows on as the next stage. In this case a Schmitt trigger can be used to create a 'deadband' (Figure 4.60). This has the effect of removing an uncertain area and makes for more positive switching than is possible with a transistor or amplifier alone. Figure 4.61 shows the symbol for a Schmitt trigger. Note how the symbol within the NOT gate is a representation of the graph.

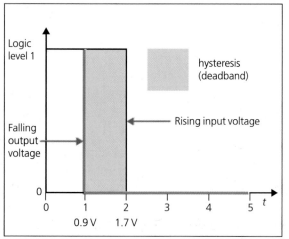

Fig. 4.60 *Graph to show the action of a Schmitt trigger*

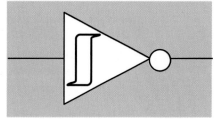

Fig. 4.61 *Schmitt trigger symbol*

Using a Schmitt trigger and an analogue sensor

A voltage divider that includes a sensor that has a variable resistance does not always provide a signal that is decisive enough for digital circuits. Figure 4.62 shows one arrangement of a Schmitt trigger with an LDR that will give a definite on or off signal even though the light levels vary in an analogue fashion. This is a simple example of an analogue to digital converter. Note that the signal is also inverted. Figure 4.63 shows a similar circuit where an adjustable light level sensor is followed by a Schmitt trigger. Notice that the schmitt trigger inverts the signal again.

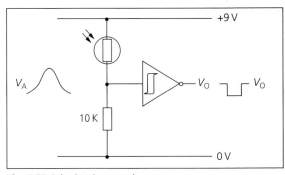

Fig. 4.62 *Schmitt trigger and an analogue sensor*

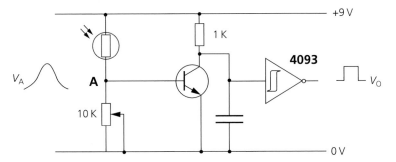

Fig. 4.63 *Adjustable light level sensor followed by a Schmitt trigger*

Switch bounce and a Schmitt trigger solution

Sometimes it is necessary to remedy a problem known as 'switch bounce'. Mechanical switches rely on small conductors touching when moved together to make a connection. When the two conductors are very close the current can jump the gap and cause not just one pulse to be made but a series of very quick on and off signals (Figure 4.64). This can be disastrous when these signals are fed into a circuit capable of registering very fast signals. For example, a counting circuit could register not just one key press but many and add them to its count.

Should you include switch de-bouncing when designing a system? For much school-based work this is not necessary, but it is a problem that you will need to be aware of. For most systems it is quite easy to add a Schmitt trigger (Figure 4.65) after some initial modelling of your design if it proves to be necessary.

Remembering a signal and de-bouncing it

An alternative method of providing a crisp 'clean' digital pulse from a mechanical switch is to use a pair of logic gates (see Chapter 7) to make an SR latch. This can be an attractive solution if you have a pair of spare NAND gates (or NOR gates if the switch and resistors are swapped round). This method is shown in Figures 4.66 and 4.67.

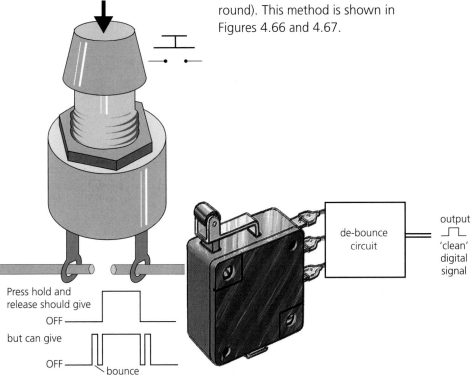

Fig. 4.64 *The problem of switch bounce*

Fig. 4.66 *Using logic gates to de-bounce a signal*

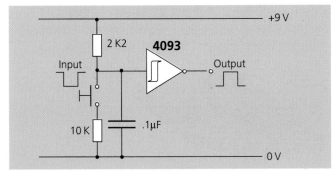

Fig. 4.65 *A Schmitt trigger solution to de-bounce a signal*

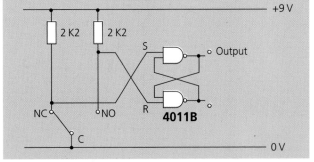

Fig. 4.67 *Circuit for logic gate method of de-bouncing*

Putting it into practice

1. A bimetallic strip forms part of many temperature sensors. Explain clearly how they work and give some examples of domestic appliances that use these strips.

2. When a car or refrigerator door is opened a switch operates a light. Explain what sort of switch is used and how it works.

3. A reed switch is a magnetic switch. Why is it not suitable for sensing the number of turns that an anemometer (an instrument for measuring wind speed) makes in a minute?

4. A weather vane needs a set of eight sensors to detect the position of a rotating shaft. Suggest and justify your choice of sensor for this.

5. To sense atmospheric pressure a sealed flexible metal container is used. The vacuum inside the metal case means that it changes size as the pressure on the outside varies (Figure 4.68). Show how this movement can be converted into an electrical signal using either a strain gauge OR a variable resistor.

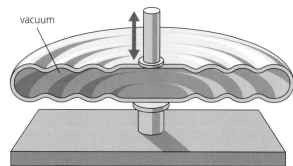

vacuum

Fig. 4.68

6. To record the number of hours of sunshine, a sensor is needed as part of a voltage divider. Show by using a diagram how this voltage divider could be made so that strong sunlight would produce a high output signal and dull light a low voltage signal.

7. When would a membrane switch be a useful method of making a switch?

8. Figure 4.69 shows a voltage divider that includes an NTC thermistor. What does NTC mean? Copy the graph and complete it to show how the output voltage would vary if the sensor was first cooled then heated.

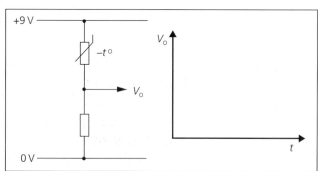

Fig. 4.69

9. Describe what is meant by switch bounce. Why is this a problem in fast counting circuits?

10. Draw two remedies for switch bounce.

11. A weather station needs to record the amounts of rainfall that occur each day. List some of the design problems that an electronic solution would have to take into account.

12. How is a relay able to act as an interface (Figure 4.70) between two electronic circuits?

Fig. 4.70

13. A diode is commonly found connected across the coil connections of a relay (Figure 4.71). Why is this?

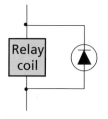

Fig. 4.71

14. A student has an idea that involves making a simple card reader. The card will have a series of black and white stripes (Figure 4.72) on it to carry a code (like some library cards).

Fig. 4.72

After some research she finds that supermarket bar code readers use low power lasers to do this. However, lasers are too expensive for her project. Can you suggest a more appropriate solution?

15. An observant student notices that car wash tokens are just rectangles of plastic with a pattern of holes drilled into them (Figure 4.73). Suggest how the car wash senses which programme has been purchased with the token. Suggest how the sensor works.

Fig. 4.73

5·Amplification

TRANSISTORS

The transistor is probably the most important component used in electronics today. You will recognise its use as a discrete (separate) component, but it is also to be found in integrated circuits in which there may be several thousand. Why are transistors used in electronic circuits? Many of the sensors described in this book only provide a very small output current or voltage. To provide a practical working circuit it may be necessary for the designer to amplify this current or voltage in order to drive an output device, e.g. a bulb or light emitting diode (LED).

Fig. 5.1

Types and identification

There are two types of transistor:

  i) the bipolar (NPN and PNP)
  ii) the field effect (FET).

Both types come in a variety of encapsulations (styles of case in which the transistors are packaged) and each has three connections.

These connections are very important as they must be connected in the correct way if the transistor is to work. The symbols and connections for these types of transistor are shown in Figure 5.2.

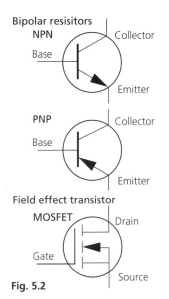

Fig. 5.2

Which transistor to use?

As can be seen from Figure 5.2, you have the choice of two types of transistor: bipolar and field effect. The bipolar is the more commonly used transistor in school projects and you will find many examples of its use in this and other books.

The bipolar transistor

There are two kinds of bipolar transistor: the NPN and the PNP. These terms describe the structure, a sandwich of N (negative)-type and P (positive) -type material. Your choice will depend on which way you want the current to flow through the transistor, as shown in Figure 5.3. This choice will often be NPN transistor.

Fig. 5.3

Each transistor has three connections (legs): the emitter (e), the base (b) and the collector (c). Once you have chosen the type of transistor, you will need to identify its encapsulation as well as the position of its connections. This information will usually be found in a supplier's catalogue.

A common transistor used in schools is the BC108. This comes in the TO18 case. The diagram of the transistor in Figure 5.4 shows the position of the legs when viewed from underneath the case.

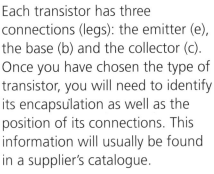
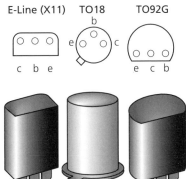

Fig. 5.4

Design issues – using transistors

1. What type of transistor will be needed?
2. Which leg is the emitter, which leg is the base and which leg is the collector?
3. How much current will the transistor be expected to carry through the collector/emitter connections?
4. How will you bias the base of the transistor and how can you work out the resistor values needed?
5. Will the transistor act as a voltage source or a current source?

Deltronics is an electronics company situated in Carmarthenshire in Wales. They design and make a wide range of electronic equipment for a number of companies and also sell directly to schools. For a number of years Deltronics have made computer control interfaces (sometimes called 'buffer boxes'). Computers are expensive pieces of equipment and can be

damaged if too much current is drawn from their input/output ports (connections). Buffer boxes enable the small current signals from a personal computer to be amplified to provide much larger current outputs. This increase in current is needed if the computer is to be able to switch on electrical devices such as bulbs, relays, motors, etc. It is important that any interface is designed to ensure that no damage will occur to the computer when it is used to switch on these relatively high current devices.

How the transistor works

Figure 5.5 shows a simple schematic view of a transistor circuit when it is to be used as a switch. Figure 5.6 shows a light sensing circuit. In this example R_1 is a variable resistor, R_2 is the light sensor (see Chapter 4) and R_3 is a resistor in series with an LED.

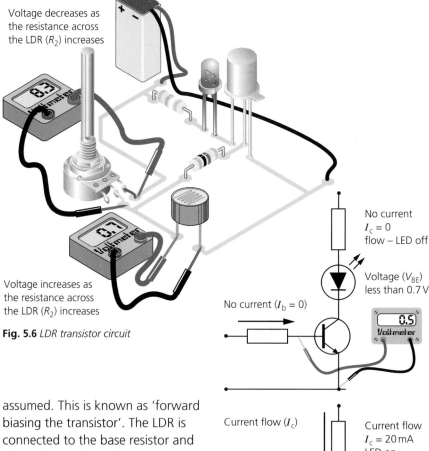

Voltage decreases as the resistance across the LDR (R_2) increases

Voltage increases as the resistance across the LDR (R_2) increases

Fig. 5.6 *LDR transistor circuit*

No current $I_c = 0$ flow – LED off

Voltage (V_{BE}) less than 0.7 V

No current ($I_b = 0$)

0.5 *Voltmeter*

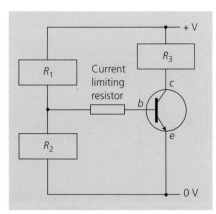

Fig. 5.5 *Transistor circuit switch*

Biasing the transistor

The light sensor (LDR) and the variable resistor form a potential (voltage) divider (see Chapter 4, page 30). As the light decreases the resistance of the LDR increases. As a result the voltage across it increases (see Figure 5.6). In order to 'switch on' a transistor a voltage between 0.6 V and 0.8 V is required between the base and the emitter (V_{BE}) as shown in Figure 5.7. For most practical purposes a value of 0.7 V is

assumed. This is known as 'forward biasing the transistor'. The LDR is connected to the base resistor and the emitter. When the voltage across the LDR is above 0.7 V current will flow into the base of the transistor. This will 'switch on' the transistor and current will then flow between the collector and the emitter. This current flow would light up the LED providing enough current flows into the base when the voltage V_{BE} is above 0.7 V (Figure 5.7).

Current flow (I_c)

Current flow ($I_b > 0$)

Current flow $I_c = 20$ mA LED on

Voltage (V_{BE}) 0.7 V

0.7 *Voltmeter*

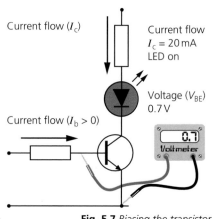

Fig. 5.7 *Biasing the transistor*

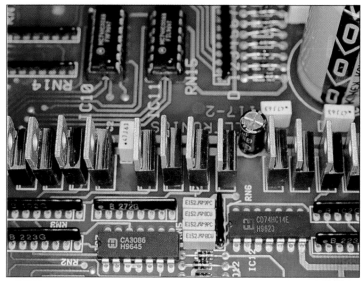

To achieve this amplification Deltronics have made use of transistors in their buffer boxes. The types of transistors used in the buffer box shown in the photo on the left are bipolar transistors, of which both NPN and PNP types have been used. A transistor array (a number of single transistors in one package) is used to amplify the signal which in turn switches on a power darlington transistor. This power darlington transistor uses a current source provided by the interface's own internal mains power supply, which can provide 6 volts or 12 volts with a current rating of about 2 amps. It can be seen from the photo on the right that the buffer box uses a large number of transistors. In fact there is a total of 40 transistors used to amplify the eight output lines and the four motor control circuits.

CHOOSING THE TRANSISTOR

The base resistor

If there was no resistor in series with the base of the transistor, the current flow into the transistor could become excessive. When constructing a transistor switching circuit a base current limiting resistor should always be included. For most practical purposes a value of between 1K and 2K2 should be acceptable.

The collector current

When choosing a transistor it is important to know what current is expected to flow into the collector (I_c). For example, a standard LED typically has a maximum current rating of 20 mA.

Transistor gain

The values of I_c and I_b are used to find out what gain (h_{FE}) is required. For example, in a circuit where the collector current (I_c) was calculated to be 20 mA and the base current (I_b) 0.05 mA:

$$I_c = 20\,\text{mA} \qquad I_b = 0.05\,\text{mA}$$
$$\text{Gain} = I_c \div I_b = 20 \div 0.05 = 400$$

When the calculations have been made, look in the supplier's catalogue at the transistor data from which you can make your choice. For the circuit shown in Figure 5.6 the specification could be:

Type: NPN
V_{ce} (max): 9 V
I_c (max): 20 mA
h_{FE}(min): 400

A transistor that matches this specification could be the BC108.

Transistor gain

$$h_{FE} = \frac{I_c}{I_b}$$

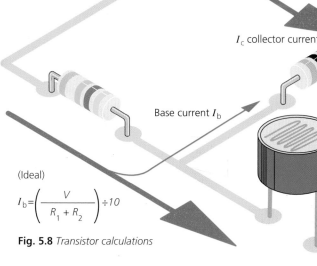

I_c collector current

Base resistor

Base current I_b

Emitter current
$I_e = I_c + I_b$

(Ideal)

$$I_b = \left(\frac{V}{R_1 + R_2}\right) \div 10$$

Fig. 5.8 *Transistor calculations*

Part of Deltronics' product range includes sensors. Most of the sensors they produce can be connected to the buffer box shown on page 44, but some require additional electronics to amplify their output signal. Two such sensors are the pH probe and the magnetic field probe (which you can see on the right). The magnetic field probe has been designed so that the amplifier is built into the casing whereas the pH probe has a separate external amplifier (see bottom right). The design problem faced by Deltronics when designing the circuits for these probes was different to that of the buffer box. Whereas the buffer box required high current outputs, the probes required the signal output to be amplified and any variations in the strength of the magnetic field or pH level to be shown as an increase or decrease in voltage levels.

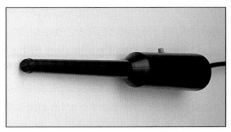

Magnetic field probe

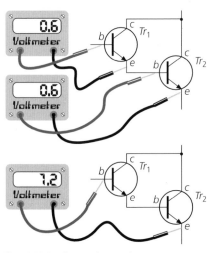

pH Probe amplifier

pH Probe

DARLINGTON PAIR

The variation of gain (h_{FE}) between types of transistors can be anything between 40 and 800. Often the gain required will be much more than that obtained by the use of a single transistor. In the circuit shown in Figure 5.9 initial calculations showed that a gain of 13000 was required to amplify the current so that the relay would operate. This gain is far more than could be obtained by a single transistor. The circuit solution shown in Figure 5.9. makes use of a transistor configuration called a Darlington pair.

This arrangement of transistors increases the gain by the product of each discrete transistor. For example, if Tr_1 and Tr_2 each have an h_{FE} of 150 then the gain of this arrangement is 150 × 150 = 22500.

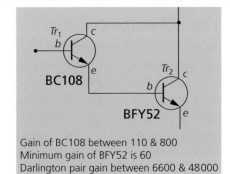

Gain of BC108 between 110 & 800
Minimum gain of BFY52 is 60
Darlington pair gain between 6600 & 48000

Fig. 5.10 *Darlington pair*

The two transistors do not have to be of the same type. On examining transistor data sheets it will be found that transistors that can carry large currents do not have a high gain (h_{FE}). It can be seen from the list of transistors in the extension section on page 51 that the BFY52 can drive a current of 1 A, but it only has a gain of 60. A useful combination could be a BC108

coupled with a BFY52 (Figure 5.10) which would have a minimum gain of 6600 (110 × 60) and a possible gain of 48000 (800 × 60) and would be able to drive a current of 1 A.

Biasing the Darlington pair

A single silicon transistor requires a minimum voltage of 0.6 V before current is able to flow between the collector and emitter. When two transistors are connected together to form a Darlington pair the base emitter connections of each transistor act like a potential divider. This means that 1.2 V is required to bias the transistors (Figure 5.11).

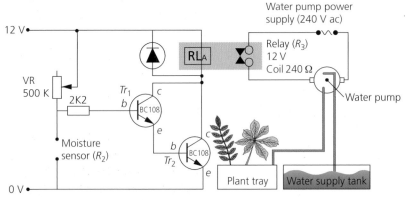

Fig. 5.9 *A moisture sensor system*

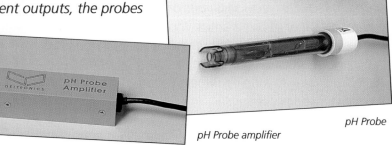

Fig. 5.11 *Darlington base voltage*

Deltronics' solution to the problem was to use operational amplifiers (see page 48). Both circuits are principally the same and measure the difference between two input voltages. This difference is controlled to provide an output that will be measured by the analogue interface connected to the computer. It is also worth noting on the pH probe circuit (which you can see on the right) how one of the operational amplifiers is used as a buffer by using a voltage follower configuration (see page 50). This is because the pH probe has a high impedance.

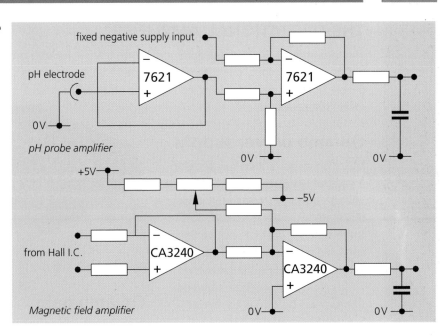

TYPES OF TRANSISTOR SWITCHES

There are two types of transistor switching circuits: a voltage switch and a current switch. When using the transistor as a voltage switch (Figure 5.12a), the load is a resistor and a connection is made between this and the collector. If the transistor circuit is to be a current switch (Figure 5.12b), then the load will be an output device such as a bulb, LED, relay etc. The voltage switch can be used to provide a voltage source for another component, such as a transistor, a 555 timer (see Chapter 6), or an input for a logic gate (see Chapter 7). It is important to understand that when the transistor is forward biased and is turned on the voltage output will be low. This is illustrated in Figure 5.13. The circuit in Figure 5.14 shows a transistor voltage switch used as an inverter. When *Tr1* is off *Tr2* is on and vice versa.

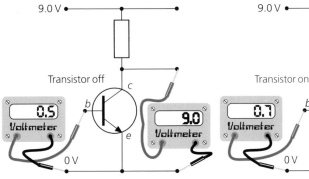

Fig. 5.13 *Transistor as a voltage switch*

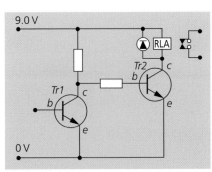

Fig. 5.14 *Voltage switch inverter*

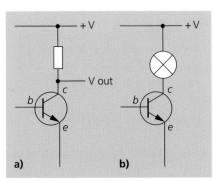

Fig. 5.12 *Transistor outputs*

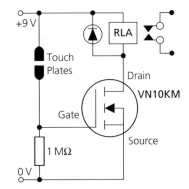

Fig. 5.15 *Touch switch*

Field effect transistors (FET)

The bipolar transistor amplifies the current at its base in order to gain an increase in voltage or current. The FET amplifies the voltage at its gate in order to gain an increase in voltage or current. One of the advantages of the FET is that very little current is drawn into the gate compared to that of the base of a bipolar transistor.

Bridging the touch plates shown in the circuit of Figure 5.15, the voltage at the gate will increase which will then energise the relay.

The voltage required to switch on the FET will typically be between 0.8 V and 2.0 V. Care must be taken when handling MOSFET as they can be damaged by static electricity.

THE OPERATIONAL AMPLIFIER

The 'op amp', to use its more common name, is an integrated circuit device that is used to amplify the difference between two input voltages. The 741 (Figure 5.16) is one of the most common op amps and comes in an 8-pin dual in line (DIL) package.

Op amp power supply

Many op amps, but not all, require a positive ($+V_s$) and negative ($-V_s$) voltage supply. Power supply units (PSU) are available which provide these dual supplies of positive and negative but two batteries can be used by connecting them in series. The common connection between the two will be zero volts. Figure 5.17 shows how this is done.

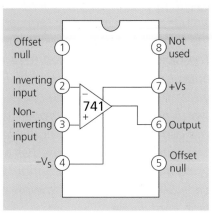

Fig. 5.16 *The 741 op amp*

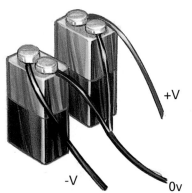

Fig. 5.17 *Dual power supply*

Op amp inputs

The op amp has two inputs, the inverting input and the non-inverting input. The + and – symbols shown at the input connections in Figure 5.18 should not be confused with the power supply connections. These symbols indicate the state of the resulting output (V_O) which is dependent on the differences between these two inputs. There are three possible states:

   i) if $V_I > V_N$ then V_O is negative
   ii) if $V_I < V_N$ then V_O is positive
   iii) if $V_I = V_N$ then V_O is zero

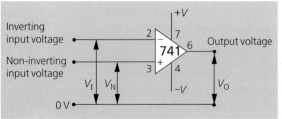

Fig. 5.18 *Op amp inputs*

Op amp gain

The voltage difference between the two inputs is amplified to produce a voltage gain(A_O). This voltage gain (A_O) can be as high as 100 000 (10^5) times. However, the output voltage cannot be any greater than the power supply voltages. In practice the 741 can only output a voltage to within about ±2 V of its power supply connections.

Therefore, if $+V_s$ at pin 7 is +9 V then the output cannot be greater than +7 V. Op amps such as the 3140 can provide outputs which are very close to their $+Vs$ and $-Vs$ but these are more expensive. The voltage output is calculated using the equation:

$$V_O = A_O \times (V_N - V_I)$$

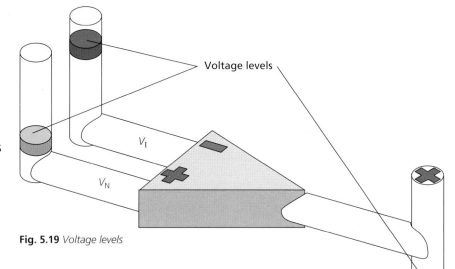

Fig. 5.19 *Voltage levels*

> ## Design issues – using op amps
> 1. Will a general purpose op amp like the 741 do what is needed?
> 2. What type of power supply and voltage will be needed?
> 3. Will the current capacity of the op amp be sufficient or will additional components be needed?
> 4. How will the op amp be used: as a comparator, a voltage amplifier or a differential amplifier?
> 5. Will the op amp require feedback? If so will it be positive or negative and how much?

THE OP AMP COMPARATOR

When the op amp is used as a comparator, it performs a similar function to a transistor when used as a switch. The two input voltages are compared. If one is more positive or negative than the other the output is turned fully on (saturated) or off depending upon the result (see page 48 under 'Op amp inputs').

Figure 5.20 shows an op amp being used as a comparator in a moisture sensor circuit.

The design and calculations required for this circuit are quite simple. Using the value of 20 K for the moisture sensor all other resistor values, to the inverting and non-inverting inputs, can be the same. The potential dividers (the two 20 K fixed resistors and the moisture sensor with the variable resistor) are arranged to split the supply voltage equally. If the moisture is at just the right level both potential dividers will have an output of 6 V. For this condition:

$V_I = V_N$ therefore V_O is zero

If the moisture level is low then the moisture sensor's resistance will increase. This will cause the inverting input voltage to drop and be lower than the non-inverting input voltage. Therefore:

$V_I < V_N$ and V_O will be positive.

If V_O is positive the transistor will be turned on, energising the relay.

Comparator inputs/outputs/gain

The gain of the op amp is impressive. But what is the difference required at the inputs (V_N and V_I) to switch the op amp fully on? Remember:

$$V_O = A_O \times (V_N - V_I)$$

Therefore, the difference:

$$V_N - V_I = V_O \div A_O$$

If the output is 10 V and the gain is 100 000 then:

$$V_N - V_I = 10 \div 100\,000$$

$$= 0.0001\,V\ (0.1\,mV)$$

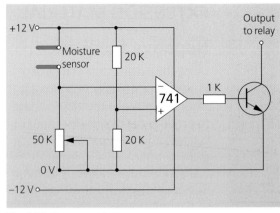

Fig. 5.20 *Op amp moisture sensor*

Comparator array

Op amps do not just come in single form. The LM324 and LM348 are quad op amps, which means there are four op amps per integrated circuit (IC). The LM324 (Figure 5.21) is designed for a single power supply whereas the LM348 is for the more common dual supply. When a circuit requires more than one amp these devices should be considered. The circuit shown in Figure 5.22 is a moisture level sensor. Each of the op amps is used as a comparator which will light up an LED for different levels of moisture. This is determined by the value of the resistors in series with non-inverting inputs. The arrangement used in this circuit will turn on the LEDs when the moisture sensor is between the values of 10 K and 22 K. Adjustment is provided by use of the 20 K variable resistor.

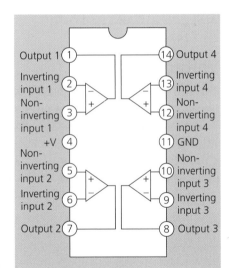

Fig. 5.21 *The 324 op amp*

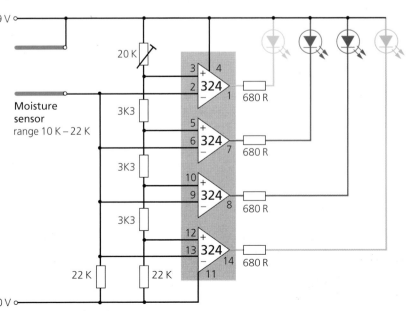

Fig. 5.22 *The LM324 Quad op amp used in a moisture level sensor circuit*

EXTENSION MATERIAL

Negative feedback

Using the op amp as a comparator is useful but it simply amplifies any small difference in the input voltage to produce the maximum output voltage. This is known as open loop gain. By using negative feedback we can gain greater control of the op amp and amplify the input signals (voltage) by specific amounts.

Negative feedback works by feeding back some of the output of the op amp to the inverting input. Figure 5.23 shows two op amp circuits: (a) an inverting amplifier and (b) a non-inverting amplifier. As the name suggests the inverting amplifier circuit will invert the polarity of its output to that of the input. Therefore, if the input is negative the output will be positive and vice versa. With the non-inverting amplifier the output polarity will remain the same as the input polarity. The gain for the two circuits is given by:

$$\text{Inverting amplifier} = -Rf \div Ri$$

For example, if $Rf = 100\,\text{K}\Omega$ and $Ri = 10\,\text{K}\Omega$ then the gain would be $-100 \div 10 = -10$. If the input (Vin) was 0.5 V, then the output would be −5.0 V.

$$\text{Non-inverting amplifier} = 1 + (Rf \div Ri)$$

For example, if $Rf = 100\,\text{K}\Omega$ and $Ri = 10\,\text{K}\Omega$ then the gain would be $1 + (100 \div 10) = 11$. If the input (Vin) was 0.5 V, then the output would be 5.5 V.

Using negative feedback

Figure 5.24 shows a moisture sensor circuit which produces a range voltages at the output of the op amp. This voltage range is fed into an LED bar graph display driver IC (LM3914) which is wired to produce a dot display (only one LED is lit at any one time).

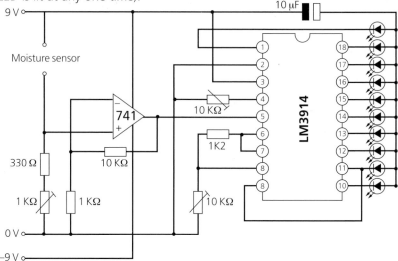

Fig. 5.24 *Moisture sensor circuit*

Voltage follower

If all the output is fed back directly to the inverting input then a special kind of negative feedback circuit is produced. The circuit is shown in Figure 5.25. The voltage gain is very close to 1 and therefore the output voltage is virtually the same as the input voltage at the non-inverting input. This circuit is useful as a buffer amplifier when a very high impedance is needed. An example of where it could be used is the input terminal of a voltmeter where it is important not to draw current from the circuit being tested.

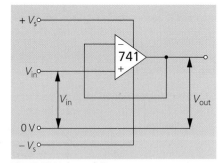

Fig. 5.25 *Voltage follower*

Summing (adder) op amp

The op amp circuit shown in Figure 5.26 is used to 'add' a number of input voltages. 'Sound mixers', microphones, etc. use this type of circuit.

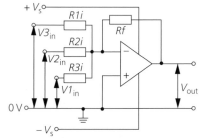

If the input resistors are unequal then:

$$\frac{-V_{out}}{Rf} = \left(\frac{V1_{in}}{R1i}\right) + \frac{V2_{in}}{R2i} + \frac{V3_{in}}{R3i}$$

if they are equal then:

$$V_{out} = \frac{RF}{Ri}\left(V1_{in} + V2_{in} + V3_{in}\right)$$

where $Ri = \left(R1_i + R2_i + R3_i\right)$

Fig. 5.26 *Summing amplifier*

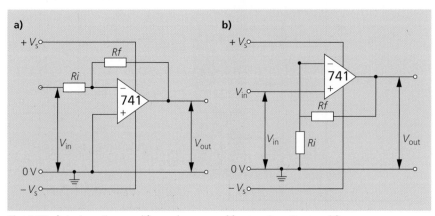

Fig. 5.23 a) *An inverting amplifier and*   **b)** *a non-inverting amplifier*

Transistor calculations and formulas

When designing transistor circuits for the first time the amount of information and calculations can be daunting. However, using a few simple calculations, designing your own circuits from scratch will help ensure that your circuit meets the precise design considerations which you have specified and works efficiently.

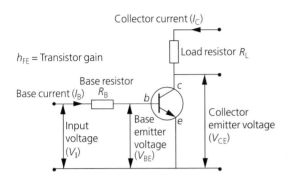

$$V_I = I_B R_B + V_{BE}$$

$$I_B = \frac{V_I - V_{BE}}{R_B}$$

$$R_B = \frac{V_I - V_{BE}}{I_B}$$

$$I_C = \frac{V_{CC}}{R_L}$$

$$h_{FE} = \frac{I_C}{I_B}$$

$$V_{CE} = V_{CC} - I_C R_L$$

Fig. 5.27

Fig. 5.28 *Transistor with heatsinks*

Where high currents pass between the collector and the emitter excessive heat may be generated and this must be dissipated or damage to the transistor may occur. Heatsinks are used to help dissipate the heat. They come in many forms one of which is illustrated in Figure 5.28.

Application:
Transistors can often be interchanged with other types. However, some have special properties. This information will indicate its main use and help in deciding if it is suitable for the purpose intended.

NPN transistor data

Type	Case	Ic (max) mA	VCE (max) V	hFE min/max	Power mW	Application
BC108	TO18	100	20	110–800	300	General
2N3035	TO39	700	40	50–250	5000	General
BFY52	TO39	1000	20	60 min	800	General
ZTX300	E-Line	500	25	50–300	300	General

PNP transistor data

Type	Case	Ic (max) mA	VCE (max) V	hFE min/max	Power mW	Application
BC178	TO18	100	25	125–500	300	General
2N2907A	TO18	600	60	100–300	400	General
ZTX500	E-Line	500	25	50–300	300	General

Transistor selection

The tables shown above contain the sort of information which must be considered before selecting a suitable transistor.

The case:
This will indicate the shape and physical size of the transistor to be used and the position of the connections.

I_C (max):
It is important that you calculate the amount of current that will pass through the collector. Check and make sure that the transistor is capable of passing this amount of current.

V_{CE} (max):
You must make sure that this voltage is larger than that of your power supply.

Power (mW):
If the circuit is designed so that the transistor switches on quickly then the power rating will not normally need to be considered, with the exception of those circuits passing high currents. The formula for power is:

Power = V_{CE} (0.7 V) × I_C (45mA)

Try this:

For the specification below choose two transistors to make a Darlington pair.

Material	– NPN
Case	– not too large
I_C (max)	– 600 mA
V_{CE} (max)	– >12 V
h_{FE} (min)	– Tr1 × Tr2 => 5000
Power	– 0.7 V × 45 mA (typical)
Application	– general purpose

Summary of Transistor Selection Calculations

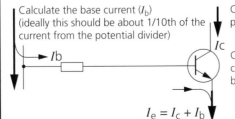

Calculate the base current (I_b) (ideally this should be about 1/10th of the current from the potential divider)

Calculate the current that will pass through the collector (I_c)

Calculate the gain (h_{FE}) by dividing the current to pass through the collector (I_c) by the base current (I_b)

$$h_{FE} = I_c / I_b$$

$$I_e = I_c + I_b$$

Check to make sure the transistor will be turned on quickly. When you multiply $h_{FE} × I_b$ the answer should be greater than the value required for I_c

Fig. 5.29

Putting it into practice

The diagram shown in Fig. 5.30 is of a transistor switching circuit.

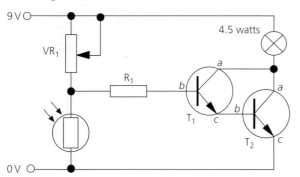

Fig. 5.30

1. Will the light bulb come on when it is light or when it is dark?

2. Why should a resistor R_1 always be included in a transistor switching circuit?

3. What is this arrangement of transistor called?

4. If the two transistors are of the silicon type what would be the minimum base voltage required to turn on the bulb?

5. If the two transistors were replaced by a single transistor the emitter base voltage would change. Explain why.

6. Briefly describe the function of VR_1 within this circuit.

7. The transistor T_1, has a gain of 300 and transistor T_2 has a gain of 40. What is the hfe of this transistor arrangement?

8. The designer has used two different transistors in the circuit in order to maximise the gain. Explain why.

9. Which of the transistors shown in the data table (Fig. 5.31) would not be suitable for the circuit shown in Fig. 5.30?

Transistor	Type	hFE	Ic (MA)	Vce
BC 107	NPN	110–450	100	45
ZTX500	PNP	50–300	500	25
BFY 51	NPN	40	1000	30
2N2905	PNP	100–300	600	60
ZTX300	NPN	50–300	500	25
ZTX651	NPN	100–300	2000	60

Fig. 5.31

10. Which transistor from those that could be used has the highest gain?

11. Which transistors from those listed would you use for **a)** T1 and **b)** T2?

12. Choose two suitable transistors from those in the data table and calculate the minimum and maximum possible gain? Show your workings.

13. If the operational amplifier shown in Fig. 5.32 is used as an open loop differential amplifier and V_1 and V_2 are equal the output at V_0 should be 0V. In practice this is almost impossible to achieve. Explain why.

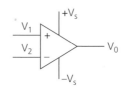

Fig. 5.32

14. What is the gain of the operational amplifier shown in Fig. 5.33?

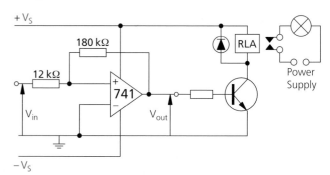

Fig. 5.33

15. If the input voltage Vin is 60mV, what would be the output voltage?

16. Give two advantages of negative feedback systems when using an operational amplifier.

17. Why is the transistor necessary to drive the relay?

18. What is the minimum supply voltage that would be required if the maximum input voltage was to be 1 volt and the designer of the circuit did not wish the 741 to reach saturation.

19. What voltage would you expect to find at each of the inverting inputs in the circuit shown in Fig. 5.34?

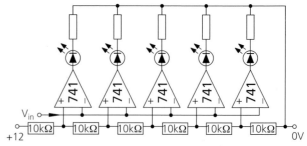

Fig 5.34

20. Explain what happens as the voltage at Vin is increased from 0V to +12 V.

21. The 741 integrated circuits in Figures 5.33 and 5.34 are being used in two different ways. By what name are these two applications known?

6·Timers and timing

TIMING

Often you need to be able to set a time period while an output is turned on. An example of this is the timer on a microwave oven (Figure 6.1). Alternatively, a device may need to be off for a set time until it needs to come on. Problems like these need a type of timer called a monostable.

Synchronizing time

To cope with the problem of providing a stream of pulses or clock beats a second type of timer is needed. This is known as an astable and it can be likened to a conductor beating time to an orchestra.

A very fast astable is to be found at the heart of a computer (Figure 6.2). It is called a clock and it controls the pace of operations inside the machine. Computer clock frequencies are quoted in MHz.

How do circuits keep time?

At the heart of all timing circuits there has to be some form of control (which can be compared to the pendulum on a mechanical clock). Most timing circuits that you will meet use a resistor and capacitor to control the timing. The use of resistors and capacitors is explained on pages 54–55.

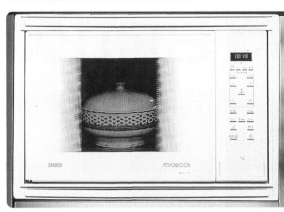

Fig. 6.1 *A microwave oven uses a timer called a monostable*

Fig. 6.2 *A computer uses a very fast astable called a 'clock'*

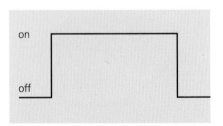

Fig. 6.3

Monostables

Monostables are used to time a set period, as with an egg timer. This is what we would normally associate with a timer. At the end of the set time the state of the output changes. For example, an LED which was off comes on and will then go off again after the set time. This can be shown by means of a timing diagram (Figure 6.3).

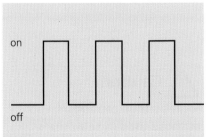

Fig. 6.4

Astables

In electronics a circuit that gives a regular pulsing signal is also called a timer. This too can be shown by means of a diagram (Figure 6.4).

The frequency (speed of pulsing) can vary from very small fractions of a second to days or months. The unit used to measure frequency is the Hertz (Hz), where 1 Hz = 1 pulse per second. This beat signal is also referred to as a clock pulse and is abbreviated to CK or CLK on diagrams.

▷ Design issues – timers

When designing you may need to consider …

1. Whether you will need an astable or a monostable.

2. How fast an astable will need to pulse.

3. How long a monostable will have to time.

4. How accurate the timer will need to be. This may later affect the type of timer that you can use.

5. What will trigger (start) the timer and if it will need to be reset (cancelled).

6. What the eventual output of the timer will be.

SEIKO

Seiko are well known for producing precision timepieces. They also produce complete timing systems for sporting events providing athletes, trackside spectators, judges and television viewers with a wealth of timing data. Each sport requires a tailor-made system which must conform to the stringent competition rules for each event. For example, systems for track events that use starting blocks have to incorporate advanced sensors to detect the pressure that an athlete places on the blocks. This is monitored and graphed on a computer and used to detect false starts.

World class athletics demands that the timing systems used must be 100% reliable, even when the weather conditions at winter events may cause the temperature to drop to –20°C. Electronic equipment must be waterproofed, and cabling and displays must be reliable at sub-zero temperatures if accurate data is to be obtained.

TIME DELAYS

Using a resistor and capacitor to create a delay

The use of a resistor and a capacitor is at the heart of a great many timing circuits. They are used to regulate the action of the timer.

A capacitor can store an electric charge. You can think of a capacitor as having the ability to behave like a short-term rechargeable battery. If you run down or empty a battery it is said to be discharged and when filled again we say that it has been fully charged. This is the same with a capacitor. The delay is created by the fact that it takes time to charge the capacitor.

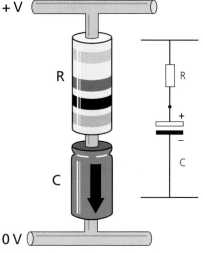

Tap = resistor

Bucket = capacitor

Fig. 6.5 *Using a resistor and capacitor*

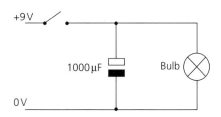

To increase the time taken to charge a capacitor you can either increase the size of the capacitor or restrict the flow of current into it by using a resistor. The larger the value of resistor, the slower the flow of current into the capacitor. This can be compared to slowing the flow of water into a bucket by using a tap (Figure 6.5).

> ## ⚠ Caution!
>
> High-voltage capacitors, such as those used in televisions and some camera flash units, can contain a very high charge, which can be dangerous. Do not touch the leads of these items, even if the power is off!

> ### Try this:
>
> Set up the circuit shown in Figure 6.6. Check that the capacitor is connected the correct way round. Then switch on. What happens? Now switch off and see what happens. Try to explain your results. Remember that a capacitor can act like a short-term battery.

+9 V

1000 μF   Bulb

0 V

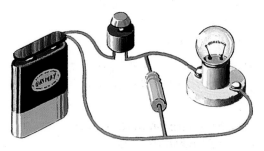

Fig. 6.6

The timing system for a downhill skiing race is triggered when the skier passes through the start gate (a flexible bar connected to a switch). You can see this in the photo on the left. The progress of the skier is monitored by measuring times at intermediate stages of the race. This helps to inform spectators and enables comparisons to be made between skiers as the event proceeds. The timings are made using photo-electric beams which are positioned across the track. These sensors are carefully aligned and need to be kept free of build-ups of snow and ice. The system constantly monitors the condition of the sensors and is able to switch to back-up units if problems occur.

The data produced is processed by computer and relayed instantly to giant scoreboards and to television networks world-wide. On the right you can see a diagram of a complete timing system used for Alpine ski events.

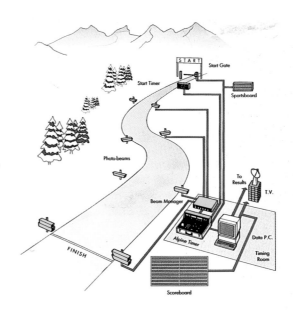

Checking a capacitor

To see how 'full' a capacitor is and how fast it is charging, use the display of a voltmeter connected in parallel with the capacitor (Figure 6.7). By detecting when a set voltage has been reached it is possible to create time delays. One way of detecting a set level is to use a transistor (or Darlington pair, see Figure 6.8).

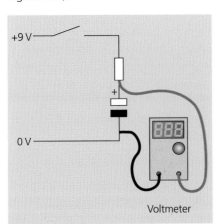

Fig. 6.7 *Using a voltmeter to see how fast a capacitor is charging*

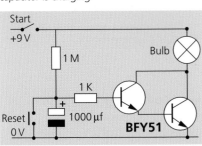

Fig. 6.8 *Using a Darlington pair to detect the charge level*

Resistor/capacitor network (monostable)

Figure 6.8 shows a Darlington pair (see Chapter 5) used to sense when the voltage across the capacitor reaches 1.2 volts. Remember, this can be imagined as a bucket filling (Figure 6.9). The level in the capacitor ('bucket') starts at 0 V and rises until eventually it is full (at 9 V). In this circuit, however, a level of 1.2 V is being used to trigger the Darlington pair turning on the output. This can be thought of as a hole in the side of the bucket which will indicate when 1.2 V has been reached.

Fig. 6.9

Discharging a capacitor

To discharge or empty a capacitor you can simply short circuit it or you can discharge it through a resistor.

Figure 6.10 shows a circuit that allows you to use either of these options. Which route do you think will empty the capacitor more quickly, A or B?

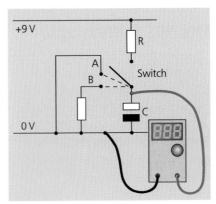

Fig. 6.10

Try this:

Using the circuit shown in Figure 6.8, try to predict the time delay that will result if the values are R = 1 Mega Ohm and C = 1000 µF.

The formula t = CR will predict the time taken to charge to 6 V not 1.2 V.)

Use the extension material on pages 62–63 to help you.

A TIMER IN A 'CHIP'

The 555 integrated circuit

An integrated circuit (IC) is simply a package that includes an array of components on a silicon 'chip'. If you have not met this idea before then turn to page 118 for more basic facts about ICs.

The 555 or triple 5 timer IC (Figure 6.11) is a very versatile chip which first appeared in 1972. Since then it has become a firm favourite with electronic designers.

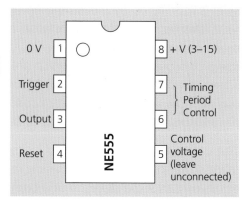

Fig. 6.11 *The 555 integrated circuit*

555 variations

There are some very ingenious uses to which a 555 can be put, but it has two main functions: that of astable and monostable timer. Although it contains the equivalent of forty transistors and resistors it still needs an external resistor and capacitor to give the times required.

There are some very useful books that feature the 555 timer alone but this chapter gives some basic starting points.

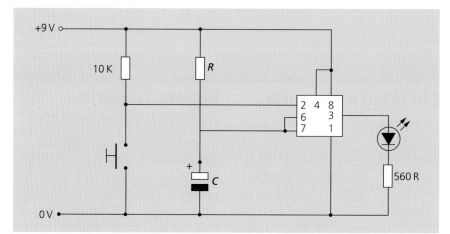

Fig. 6.12

The 555 monostable

Compare the circuit shown in Figure 6.12 with the pcb layout in Figure 6.13. Notice that the layout of the pins in Figure 6.12 is not in a logical order. This is often true with circuit diagrams that include ICs. Make sure that you remember this when designing a circuit layout.

To alter the time period, vary the values of R and C (see the extension material on page 62 for the formula).

+9 V

Trigger input   1

Output

0 V

Fig. 6.13 *A possible pcb layout*

Both these components need to be selected from a range of fixed values (preferred values) that can be purchased. Check these in the reference section (pages 112 and 114).

Limitations

The 555 monostable is often quoted as having very long theoretical time delays but in practice they are limited to about 20 minutes maximum. (For longer times see page 63.) However, once set up the delays are repeatable and are not affected by changes in the voltage of the battery.

Resetting

The circuit shown in Figure 6.12 can form the basis of many variations which can start an output, or turn it on for set times. It is also possible to cancel the action of the timer by resetting. To cancel the timing a connection is made to pin 4 (see Figure 6.14).

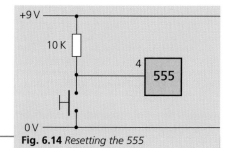

Fig. 6.14 *Resetting the 555*

Hints:

For most work it is good enough to use the formula $t = C \times R$ instead of $t = 1.1\,CR$ (see extension material on page 62).
If you must have a fairly exact time period, then use a variable resistor so that the time can be adjusted.

MANIPULATING THE BASIC MONOSTABLE CIRCUIT

555 monostable combinations

To make some of the more common combinations of input and output using a 555 choose one of the input (triggering) options and one of the output options shown below. Connect these to pins 2 and 3 respectively.

Input (triggering) options

Some triggering options (which all connect pin 2 to 0 V):

Output options

Some of the output options that can be connected to pin 3:

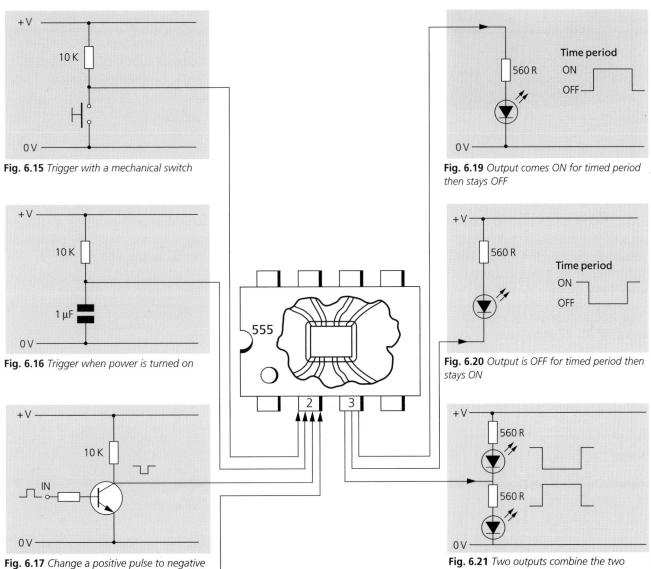

Fig. 6.15 *Trigger with a mechanical switch*

Fig. 6.16 *Trigger when power is turned on*

Fig. 6.17 *Change a positive pulse to negative (simple NOT gate action)*

Fig. 6.19 *Output comes ON for timed period then stays OFF*

Fig. 6.20 *Output is OFF for timed period then stays ON*

Fig. 6.21 *Two outputs combine the two options at the same time*

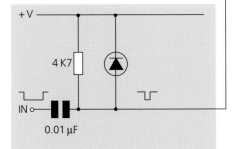

Fig. 6.18 *Convert a long pulse to a short useful pulse to avoid re-triggering the 555*

Try this:

It is possible to use the information in this section to design a quiz timer. Aim to design a timer to signal that 'time is up'. Decide first what would be desirable on such a timer and then check that your solution has the following.

1. Your circuit will need to have values for a resistor and capacitor, to control the time delay.
2. Show what will start the timer. (See also Chapter 4 on Sensing and switching).
3. Will it be necessary to reset the timer? Why is this so?
4. Show on your circuit an output that you think might be suitable. (See also Chapter 8 on Output devices.)

PROVIDING CLOCK PULSES

It does not seem strange to us today that clocks in say London and Aberdeen should display the same time. However, this has not always been the case. The necessity for a universal time first became apparent with the spread of the railway network.

Today 'real time' is defined by a laboratory in Paris (BIPM). This time standard, called Universal Time, is available in Britain from the National Physical Laboratory (NPL). The NPL transmits a time signal as a longwave radio signal at a frequency of 60 kHz. This signal enables radio-controlled clocks to remain in time with the NPL clock. The time signal is briefly turned off every second for either 1/10 of a second or 1/5 of a second. The duration of the pause is used to form a binary code to signify the occurrence of each second, minute, hour, etc. (The code uses the 1/5 sec breaks as a binary 1 and the 1/10 sec breaks as a binary 0.)

The 555 astable

The 555 chip is also used to build an astable. It is capable of providing a regular clock pulse from pin 3. The frequency of the pulses is usually given in Hz (pulses per second).

To alter the frequency change the values of *R1*, *R2* and *C* (see Figure 6.22). *R* is in Mega Ohms and *C* in µF (see the extension material on page 62 for the formula to use).

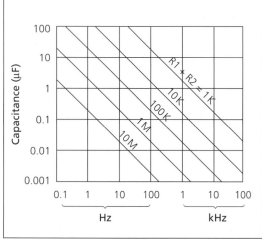

Fig. 6.22 *Graph to approximate values for C, R1 and R2*

This formula becomes much less reliable as the value of the capacitor gets larger. For more accurate results, use a preset or cermet resistor for *R2*, then fine tune the circuit using an oscilloscope (see the extension material on page 62.)

The 555 astable circuit

Figure 6.23 shows a 555 astable circuit, which for most purposes is accurate enough. However, if much greater accuracy is needed then a crystal-based astable can be used (see the extension material on page 63.)

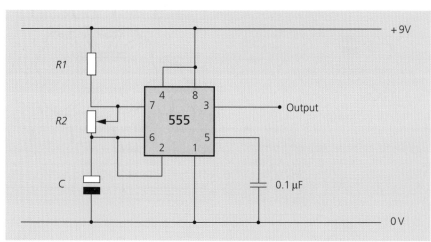

Fig. 6.23 *A 555 astable circuit*

Practical layout for a PCB

As with the monostable, the component layout for a printed circuit board (PCB) has to be slightly different to the circuit diagram. Don't forget that ideally you should always model the circuit to check that it operates correctly and will work with other parts of your system. Figure 6.24 shows a possible PCB layout for an astable.

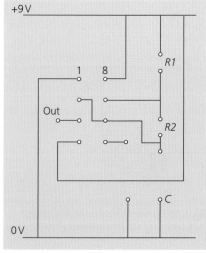

Fig. 6.24 *Component side view*

The code bits are weighted according to the position in the string of numbers being sent. The day codes, for example, are weighted 4, 2 and 1 (e.g. Tuesday would be 010).

As a consequence radio-controlled clocks are able to tune into this signal which is kept to within 1 millionth of a second of 'real time'.

Once turned on radio-controlled clocks and watches should never need adjustment. They will automatically keep in time with the transmitter even changing to suit the transfers between 'Winter' and 'Summer' time. One company that make such clocks is Junghans.

To conserve power most clocks only sample the time signal. To sample the time signal the receiver has to be turned on for a period that will capture sufficient information to regulate the clock with the hour, month, year etc.

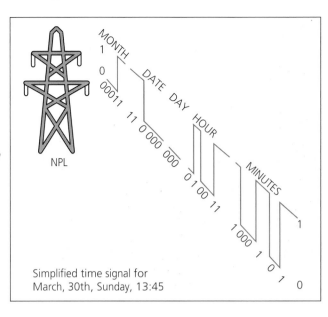

Simplified time signal for March, 30th, Sunday, 13:45

Variations available when using the 555 astable

Using an LDR

Try using an LDR instead of *R2* (Figure 6.25). The output frequency will then depend on the light falling on the sensor.

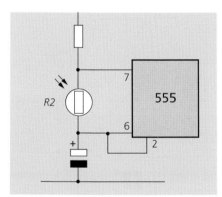

Fig. 6.25 *Using an LDR*

Output to a loudspeaker

By choosing very fast frequencies and adding a capacitor and loudspeaker it is possible to produce a reasonable tone circuit (Figure 6.26).

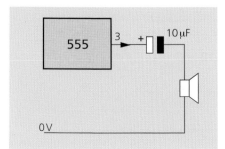

Fig. 6.26 *Output to a loudspeaker*

Using two outputs

Try using two outputs at the same time, one connected from pin 3 to + V and the other to 0 V (Figure 6.27). They should then alternate.

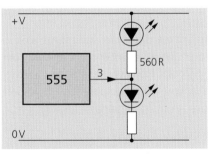

Fig. 6.27 *Using two outputs at the same time*

High current outputs

To pulse outputs that require higher current use a single transistor, Darlington pair of transistors (see Chapter 5) or a relay (Figure 6.28).

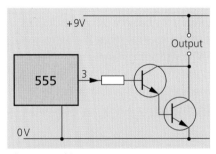

Fig. 6.28 *Pulsing outputs*

555 problems

In both astable and monostable modes the 555 can be affected by electrical interference ('noise' or spikes) from the power supply lines. This can occur when switching on the power and can cause the circuit to trigger prematurely.

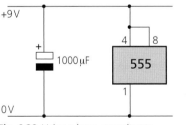

Fig. 6.29 *Using a large capacitor to overcome noise problems*

It can also cause noise for other circuits. If this becomes a problem then insert a large capacitor between the + V and 0 V lines (Figure 6.29).

If you find that the timing of the 555 is still inaccurate then make sure that your power supply is 'smoothed' or better still use a battery and recheck.

When wired as a monostable, the 555 can be too sensitive. To reduce this problem keep any wires to pin 2 as short as possible and if possible twist the pair of trigger wires together.

Quartz crystals enable very cheap clocks and watches to perform with almost the same precision as expensive rotary movements. Quartz crystals are therefore used in nearly all electronic timepieces. They are used at the heart of the timing circuit to provide a steady stream of fast pulses. This is achieved by slicing quartz crystals very thinly and putting a conductive layer on each side of the slice. When quartz is squeezed it produces a small voltage, the reverse is also true – i.e. when a voltage is applied across the crystal it changes shape (this is known as the piezo electric effect). The way the crystal is sliced effects the frequency at which it vibrates. Changes in temperature have a negligible effect on quartz crystals and most clocks and watches are accurate to within at least half a second a day.

To be used in timepieces a crystal is cut that will vibrate at the frequency of 32,768 Hz (this is a binary multiple). To slow down the very fast pulses into a usable form a divider circuit is used.

ALTERNATIVES TO USING A 555

Although the 555 is a very useful IC, it is often easier to use another method. For example, an astable can be made from two NOT gates which might be spare in a logic IC from another part of the system. Or a more complex chip may save on design time, number of components and circuit space.

LED flasher IC LM3909

This IC (Figure 6.30) was developed initially for battery powered devices in order to show that the battery was still functioning. One use has been in domestic smoke alarms. It will run for many months flashing an LED brightly using a very small current.

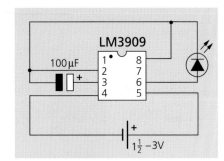

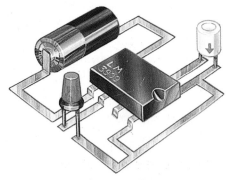

Fig. 6.30 *LED flasher IC LM3909*

Using a pair of NOT gates to make an astable

Logic gate astables can be used to replace 555 astables. This at first might seem to make little sense as a logic gate IC is larger than an eight-pin 555 chip. However, it is often the case that you will have spare logic gates left over from other parts of your system.

Figure 6.31 shows a pair of NOT gates used to make an astable. It is also common to use a pair of NAND gates (Figure 6.32). (If this is unfamiliar, refer to Chapter 7.)

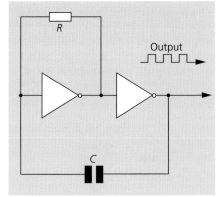

Fig. 6.31 *Using a pair of NOT gates*

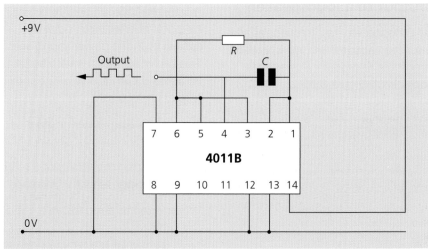

Fig. 6.32 *Using a pair of NAND gates*

By repeatedly dividing by two (fifteen times) a frequency of 1 Hz is obtained. The 1 Hz can then be used to change a display showing seconds elapsed. Further division enables extra digits to be updated. For instance, dividing the 1 Hz output by ten will give a signal that can change a display showing tens of seconds and so on.

The output from quartz-controlled clocks can either be in the form of the changing digits on a Liquid Crystal Display (LCD) or the more traditional analogue display, which uses rotating hands. Quartz clocks that have hands do not need as much electronic control as LCD clocks, because once the 1 Hz signal has been generated it is then fed to a motor that drives the hands of the clock. The division of seconds into minutes and hours is done mechanically using a gear train.

Inside a quartz watch

Divider chains

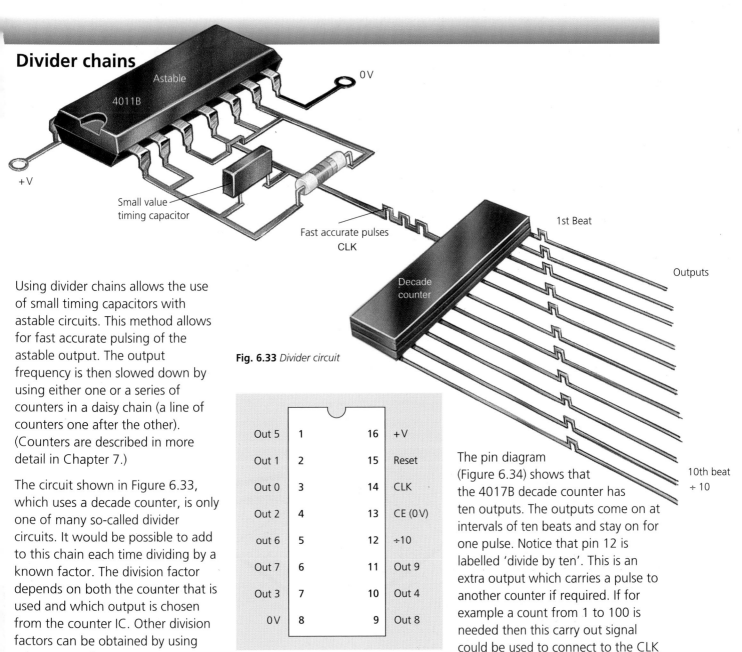

Fig. 6.33 *Divider circuit*

Using divider chains allows the use of small timing capacitors with astable circuits. This method allows for fast accurate pulsing of the astable output. The output frequency is then slowed down by using either one or a series of counters in a daisy chain (a line of counters one after the other). (Counters are described in more detail in Chapter 7.)

The circuit shown in Figure 6.33, which uses a decade counter, is only one of many so-called divider circuits. It would be possible to add to this chain each time dividing by a known factor. The division factor depends on both the counter that is used and which output is chosen from the counter IC. Other division factors can be obtained by using other types of counter.

Out 5	1	16	+V
Out 1	2	15	Reset
Out 0	3	14	CLK
Out 2	4	13	CE (0 V)
out 6	5	12	÷10
Out 7	6	11	Out 9
Out 3	7	10	Out 4
0V	8	9	Out 8

Fig. 6.34 *Pin diagram for 4017B decade counter*

The pin diagram (Figure 6.34) shows that the 4017B decade counter has ten outputs. The outputs come on at intervals of ten beats and stay on for one pulse. Notice that pin 12 is labelled 'divide by ten'. This is an extra output which carries a pulse to another counter if required. If for example a count from 1 to 100 is needed then this carry out signal could be used to connect to the CLK pin of a second decade counter IC.

TIMERS – EXTENSION MATERIAL

Motor speed control

A common problem found in project work using DC electric motors is that although they work well at high speed they tend to lack power when used to drive useful loads. One solution is to add a gearbox and slow the output mechanically. Another solution is to switch the motor on and off rapidly using an astable (Figure 6.35). The amount of time that the motor is 'ON' can be varied compared with the 'OFF' times. This is called the 'mark to space ratio'. The longer the 'OFF' periods are then the slower the motor revolves.

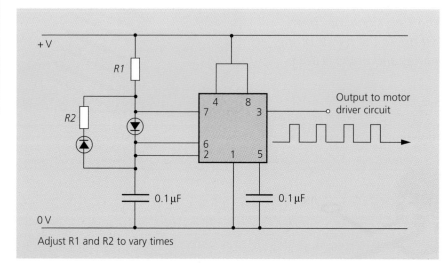

Fig. 6.35 *Motor speed control using an astable*

Timing formulae

Units: use Mega Ohms for *R* and μF for *C*.

To find how long a capacitor will take to charge through a resistor to two thirds full use:

$$t \text{ (in seconds)} = C \times R$$

This is known as the time constant.

To find the on time of a 555 monostable use:

$$t = 1.1RC$$

However, for most work it is quite accurate enough to use just *RC*.

To find the frequency of a 555 astable use:

$$f = \frac{1.44}{(R1 + 2R2) \times C}$$

Graphing the results

If you were to plot a graph of the voltage across a capacitor as it charges through a resistor then you could expect to get a result similar to that shown in Figure 6.36. If you did the same for a capacitor discharging through a resistor then the result would be as shown in Figure 6.37.

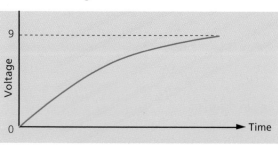

Fig. 6.36 *A capacitor charging*

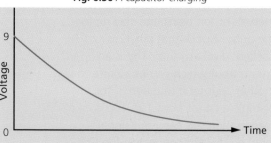

Fig. 6.37 *A capacitor discharging*

Calibrating an RC based timer

If an oscilloscope is available then it is possible to adjust the timing values of your resistor so that a guaranteed output frequency or delay is given (Figure 6.38).

A very fine adjustment is possible if a cermet resistor is used in the place of a normal variable resistor. With this type of resistor you make adjustments with a small screwdriver and need more turns/ travel than a preset resistor.

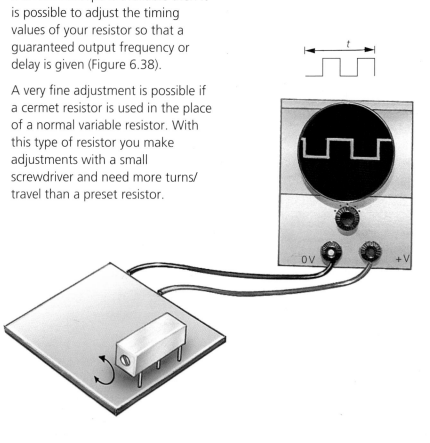

Fig. 6.38 *Calibrating a timer for greater accuracy*

More precision

Using a quartz crystal

A quartz crystal can be used instead of the resistor and capacitor combination. These crystals vibrate at very exact frequencies and are available in the range 10 kHz to 10 MHz. They are exact to about 0.001% or better if kept at an even temperature.

Using a fast astable

Figure 6.39 shows how a fast astable can be used to time a certain period. Obviously to gain a reasonable length of time it will be necessary to divide this frequency and detect when a certain number of pulses have been supplied. To do this you need to use one or more counters.

Using logic can help in detecting when a certain number has been reached (see Figure 6.39).

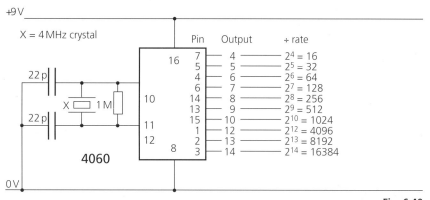

Fig. 6.39

Using a quartz crystal and a 14 bit 4060BE counter

When making a crystal-based oscillator (astable) the 4060BE counter is very useful as it contains a pair of NOT gates which can be used as shown in Figure 6.40. The counter can count up to 16384. However, the IC does not give every binary output – the outputs 2,4,8 and 2048 are missing. (To see how binary counting works refer to Chapter 7.)

Pin	Output	÷ rate
7	4	$2^4 = 16$
5	5	$2^5 = 32$
4	6	$2^6 = 64$
6	7	$2^7 = 128$
14	8	$2^8 = 256$
13	9	$2^9 = 512$
15	10	$2^{10} = 1024$
1	12	$2^{12} = 4096$
2	13	$2^{13} = 8192$
3	14	$2^{14} = 16384$

X = 4 MHz crystal

Fig. 6.40

A programmable timer using a UA2440

It is often convenient to be able to select timing values. The timer shown in Figure 6.41 incorporates an oscillator (astable) which needs you to add an external resistor and capacitor. The eight-bit counter inside the IC counts up to 255. Any multiple from 1 to 255 can be selected using switches. The timer can either be made to start again (in astable mode) by leaving out the 47 K resistor or left to reset itself and wait to be triggered. If you want the timer to start as soon as the power is turned on then add the extra trigger circuit in Figure 6.42.

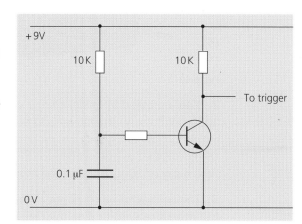

Fig. 6.42 *Power on trigger*

Values for Ct and Rt

Rt can be between 0.001 M Ohms and 10 M Ohms and *Ct* between 0.01 μF and 1000 μF.

If only pin 6 (value 32) switch is closed and *Ct* = 1000 μF and *Rt* = 1 M Ohm then the time period equals

$$1 \times 1000 \times 32 = 32\,000\,\text{sec}$$
$$= 8\,\text{hours }53\,\text{min }20\,\text{sec.}$$

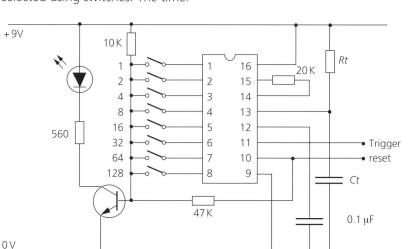

Fig. 6.41 *Time period = Rt × Ct × sum of closed switches*

Putting it into practice

To save energy the owner of a small block of flats wants to prevent the corridor lights from being left on all night. One solution might be to allow the lights to come on for a set time once a button has been pressed. A button could be sited on each floor of the building.

1. A number of press buttons are to be used. Each button should be capable of turning on the timer. To trigger and turn on the timer it is necessary to join the two trigger inputs briefly. Copy and complete Figure 6.43 so that any of the buttons can make the timer work.

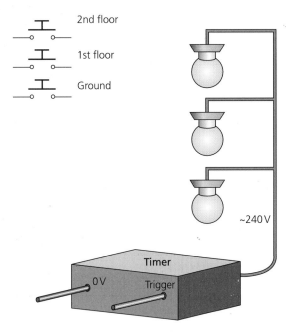

Fig. 6.43

2. You are asked to model a timer using a 555 circuit and a 9 V battery. The model is to be used to show the residents how the system will work. Draw a diagram of the circuit that will be needed for the model. Include a time delay of 30 seconds for the model.

3. The contractor who will put in the system says that it will need a relay to turn on the mains electricity. Explain how a relay will do this using a diagram to help. (Refer to Chapter 8 to help you.)

4. Some of the residents have expressed doubts about the system. It is feared that it could lead to people being left on the stairs when the lights go out. It also becomes clear that the lights had previously been left on to deter vandals.

Devise a system that uses a long-period timer to come on for a period of one hour (which corresponds to the period of highest risk when the caretaker is off duty). This will be a separate timer from the previous tasks and can only be triggered by the caretaker (see Figure 6.44).

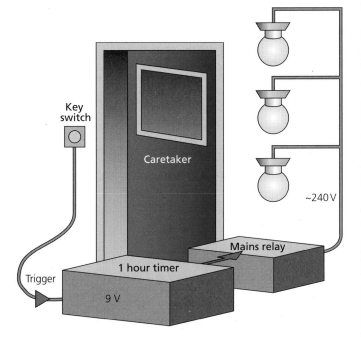

Fig. 6.44

5. After seeing the model and listening to the residents' views it is now agreed to go ahead with a system that includes features to please both the owner and residents (Figure 6.45). Draw a circuit diagram that combines the circuit used for the model of task 2 and includes the longer timer from task 4.

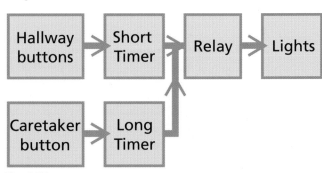

Fig. 6.45

7·Decisions, counting and memory

DECISIONS

Decision making in digital electronics is a bit like playing Twenty Questions, where you are only allowed to answer yes or no.

These yes or no states (answers) are the results of conditions that have to be met. For example: has the switch been pressed? Is the level of light in a photographer's darkroom too bright? Is the temperature of a liquid in a scientific experiment too low? Is the moisture content of the soil in a flower pot too low? Providing you know which switch, or the level of light, temperature or moisture needed then you can answer these questions with yes or no.

Fig. 7.1 *Automatic doors requiring a decision making circuit*

Depending on the answer, 'yes' or 'no', a predetermined (fixed) event will take place. The event that is to take place will have been determined by the circuit designer.

Some circuits will only require one condition to be met but many will require two or more. Figure 7.1 shows the automatic doors into a supermarket. This circuit could be designed so that the decision being made could be expressed in the following way: Is someone in front of the doors? Are the doors open? Are the doors closed? Is someone walking through the doors?

Try this:

Using the examples below write the questions you would ask in order to be able to answer either yes or no.

1. What conditions might be required for the control of a greenhouse?
2. In the event of a fire in a block of flats the lift should not be used. What conditions would you check in order to ensure that no one uses the lift but also to ensure that anyone in the lift when the alarm is raised is able to get out safely?
3. Domestic outside security lights are normally only turned on when certain conditions are met. What are these conditions?

The way in which electronic systems recognise these yes or no answers is to use circuit conditions which are either on or off. Circuits which work on the principle of being on or off are known as digital systems. It is important to remember that a digital system requires the state or condition to be answered by a simple answer of yes or no, as in the examples given above. Although the incoming information may be variable, the output needed for digital electronics will always be one of two states. For example, the answer to the question 'Is the temperature of the liquid greater than 80°C?' will always be yes or no even though the incoming information is variable, i.e. the temperature could be 69, 74 or 82°C.

▷ Design issues – decision making

1. What conditions must be met in order to get a 'yes' or 'no' decision?
2. Will all the conditions have to be met or only certain combinations in order for the decision to be made?
3. Will the conditions be checked constantly or at regular timed intervals?

4. What do you want to happen when the decision has been made, and what electronic output will be required to achieve this?
5. Will the conditions be decisive or is there a possibility that the condition could 'flicker' between a yes or no decision, e.g. a light source having to reach a certain level?

The 'Digital Age' is upon us. The impact of the compact disc, as one of the most successful consumer products of the 1980s, demonstrated many of the shortcomings of analogue technology. In broadcasting, analogue technology is being pushed to its limit through the industry's use of satellite and cable to provide more channels. Although such developments have transformed listening and viewing for many people, the limits of analogue technology are becoming a barrier to further expansion. Companies such as the BBC are, therefore, exploring and developing in the area of digital technology.

Digital signals are much more resistant to interference than analogue signals. This, along with new coding techniques used with digital technology means that the number of services can be greatly increased. Indeed, if the full potential of digital technology is realised, then the production, scheduling and transmission of audio-visual services will be revolutionised.

LOGIC GATES

Using electronic circuits to make decisions is very useful when designing systems. These circuits are not necessarily complex. The light bulb and push-to-make switch shown in Figure 7.2 can be thought of as a circuit in which a decision is being made. If the switch is pressed, turn on the light.

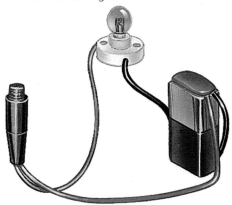

Fig. 7.2 *Simple circuit in which a decision is being made*

The circuits shown in Figure 7.3 each have two push-to-make switches. The way in which the two switches are connected together will determine when the light bulbs come on.

For the bulb to come on in the first circuit, both switches would have to be pressed at the same time. To light the bulb in the second circuit either or both of the switches have to be pressed.

The decisions being made in these two examples can be expressed in the following way. For the first circuit you might say: only turn on the bulb if switch one AND switch two are pressed. For the second circuit you might say: only switch on the bulb if switch one OR switch two OR both switches are pressed.

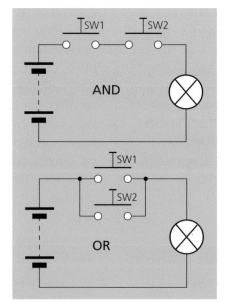

Fig. 7.3

The decision to turn on the bulb in first circuit was made by the AND condition whilst the second circuit needed an OR condition. These AND and OR expressions are known as logic gates and are represented by symbols shown in Figure 7.4. A and B are the input connections and Q is the output connection. Just as the output of a digital circuit can only be ON or OFF, the same is true of the inputs. If an input or output is ON then it is said to be 'high' or at logic 1. If the input or output is OFF then it is 'low' or at logic 0. With a two-input gate there are only four possible input conditions and these can be represented by a truth table. Figure 7.5 shows the truth table for these two gates.

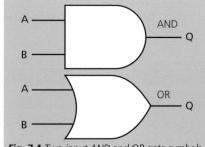

Fig. 7.4 *Two input AND and OR gate symbols*

Try this:

1. List all the possible input conditions of a three-input gate?
2. Write the truth table for a three-input OR gate.
3. Write the truth table for a three-input AND gate.

For customers, the most important change will be in the flexibility of services available. The two main constraints of analogue technology – channel scarcity and the lack of control by the audience – will disappear. Consumer choice will increase and, eventually, audiences may even be able to schedule their own programmes. There would be access to:

- television and radio services from all over the world
- movies on-demand
- music on-demand on radio
- a myriad of live sporting events
- new rock and pop videos at the moment of release
- home learning
- individual television programmes ordered from television libraries
- news on-demand

The AND gate

A	B	Q
0	0	0
0	1	0
1	0	0
1	1	1

The OR gate

A	B	Q
0	0	0
0	1	1
1	0	1
1	1	1

Fig. 7.5 *Truth tables*

The outputs to these gates can be inverted (changed around). This is done by using a NOT gate (Figure 7.6).

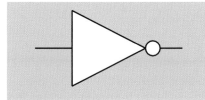

Fig. 7.6 *The NOT gate*

When a NOT gate is connected to the output of an AND gate it makes another type of logic gate called a NAND gate (NotAND). Connecting a NOT gate to the output of an OR gate will make a NOR gate (NotOR). These gates and their truth tables are shown in Figure 7.7. To simplify the symbols for these gates the triangle is removed and the small circle is placed on the output connection.

A logic gate where the output is at logic 1 if one or other of the inputs is on, but not both, is an eXclusive OR gate – XOR. The inverse gate to this is an eXclusive NOR gate – XNOR. These gates are shown in Figure 7.8.

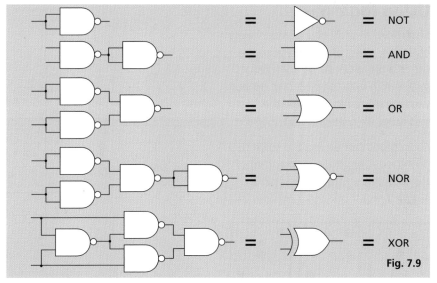

Fig. 7.9

Making logic gates from two-input NAND gates

It is possible to make up all the logic gates from two-input NAND gates, as shown in Figure 7.9.

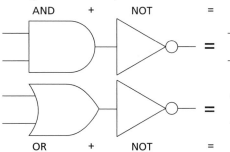

Fig. 7.7 *NAND and NOR gates and their truth tables*

A	B	Q
0	0	1
0	1	1
1	0	1
1	1	0

A	B	Q
0	0	1
0	1	0
1	0	0
1	1	0

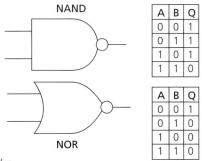

Fig. 7.8 *XOR and XNOR gates and their truth tables*

A	B	Q
0	0	0
0	1	1
1	0	1
1	1	0

A	B	Q
0	0	1
0	1	0
1	0	0
1	1	1

Digital techniques will allow many more services to be transmitted on existing delivery systems. New services will be added to those currently available on terrestrial cable, satellite and telecommunications systems (see the diagram on the right). Digital broadcasting systems will be exceedingly flexible. Operators will be able to choose between increasing the number of channels they offer or improving the quality of the pictures delivered – up to the point where television pictures may, ultimately, be as good as those in the cinema.

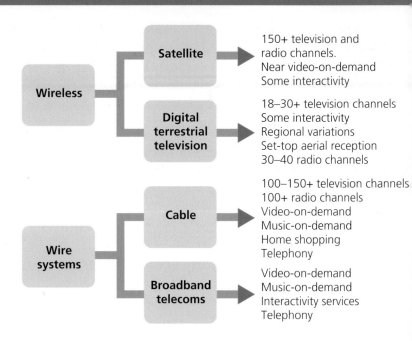

Wireless → Satellite: 150+ television and radio channels. Near video-on-demand. Some interactivity

Wireless → Digital terrestrial television: 18–30+ television channels. Some interactivity. Regional variations. Set-top aerial reception. 30–40 radio channels

Wire systems → Cable: 100–150+ television channels. 100+ radio channels. Video-on-demand. Music-on-demand. Home shopping. Telephony

Wire systems → Broadband telecoms: Video-on-demand. Music-on-demand. Interactivity services. Telephony

Using logic gates

Situation: a family plays a wide variety of games, many of which require the use of a die (dice). As part of a games system they want an electronic die but wish the display to represent the traditional die pattern (Figure 7.10).

Logic gates can be used to solve this problem. A block circuit diagram of the possible solutions is shown in Figure 7.11.

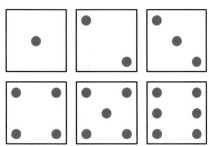

Fig. 7.10 *Die pattern*

System 1 generates six numbers (0–5 or 1–6). This is to be represented as a three-bit binary number – 0 0 0 to 1 0 1 (0–5). (See the extension material on page 79 for an explanation of binary numbering.)

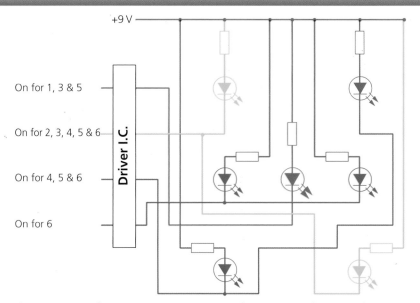

On for 1, 3 & 5

On for 2, 3, 4, 5 & 6

On for 4, 5 & 6

On for 6

+9 V

Driver I.C.

Fig. 7.12 *Layout of LED array*

System 2 uses combinational logic (a number of logic gates connected together) to interpret the binary number so that it will light up the correct LEDs.

System 3 will be an array (arrangement) of LEDs that will represent the spots of the die. A layout of the LED array is shown in Figure 7.12.

There are mathematical ways, using Boolean algebra, to work out the logic required for circuits such as this but for small combinational logic a step by step approach can be used to carefully analyse the logic required. Truth tables are used as part of this analysis. The truth table for the die is shown in Figure 7.13.

System 1 Inputs			System 3 Outputs			
C msb	B	A lsb				
0	0	0	On	Off	Off	Off
0	0	1	Off	On	Off	Off
0	1	0	On	On	Off	Off
0	1	1	Off	On	On	Off
1	0	0	On	On	On	Off
1	0	1	Off	On	On	On

Fig. 7.13 *Die truth table*

System 1:	System 2:	System 3:
Generate a number which represents the values of one to six inclusive (e.g 0–5 or 1–6).	Process the number to provide a driver for an LED display.	LED display which represents the dots of a die.

Fig. 7.11 *Block diagram of possible solutions*

At the same time, the equipment used to receive these services – in the home, school and workplace – will grow in sophistication and capability. These changes will happen gradually, but over time consumers will be able to re-equip their homes with a variety of audio-visual equipment, such as:

- *television sets offering the benefits of large flat screens and high definition picture quality*
- *built-in computer capability enabling viewers to interact with broadcasts in the same way as they do with a computer disc*
- *personal computers with the ability to receive audio visual signals, so making it easier to call up the latest television news, or download educational programmes or other multimedia*

As with all technological developments, change will take time but the 'Digital Age' is here.

The logic

The middle LED (colour red) is the inverse (opposite) of the input A (lsb).

The red LED is NOT the output of input A.

The green LEDs only come on when the input C (msb) AND the input A (lsb) is at logic 1 (Figure 7.14).

The yellow LEDs are only off when each of the three inputs are at logic 0. Therefore, if input A OR input B OR input C are at logic 1 then the yellow LEDs are on. A three-input OR gate could be used for this or two two-input OR gates (Figure 7.15).

The blue LEDs are on when input A (lsb) AND input B are at logic 1 OR if input C is at logic 1 (Figure 7.16).

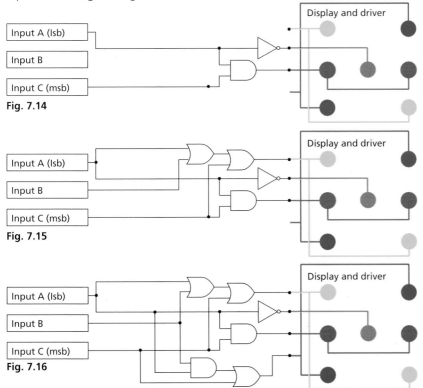

Fig. 7.14

Fig. 7.15

Fig. 7.16

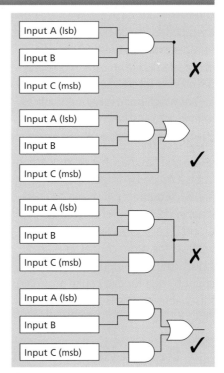

Fig. 7.17

Connections with logic gates

You might be forgiven for thinking that there is no need for the OR gate which controls the operation of the blue LEDs between the inputs A and B and the input C. It must be remembered that the outputs from logic gates must not be connected directly to the outputs from other devices, including other logic gates (Figure 7.17).

COUNTING

System 1 in the electronic die problem (page 68) required a sequence of binary numbers from (000, 001, 010, 011, 100, 101). When counting, each change of number is activated by a single clock pulse (Figure 7.18).

Counters can be made using logic gates. The logic gates are connected to form devices called flip-flops (see page 74) which in turn are connected together to make counters. However, because counters are so often used there are a variety of dedicated counter ICs available that can be used for many applications. The problem for the designer is which one to use.

The CMOS 4518B IC is a divide-by-ten counter (Figure 7.19). Counters are often described as 'divide-by-<number>'. The number indicates the total possible count, starting from zero. A divide-by-ten counter means that it counts from 0 to 9 at which point it will automatically reset to zero and begin the count again.

The 4520B (Figure 7.20) is a similar device and has the same pin connections but is a divide-by-sixteen counter. It has two counters which can be used independently. The connections A, B, C and D each provide a binary output, while all the other connections are inputs. The clock input increases the count by one for each pulse providing the enable input is high and the reset input is low.

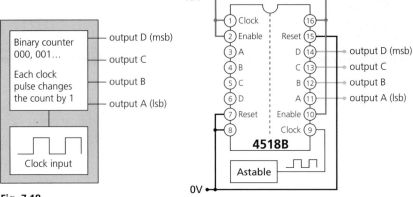

Fig. 7.18

Fig. 7.19 *CMOS 4518B counter*

Resetting the counter

To reset the counter back to zero before the end of its full count (0–9 or 0–15) the reset input (7 or 15) is made high (logic 1). To reset the counter back to zero at a specific number a logic gate system may be needed. For example, how would you reset the counter back to zero after a count of 5? The outputs C and B go high on a value of 6. These outputs would be connected to an AND gate with its output connected to the reset input. As soon as the counter tries to increase to six the counter will reset to zero (Figure 7.21).

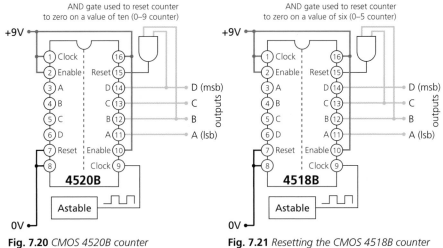

Fig. 7.20 *CMOS 4520B counter*

Fig. 7.21 *Resetting the CMOS 4518B counter*

Design issues – counting

1. Do you want the circuit to count the number of times a condition has been met, or an event has taken place or to count periods of time, e.g. in seconds or minutes?

2. Do you want your system to check how many times a condition has been met or an event has taken place during a specific time period?

3. Which input is used for the clock pulse to enable the counter to change its outputs by one?

4. Do you want the counter system be reset to zero? When would the counter be reset? Will the reset be done manually or automatically?

5. Which inputs have to be high and which have to be low in order for the counter to work (remember with CMOS all inputs must be connected)?

6. Do you want your system to display the number of times a condition has been met or an event has taken place? How do you want the number displayed – numbers, lights?

7. If a number greater than that for which the counter is designed is needed, e.g. 99, how will the ICs be linked together in order to count these larger numbers (cascade count, see page 72)?

Checking the inputs

It is important to find out if an input should be positive or at ground in order for the count to take place. When using CMOS you must ensure that all inputs are connected. Unused inputs should either be connected to the positive supply or the negative (ground) supply of the power source. The wiring diagram for a die is shown in Figure 7.22. A simplified circuit diagram is shown Fig. 7.23. Study both circuits carefully and see what has been done to the input connections that are not used.

> It is very important with CMOS that all inputs are connected. Any which are not used should either be connected to ground or +V.

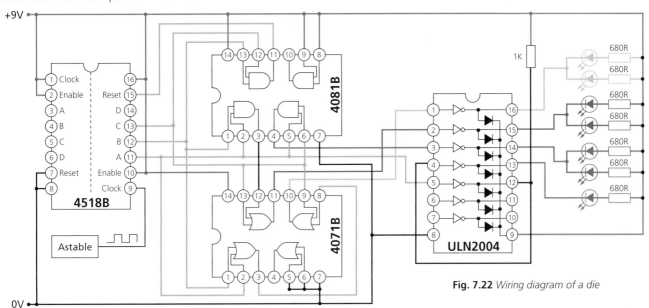

Fig. 7.22 *Wiring diagram of a die*

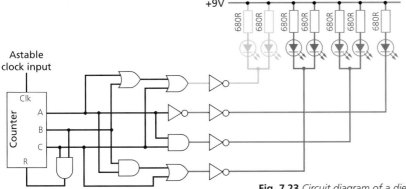

Fig. 7.23 *Circuit diagram of a die*

Decimal counting

Not all counters have binary outputs. Decimal counters are available which could be used for counting divisions or dot displays. Figure 7.25 shows a 4017 which is a divide by ten counter. Each time the clock input goes from ground to positive one of the LEDs will be turned on; all the others will be off. This could be used as a lap counter using a dot display to indicate the number of laps.

Counting down

There are times when a down count is required. Some counters are dual purpose in that they can count up or down. An example of this type of counter is the 4510 (Figure 7.24). By holding the pin 10 low the counter will decrease its count by one when the clock input goes from ground to positive.

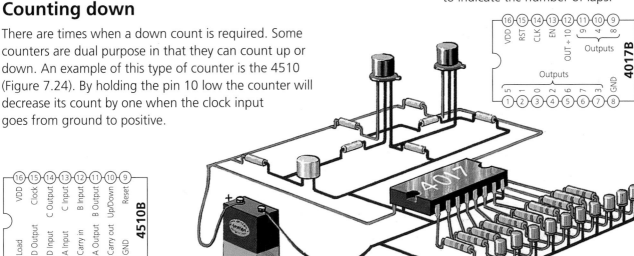

Fig. 7.24 *4510 up/down counter*

Fig. 7.25
4017 Decimal counter

71

Displaying numbers

Situation: The die project discussed earlier is to be enhanced. A family, when playing some games, wish to know the number of times a die has been 'thrown' up to maximum of 99.

It is important to draw the block diagram/s of possible solutions. The enhanced system is shown in Figure 7.26, which includes the solution to the earlier task of generating an electronic die (see page 68).

Binary coded decimal

The counter needed for system 5 is a divide-by-ten binary coded decimal BCD counter. In BCD the binary number is divided into groups of four bits. Each group of four bits counts from 0–9 only. This is shown in Figure 7.27. For more information see the extension material on page 79.

Cascading

The counter ICs described earlier do not count up to 99. Linking the counters together makes this possible. This is called cascading. The way in which you cascade the counters will depend on what sort of count you want. You may wish to count from 0 to 999, or display time (digital clock) in hours, minutes and seconds (e.g. 12:34:56). When displaying time you increase the minutes by one when the seconds count gets to sixty and return the seconds count to zero.

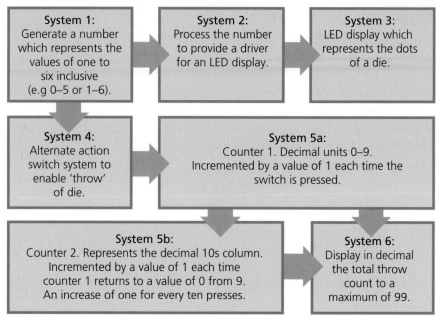

The 4518B IC has two counters and can be used to count up to 99. The wiring diagram for this is shown in Figure 7.31. You may wonder why the clock on the second counter is not used. The tens counter increases by one each time the first counter goes to zero (remember this is a decade counter and resets after 9 returning to 0). A four input NOR gate could have been used to detect this and connected to the clock input of the second counter. This would require another IC to be used and the designer should always look for ways of keeping the number of ICs to a minimum. The way in which this IC operates the use of the enable input has been exploited. It will advance the clock by one when the clock is low and the enable is made low. The D connection of the unit counter becomes low when resetting from 9 to 0.

Some of the solutions for cascading are more obvious than others. Some use 'tricks' exploiting the way the devices operate, as is the case with the CMOS 4518B and 4520B.

Fig. 7.26 *Block diagram of the enhanced die project*

The way in which counters are cascaded varies. You will need to research the relevant IC's data. Two other IC counters and methods of cascading are shown here. Note that the 4033B is a counter and seven-segment display decoder.

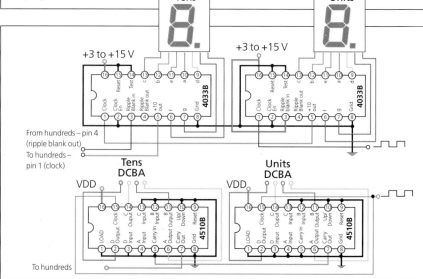

Fig. 7.28 *Cascade counting*

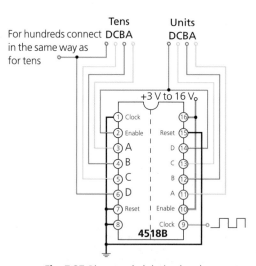

Fig. 7.27 *Binary coded decimal and cascade counting*

Decoding BCD

The problem with binary numbers is that they are difficult to interpret. You are used to counting in decimal. To overcome this problem binary numbers are converted into decimal displays. This can be done by using logic gates but, as with the counters, there are dedicated ICs, called decoders and drivers, which do this conversion (Figure 7.29). This type of device has two functions: (1) to decode the binary number which will provide the right outputs for the seven-segment display and (2) to provide the current output that is needed to light the LED segments of the display.

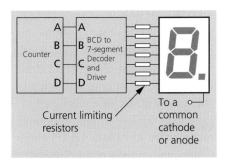

Fig. 7.29 *Decimal output IC*

The type of seven-segment display used will either be a common cathode or common anode. You will have to check the individual IC's data to find out which type is needed. The CMOS 4511B (Figure 7.30) is a BCD to seven-segment latch/driver.

The seven output pins 9 to 15 (a, b, c, d, e, f, g) go high when displaying the decimal number. Therefore, this device requires a common cathode seven-segment display. Each connection is made through a resistor. A single resistor connected to the common cathode could be used but the brightness of the output will vary depending on the number being displayed. Pins 1,

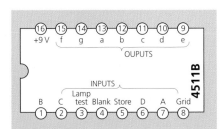

Fig. 7.30 *Segment latch and driver*

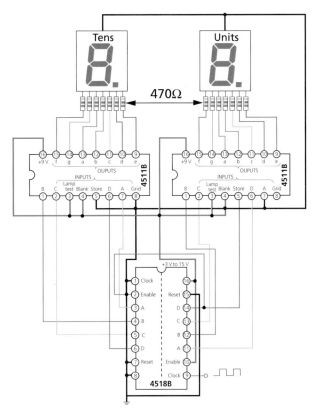

Fig. 7.31 *The die counter wiring circuit*

2, 6 and 7 are connected directly to the binary output pins of counter ICs such as pins 3,4,5 and 6 or 11,12,13 and 14 on the 4518B (Figure 7.31) or 4520B. Pin 3 is a lamp test which when connected to ground will light all the display segments. If they do not all light then there is a fault either in the seven-segment display, the circuit or the 4511B. Pin 5 is used to store the input number. If this is low then the inputs at pins 1, 2, 7 and 8 will be instantly decoded to the outputs a, b, c, d, e, f and g. When pin 4 is low the display will be blank.

Some decoders have sophisticated blanking facilities known as ripple blanking. This is useful if you do not want leading or trailing zeros. For example, if a three-digit display had a number of 050 using a ripple blanking facility this would be displayed as 50. Calculators use this facility. When you turn them on and put in a number there are no leading or trailing zeros (e.g. 00000103 is not shown). Blanking out the zeros makes the display much easier to read. The 4033B has this facility and the examples shown in Figure 7.32 use this facility.

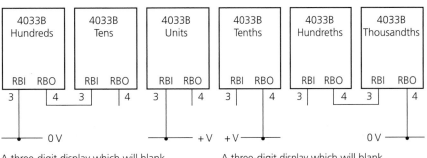

A three-digit display which will blank leading zeros, e.g. when the inputs are equivalent to 050 the 50 will be displayed, the hundreds display will be blank.

A three-digit display which will blank trailing zeros, e.g. when the inputs are equivalent to .050 the .05 will be displayed, the thousandths display will be blank.

Fig. 7.32 *Ripple blanking*

FLIP-FLOPS

Some systems require an alternate switch action. System 4 of the electronic die shown in Fig. 7.26 specifies this action. There are a number of options that could be used: a mechanical push switch, a touch switch, a temperature-activated switch, a light switch. Each has its own particular problems that the designer will have to overcome. A pull switch that is used in a bathroom is an alternate action switch. You pull once and the light is turned on. You pull a second time and the light is turned off. Mechanical push switches which have alternate actions can be purchased but they cause electrical bounce. This electrical bounce can be described as switching a circuit on to off to on very quickly. Figure 7.33 shows two graphs of current flow in a circuit which has been activated by a mechanical switch. The first is a switch without electrical bounce and the second is one with electrical bounce.

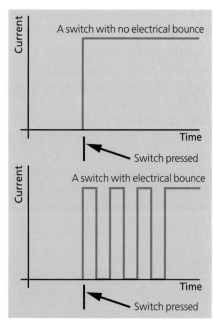

Fig. 7.33 *Switch bounce*

Digital circuits should be free of switch bounce. One way to achieve this is to use a device called a flip-flop (bistable). Flip-flops have many uses including counting, data latching (memory) and alternate switching (toggling) and are worth looking at in some detail.

Reset-set (R–S) flip-flop

Flip-flops (bistables) are one of the three types of multivibrators, the other two being astables and monostables (see Chapter 6 on Timers and timing). Flip-flops are useful devices of which the simplest form is the reset–set (R–S) flip-flop, shown in Figure 7.34.

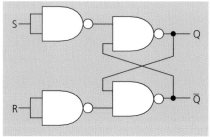

Fig. 7.34 *R–S flip-flop*

The most important thing about a flip-flop is that it is stable in one of two states. State one (high) is where $Q = 1$ and $\bar{Q} = 0$. State two (low) is where $Q = 0$ and $\bar{Q} = 1$. To help you understand the R–S flip-flop its truth table is shown in Figure 7.35.

Comment	Input		Output	
	R	S	Q	$\bar{Q}$
Start up state	0	0	1/0	0/1
Set switch pushed	0	⎍	1	0
Reset switch pushed	⎍	0	0	1
Disallowed state	1	1	0	0

Fig. 7.35 *R–S flip-flop truth table*

This type of flip-flop can be used to remove electrical switch bounce (debouncing). A circuit for this is shown in Figure 7.36. The Q output could be used to control the role of the die (Figure 7.26) if a mechanical switch was to be used.

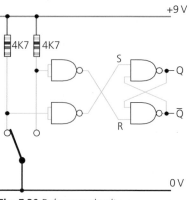

Fig. 7.36 *Debounce circuit*

Edge triggering

Flip-flops are edge triggered devices. This means that the change at the output from logic 0 to logic 1 or from logic 1 to logic 0 takes place at a point in time when the input voltage changes from low to high or high to low, respectively. This is shown in Figure 7.37.

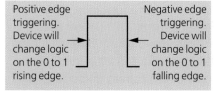

Fig. 7.37 *Edge triggering*

Thresholds

The input voltage that is needed to change the output level is called the threshold voltage. But what is the level of voltage required to make the output go to logic level 1 or to logic level 0? The answer depends on whether you are using TTL or CMOS and, if using CMOS, what supply voltage is being used. Figure 7.38 shows the input voltage levels needed to achieve logic 1 or logic 0. The areas inbetween should be avoided and passed through as quickly as possible when moving from one logic level to the other.

IC family	CMOS 4000	CMOS 4000	CMOS 74HC00	TTL 74LS00
Supply voltage	5 V	9 V	5 V	5 V

LOGIC 1

+8 V — 8.0 V

+7 V —

+6 V —

+5 V —

+4 V —

+3 V — 3.5 V / 3.5 V

DON'T KNOW

+2 V — 1.5 V / 2.0 V / 2.0 V

+1 V — 1.0 V / 0.8 V

0 V —

Fig. 7.38 *Threshold levels*

T-type (toggle) flip-flop

If a temperature sensor, light dependent resistor, touch switch or similar device were to be used, then to provide an alternate action a different type of flip-flop would be needed. The alternate action, illustrated by the description of the bathroom pull switch is called toggling (changing from one condition to another off-on: on-off). The outputs from flip-flops can be made to toggle. As with many of the devices described in this chapter flip-flops can be made from logic gates. The symbol and truth table for the T-type flip-flop is shown in Figure 7.39.

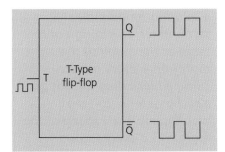

Inputs	Outputs	
T	Q	$\bar{Q}$
Pulse 1	1	0
Pulse 2	0	1
Pulse 3	1	0
Each pulse	Toggle	

Fig. 7.39 *T-type flip-flop and truth table*

As the truth table shows the T-type flip-flop has a clock input. Each pulse of the clock changes the states of the outputs. The frequency (the time it taken to change from one state to the other) of the Q output is half that of the clock input. In other words the T-type flip-flop is dividing the input clock frequency by two.

Cascading (linking together in series) T-type flip-flops will produce a binary counter. When the Q output is high it represents a binary digit of 1; when it is low is represents a binary digit of 0. This is illustrated in Figure 7.41.

You will not find T-type flip-flops in your component catalogues but you can make them from D-type flip-flops or J-K flip-flops (see below).

D-type (data) flip-flop

The D input of the D-type flip-flop determines the output of Q. If you were to make the D input logic 1 then when the clock input changed from ground to positive the output Q would change to logic 1. Figure 7.40 shows the symbol and truth table for a D type flip-flop.

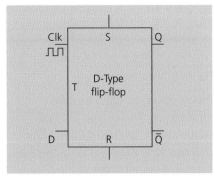

Inputs				Outputs	
S	R	Clk	D	Q	$\bar{Q}$
1	0	0/1	0/1	1	0
0	1	0/1	0/1	0	1
0	0	⌐⌐	0	0	1
0	0	⌐⌐	1	1	0

Fig. 7.40 *D-type flip-flop and truth table*

To make a D-type flip-flop into a T-type flip-flop the $\bar{Q}$ output is connected to the D input. The D input, therefore, follows the $\bar{Q}$ output. If Q is at logic 1 then $\bar{Q}$ is logic 0 as is the D input. On the next negative to positive input of the clock the output Q changes to the logic level of D, which is logic 0 and $\bar{Q}$ changes to logic level 1, changing the logic level of D. On the next negative to positive input of the clock Q changes to the logic level of D which is now 1 so Q changes to logic 1 and so on. Figure 7.41 shows a schematic drawing of a two-bit binary counter. This type of flip-flop has other uses as well as counting or toggling as will be seen later in this chapter.

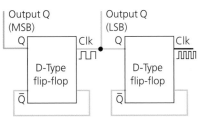

Fig. 7.41 *Two-bit binary counter*

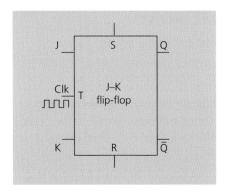

Inputs					Outputs	
S	R	Clk	D	Q	Q	$\bar{Q}$
1	0	0/1	0/1	0/1	1	0
0	1	0/1	0/1	0/1	0	1
0	0	⌐⌐	0	0	Q	$\bar{Q}$
0	0	⌐⌐	0	1	0	1
0	0	⌐⌐	1	0	1	0
0	0	⌐⌐	1	1	Toggle	

Fig. 7.42 *J–K flip-flop and truth table*

J–K flip-flop

The J–K flip-flop (Figure 7.42) is very versatile in that it can be made to operate like all the other flip-flops. This is achieved by connecting the J and K inputs in the following ways:

R–S flip-flop
Set J, K and Clk to 0 or 1

T-type flip-flop
Set J and K to 1

D-type flip-flop
Set J and K to different levels

Figure 7.43 shows how a J–K flip-flop would be used to provide the toggle switching required for counting the outputs from outputs such as a light dependent resistor, temperature sensor or touch switch.

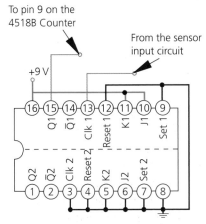

Fig. 7.43 *Sensor to counter circuit*

MEMORY

Remember the word:

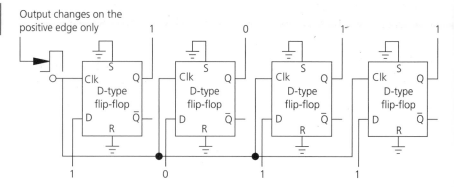

In order for you to remember this word it has been written in this book. You have then read that word and stored it in your memory. Despite other inputs that you are receiving (i.e. hearing sounds around you, seeing and reading this text) you have still remembered the word. Electronic memory systems operate in much the same way. The term 'word' is used to describe a binary number. This number may represent some item, letter or number etc. For example, the decimal number 65 (1000001 in binary) is used by computer systems to represent the letter A.

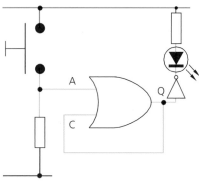

Fig. 7.44 *OR gate memory circuit*

A very simple memory circuit can be made using an OR gate. In the circuit shown in Figure 7.44 when the push switch is pressed input A of the OR goes high and therefore the output Q goes high. The output Q feeds back its output to input B. When the push switch is released A will go low but B is high so the output Q will remain high regardless of what happens to the input A. Pressing the switch wrote the 'word' to memory. The word has been stored by the OR gate. You are able to 'read the word' because the LED is turned on.

This type of circuit is called a latch and could be used in a simple burglar alarm circuit. The switch could be activated when a door or window is opened or if something is removed from a display cabinet. Closing the door or replacing the object would have no effect.

Flip-flops and memory

Output changes on the positive edge only

Fig. 7.45 *Data storage*

Flip-flops can be used to store information. The D-type flip-flop stores information by ignoring any changes to the D input until there is a positive edge trigger at the clock input. By linking D-type flip-flops together large 'words' can be stored (Figure 7.45). If you wanted to store the binary word 1011 the four data latches would be linked to a common clock. Each of the D inputs would be used to store one of the bits. When the clock pulse provides a positive edge the number is stored. With this type of memory circuit you decide when and what to store. When you want to store a 'word' put the 'word' at the D inputs and send a clock pulse which will give a positive edge. An example of where this could be used is a simple tachometer. If you wanted to know how fast a shaft was turning you could use a sensing device connected to a binary counter. The binary counter would increment by one for each turn of the shaft. This number would be fed to the D inputs. The clock would pulse once every minute and the number of turns made during the minute would be displayed thus providing the speed of the shaft in revolutions per minute.

Resetting flip-flops

It may be necessary to reset a flip-flop at any time. This reset can be done manually, automatically or using a combination of both. Some methods by which this may be done are shown in Figure 7.46.

Try this:

The example in the text gives a solution for a simple tachometer. This design only samples the speed of the motor once every minute. Using a block diagram design a tachometer circuit that would sample the speed of the motor once every second.

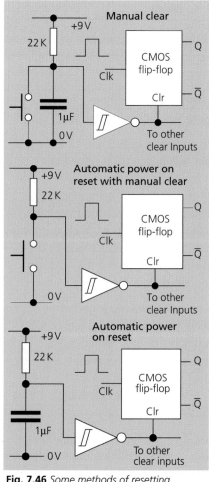

Fig. 7.46 *Some methods of resetting flip-flops*

Random access memory (RAM)

Using logic gates to solve problems that are much more complex than a die would be very difficult and require a large number of ICs. The use of static memory devices can overcome this problem.

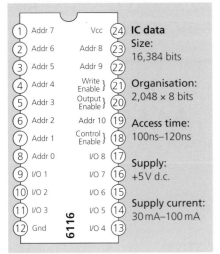

Fig. 7.47 *Static RAM*

Figure 7.47 shows the pin connections and some data for static random access memory (RAM). When purchasing these devices you need to be aware of certain information. First, do not get them confused with dynamic RAM which works differently. You need to know the RAM's size and how it organises the data stored. The device shown in Figure 7.47 can hold 16,384 bits of data (binary digits). These are organized into 2048 memory locations (addresses) of data each of 8 bits (1 byte) in length (2048 × 8 = 16,384). The access time is the time it takes once the memory address has been given for the data to appear at the output pins.

These devices are 'volatile'. This means that when the power is turned off all the stored data will be lost. You can purchase non-volatile static RAM modules, which make use of a lithium battery, but they are more expensive. However, the amount of current used by these devices is very small and a battery can be used to hold the data for quite long periods of time. Using a capacitor will provide current for short time periods while a

battery is being changed. This should enable you to hold the data indefinitely but there is always the danger that data will be lost.

If this device was used for the die described earlier then only 6 of the 2048 data lines would be required. If the seven LEDs were controlled independently then the die would be programmed as shown in Figure 7.48.

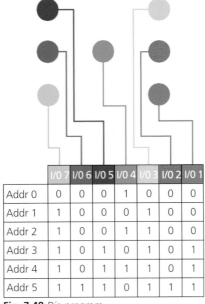

	I/O 7	I/O 6	I/O 5	I/O 4	I/O 3	I/O 2	I/O 1
Addr 0	0	0	0	1	0	0	0
Addr 1	1	0	0	0	1	0	0
Addr 2	1	0	0	1	1	0	0
Addr 3	1	0	1	0	1	0	1
Addr 4	1	0	1	1	1	0	1
Addr 5	1	1	1	0	1	1	1

Fig. 7.48 *Die program*

In order to write this information into the memory chip the output enable must first be made high. The control enable is used to disable (disconnect) the output data lines so that they stop feeding out information. This is not required for the die so this would be permanently held high. The address is set to 0000000000 by making each of the address lines a logic 0. This could be done by a set of slide switches or a binary counter. The data is then set at the I/O pins. This is done by placing a logic 1 at the bit required. In this case there would be a logic 1 at I/O pin 4 with the other data inputs at logic 0. The write enable pin is then made to go from logic 1 to logic 0. This could be done by the use of a push switch. The address line is advanced by 1 to 0000000001 and the data is set at the I/O pins (logic 1 at I/O 1 and I/O 5). The remaining memory address data is input in the same way. In order to read the data the output enable is made low. The memory address is set and the output is displayed. Figure 7.49 shows a circuit that could be used for this device.

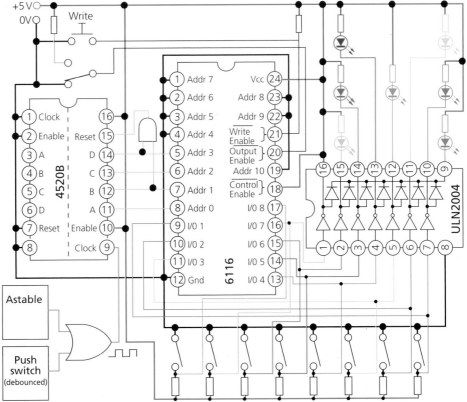

Fig. 7.49 *Die circuit using CMOS static RAM*

EXTENSION MATERIAL

Logic families

The logic gates, counters and flip-flops described in this chapter are found in integrated circuits (ICs). As a designer you will have to make a choice between the two logic families, TTL (Transistor Transistor Logic) and CMOS (Complementary Metal Oxide Semiconductor).

Using ICs from the same family will ensure compatibility enabling the inputs to be driven by direct connection to the outputs. The two main groups of these families are the 74xx and 74LSxx series (TTL) and the 4000B, 74HC and 74HCT series (CMOS). There can be some confusion when purchasing ICs for these logic families. Each has their advantages and disadvantages which are summarised in the table of characteristics opposite.

If you are using TTL it is important that a stabilised 5 V power supply is used. The 7805 regulator can be used for this purpose and provide sufficient current for most applications (1 A). The circuit for a suitable power supply is shown in Figure 7.50.

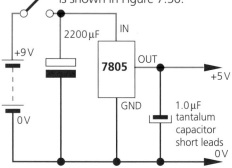

Fig. 7.50 *A 7805 regulator*

Driving outputs

TTL outputs are typically able to sink 16 mA and therefore able to drive small devices such as LEDs which do not require large amounts of current, provided a current-limiting resistor is placed in series as shown in Figure 7.51.

The current output from CMOS is dependent on the supply voltage but you may find that unless using buffer ICs such as the 4050 you will not be

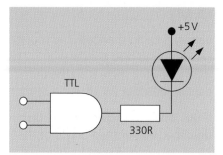

Fig. 7.51 *LED connection to TTL*

able to drive even low current devices such as an LED. Many applications will require a driver circuit that is capable of larger current outputs. There are ICs in the 4000 series that provide greater current outputs such as the 4050B. However, the use of single transistors or Darlington driver ICs (Figure 7.52) such as the ULN28030 or ULN20004 provides a solution.

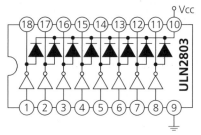

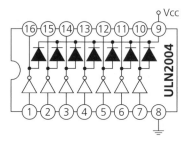

Fig. 7.52 *Darlington drivers*

Logic families – characteristics

TTL Transistor Transistor Logic

Advantages

■ Electrically robust.
■ Inputs can be left unconnected without causing problems although it is good practice to connect to 5 V supply.
■ Very fast switching. Used extensively in computer circuits although being superseded by the fast switching CMOS 74HCT series.
■ Uses less current than most CMOS ICs in high-frequency systems (not usually a consideration for circuits designed in school).

Disadvantages

■ Must have an accurate +5 V power supply.
■ Vulnerable to electrical noise.
■ Consumes more current than CMOS in low-frequency circuits.
■ Can only drive 10 TTL inputs from one output (fan out).

The TTL family come in a range known as 74xx and 74LSxx series. This number is printed onto the top surface of the IC. There are often some letters printed in front of the number; this is the manufacturer's identification.

CMOS Complementary Metal Oxide Semiconductor

Advantages

■ Can operate with a wide power supply range:
4000B +3 V to +15 V (The best performance is achieved with the supply at +9 V to +12 V); 74HC +2 V to + 6 V; 74HCT +4.5 V to 5.5 V.
■ Low current consumption on low-frequency circuits.
■ Less vulnerable to electrical noise.
■ Higher source current (typically 8 mA).
■ Can drive up to 50 CMOS inputs from one output (fan out).

Disadvantages

■ All unused inputs must be connected to either the positive or negative supply.
■ More susceptible to static electricity.

The CMOS family comes in a range known as the 4000, 74HC and 74HCT series. The code on the IC for the 4000 series will usually begin with a '4' or '14' followed by three or four figures, e.g. 4001, 4518, 14002 and end with the letter B.

Using binary numbers

Because digital electronics uses 1s and 0s binary mathematics is used to interpret the inputs, control and outputs of digital circuits. Binary is a base 2 numbering system (using two digits: 0 and 1). You normally use a base 10 (decimal) system (using ten digits: 0, 1, 2, 3, 4, 5, 6, 7, 8, 9).

With decimal the columns of numbers from right to left represent units, tens, hundreds, thousands, etc. (10^0, 10^1, 10^2, 10^3). With binary the columns from right to left represent one, two, four, eight, sixteen, thirty two, sixty four, one hundred twenty eight etc. (2^0, 2^1, 2^2, 2^3, 2^4, 2^5, 2^6, 2^7). Figure 7.53 shows the decimal value of each binary column.

Decimal value of each binary column							
MSB							LSB
128	64	32	16	8	4	2	1

Binary number							
MSB							LSB
1	1	0	0	1	0	0	1

Decimal equivalent				
1	×	128	=	128
1	×	64	=	64
0	×	16	=	0
1	×	8	=	8
0	×	4	=	0
0	×	2	=	0
1	×	1	=	1
Total			=	201

Fig. 7.53

Each individual digit of the binary number is known as a bit.

Decimal number			189		
189 ÷ 128	=	1	remainder	61
61 ÷ 64	=	0	remainder	61
61 ÷ 32	=	1	remainder	29
29 ÷ 16	=	1	remainder	13
13 ÷ 8	=	1	remainder	5
5 ÷ 4	=	1	remainder	1
1 ÷ 2	=	0	remainder	1
1 ÷ 1	=	1	remainder	0

Binary of 189 = 1 0 1 1 1 1 0 1

Fig. 7.54

The binary number shown in Figure 7.53 is an eight-bit number. Eight bits are called a byte. The 1s column is known as the LSB (least significant bit). The far left-hand column is known as the MSB (most significant bit). When represented as a power the 1s column is 2^0 and the 128s column is 2^7. For this reason you may see the bits labelled 0 – 7. Figure 7.54 shows the conversion of a decimal number to binary.

Binary coded decimal

The designer of digital circuits may need to display a numeric value but binary numbers are difficult to read and to convert to decimal numeric displays. Binary coded decimal (BCD) will simplify the display of the number. As the name suggests a combination of binary and decimal is used. The binary bits are grouped to make four-bit binary numbers each of which represents a decimal column. When using this method each four-bit binary number must be no larger than a decimal value of nine. Figure 7.55 shows how decimal values are represented in BCD.

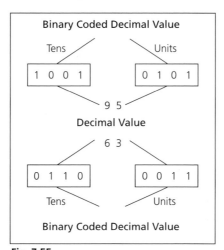

Fig. 7.55

Hexadecimal

Although not as easy to read as BCD, hexadecimal provides a very efficient way of displaying numbers. This method of numbering is used extensively in digital electronics and computer displays. Hexadecimal is a base 16 numbering system thus requiring sixteen characters. The ten decimal numbers are used plus the first six letters of the alphabet (0, 1, 2, 3, 4, 5, 6, 7, 8, 9, A, B, C, D, E and F). A has a decimal value of 10, B has a value of 11 and so on. As with BCD the binary number is separated into four-bit numbers, but with hexadecimal they are not limited to a maximum value of 9. To convert the number 9F to decimal multiply the hexadecimal value of 9 (9) by 16 = 144 and add this to the value of F (15) = 144 + 15 = 159. Figure 7.56 shows examples of hexadecimal conversion.

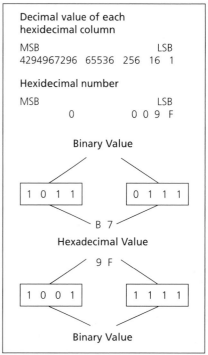

Fig. 7.56

> ### Try this:
> *Calculate the decimal value of the hexadecimal number 9F.*
>
> *What is the decimal value of the binary number 1 0 1 1 0 1 0 1?*
>
> *What would be the BCD of the above binary number?*

Putting it into practice

1. Identify five electronic products that are found in the home that make use of digital electronics.

2. For each of the products you identified in question 1, explain why digital rather than analogue electronics has been used.

3. Draw the truth table for the circuit shown in Figure 7.57.

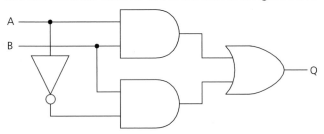

Fig. 7.57

4. Figure 7.58 shows a block diagram of a monitoring system that is being designed for a storage facility for materials that are sensitive to light and temperature. It is important, therefore, that the environment is kept at a constant temperature and is never subject to excessive light. Temperature sensor 'A' measures for low temperature. Temperature sensor 'B' measures for high temperature. Both of these sensors output logic 0 if 'true'. If the light level rises above the safety limit the sensor circuit at 'C' is logic 0. A test switch is included so that the logic and alarm system can be tested at any time. When the test switch is activated the circuit at 'D' is 'high'. A 'low' output at 'Q', will activate the alarm system.

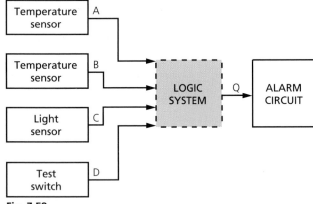

Fig. 7.58

Draw the truth table(s) showing inputs A, B, C and D and the output Q. Design a suitable logic system that will activate the alarm when any of the adverse conditions are met.

5. Explain why the designer of the monitoring system in Figure 7.58 would want the alarm circuit to be activated when the output from the logic system is 'low'?

6. The designer of the monitoring system in Figure 7.58 wishes to place a 'latch' between the logic circuit and alarm circuit. Design a latch circuit that can be 'reset' when a push button is pressed.

7. Name the logic gates used for the R–S flip flop shown in Figure 7.59.

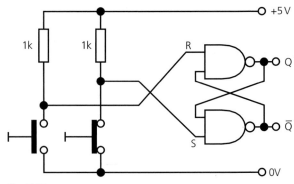

Fig. 7.59

8. Give one example where the type of flip flop shown in Figure 7.59 might be used.

9. Study Figure 7.59.
a) Explain what happens to the outputs Q and $\bar{Q}$ when the Set (S) switch is pressed.
b) Explain what happens to the outputs Q and $\bar{Q}$ when the Reset (R) switch is pressed.

10. In Figure 7.59, the outputs are activated on the 'negative edge' of the switch inputs. Explain with the aid of a diagram what is meant by this.

11. The four J–K flip flops in Figure 7.60 are connected together to form a four-bit binary counter. Explain the terms 'bit' and 'byte'.

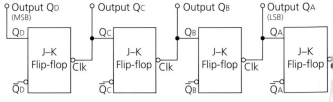

Fig. 7.60

12. Describe the sequence of events that would enable the output Qc in Figure 7.60 to go 'high'. Assume that all outputs are 'low' at the start of the sequence.

13. A TTL 7493 divide-by-sixteen counter is shown in Figure 7.61. Explain what is meant by a 'divide-by-sixteen' counter.

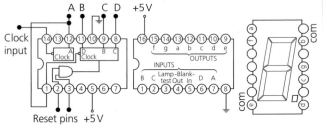

Fig. 7.61

14. Using the three components shown in Figure 7.61, draw the circuit diagram for a divide-by-ten counter to a seven segment display.

8·Output devices

To be useful electronic products have to be able to do something. Outputs (Figure 8.1) are often transducers which change electrical energy into some other form. For example, a VCR produces moving images and sound using a picture tube and a loudspeaker as output transducers.

When thinking of solutions to a design problem the output is often the easiest part to choose.

| Input(s) | → | Process | → | Output(s) |

Fig. 8.1

MAKING CHOICES: A METRONOME

Mechanical metronomes are very expensive and are far from compact. A solution to this would be to design an electronic pocket metronome.

An output such as this needs to make a sound on the beat and perhaps a different note at the end of each bar.

What will affect the choice of output device(s)?

How loud will the sound need to be?

What pitch and tone are needed?

How much space is available?

How much money from your budget can you allow?

What is the maximum current that the device can handle?

Will the output be on for long periods?

What will turn on ('drive') the output?

What are the voltage requirements of the output? Do they match those of the rest of the system?

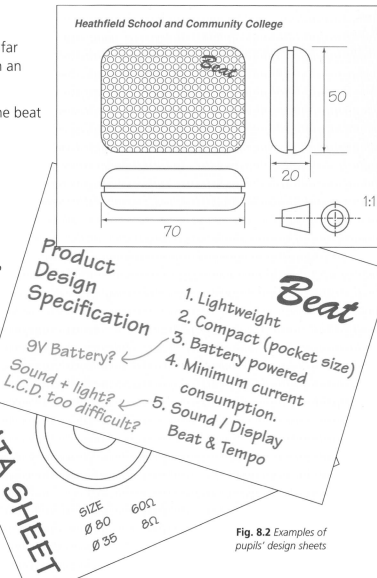

Heathfield School and Community College

Beat

50

20

70

1:1

Product Design Specification

9V Battery?

Sound + light?
L.C.D. too difficult?

Beat

1. Lightweight
2. Compact (pocket size)
3. Battery powered
4. Minimum current consumption.
5. Sound / Display Beat & Tempo

DATA SHEET

SIZE
Ø 80   60Ω
Ø 35   8Ω

Fig. 8.2 *Examples of pupils' design sheets*

Fig. 8.3 *Loudspeaker and headphones*

▷ Design issues – outputs

When designing outputs you will need to consider:

1. The amount of space available.

2. How much current the output device will need.

3. How the type of output used will affect other parts of the system.

4. Whether you need more than one form of output, for example, light and sound.

INTERFACING

One of the critical things that an electronics designer has to do is to match the different parts of a system. This is so that they are physically and electrically compatible. This process is called interfacing.

It is not unlike matching different types of toy building blocks (e.g. Lego); unless they can be connected together it is not possible to make the whole structure.

What exactly does electrical compatibility mean? The key elements that must match are the working voltage and the maximum current requirements.

Current

To decide which interface or driver circuit you need, check the current requirements of your chosen output device. This may be marked on the device itself, or you may need to refer to its data sheet or measure the current while it is running at the required voltage. If it is a motor be sure to check it when it is under load (working hard) and when it stalls (when the load becomes too much). Figure 8.4 shows how to measure the current used by an output.

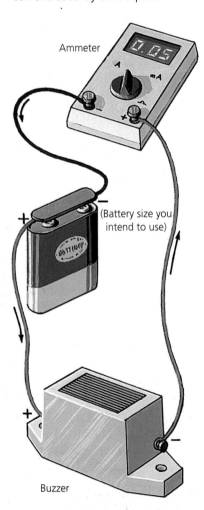

Fig. 8.4 *Measuring the current used by an output*

Choosing a transistor to turn on a load (output)

Once you know the maximum current the output device uses then you can narrow down your choice. Some approximate values for each method are shown below but check in the reference section for the maximum values of other component types.

One transistor ZTX300	500 mA maximum
Two transistor Darlington pair (BC108 and BFY51)	1 A maximum
Single Darlington transistor TIP120	5 A maximum

For greater loads use a relay. For more information about transistors refer to Chapter 7 and the reference section.

Combining eight Darlington pairs

Sometimes it is useful to be able to combine driver circuits together. One way of doing this is to use an octal (eight) Darlington driver IC. This has obvious space advantages over using sixteen separate transistors.

The ULN 2803A IC shown in Figure 8.5 has particular uses when used as an interface between input and output devices. The maximum current is 0.5 A per output (or 1 A if doubled up). For larger loads use a relay in addition to the driver IC.

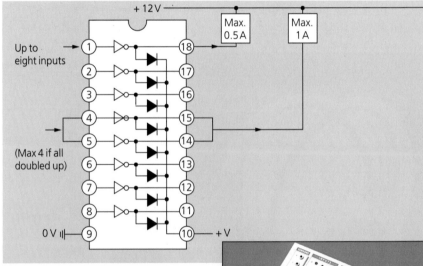

Fig. 8.5 *ULN 2803A Darlington driver IC*

Commercial interfaces (Figure 8.6) are available for use with computers. These include some protection for the computer. Additionally they may provide an interface between sensors (as well as output devices) and the computer.

Fig. 8.6 *A commercial interface*

RELAYS

A relay, as its name suggests, passes on (relays) a signal (Figure 8.7). It does this by using an electromagnet to attract a moving armature which moves the poles of a switch. As the switch is not connected electrically to the coil (the electromagnet) the switch needs its own power circuit to supply the output. Figure 8.8 shows the relay symbol with diode protection, and Figure 8.9 shows the parts of a relay.

Fig. 8.7

By using a relay you create two separate circuits which use magnetism to interface them.

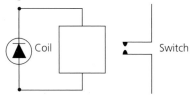

Fig. 8.8 *Relay symbol with diode protection*

Back emf

You will notice that relay coils, motors and solenoids often have a diode connected across them in parallel with the coil. This eliminates something called back electro-motive force (emf) which is a reaction to the coil being turned off. It is not necessary to know about this in detail except that back emf can be avoided by using a diode, otherwise it will destroy transistors or ICs that are meant to turn on the coil.

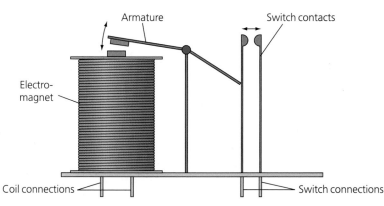

Fig. 8.9 *Inside a relay*

Uses of relays

Relays are used extensively in cars to switch on outputs that require a lot of power (voltage x current). One example of this is the use of a relay to turn on the output to a heated rear windscreen. If a device like a relay was not available then the size of the switches and wires to the instruments in the car would have to be increased substantially. Figures 8.10 and 8.11 show some examples of relays.

Fig 8.10 *An electro-mechanical relay*

Fig 8.11 *A solid state relay*

Relay ratings

When selecting a relay, you need to ensure that its specification matches the requirements of your circuit. To help select an appropriate relay for your design you should know the following terms.

Coil resistance – this affects the load placed on the circuit that turns on the coil. It is always given in Ohms.

Coil voltage – this is the recommended voltage to operate the coil (it may work at a slightly lower voltage but not as quickly).

Coil power consumption is given in mW and is the result of the product of the current (I) and voltage (V) $(P = I \times V)$.

Switch contact rating is given in amps. This is the maximum current at a given voltage that can be handled by the switch part of the relay. This will often include DC and AC voltage ratings (which will be different).

Design checklist – interfacing

1. Use a switch (see Chapter 4) if a simple mechanical switch will do.

2. Check the current that the output will need (measure it if necessary).

3. If the current needed is less than approximately 500 mA consider using one transistor.

4. If the current needed is less than 1 A consider a Darlington pair or a single Darlington transistor (maximum approx. 5 A).

5. If using lots of outputs, an IC with many Darlington pairs may help.

6. If considering a relay, what will turn on the coil? Do not forget to use a diode!

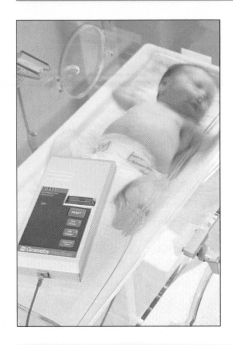

Graseby Medical are an electronics company that produce a range of infusion and respiration monitoring devices for use by health care professionals.

Electronic instruments designed for medical applications have to be designed to be fail-safe in operation and rigorously tested so that the risk of adverse effects on a patient are kept to an absolute minimum.

Graseby Medical manufacture a respiration monitor for recording infants' breathing. These monitors are intended to provide extra vigilance over infants considered at risk from Apnoea, a condition that causes the temporary ceasing of breathing.

The sensor that is used is a small pneumatic disc which is lightly fixed to the baby's abdomen. The unit monitors the air pressure changes within this sensor, and if no pressure changes are detected within 10 or 20 seconds then the unit goes into alarm mode. This means that if breathing stops for longer than 10 or 20 seconds a flashing red light will

OPTOELECTRONICS

Optoelectronics is the name given to the branch of electronics concerned with all aspects of light, including sensors, emitters and fibre optics.

The most common light output devices used are light bulbs and light emitting diodes (LEDs). As with all output devices care must be taken not to exceed the maximum current or power rating. Most LEDs are rated at 20 mA but vary according to colour and size etc. Figure 8.13 shows various types of LED.

Choosing a series resistor

To restrict the current available use a series resistor. To find the value of a resistor you need to use Ohms law (see page 112).

270 R   560 R (or 470 R)

With a 5 V supply.   With a 9 V battery.

Fig. 8.14 *Choosing a series resistor*

Types of bulb

The type of bulb that are usually found in small torches are called MES bulbs (miniature Edison screw), and are marked with both their voltage and current. Bulbs designed for cars are useful for some work but need more current. These are marked with their voltage and wattage ratings. (For small scale work car bulbs can also be used as heating devices.)

Fig 8.15

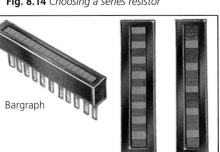

Bargraph

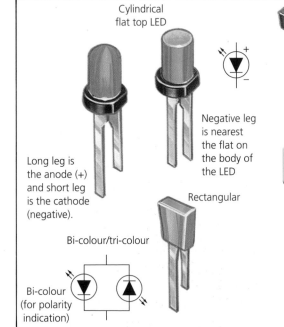

Cylindrical flat top LED

Negative leg is nearest the flat on the body of the LED

Long leg is the anode (+) and short leg is the cathode (negative).

Rectangular

Bi-colour/tri-colour

Bi-colour (for polarity indication)

Fig. 8.13 *Types of LED*

Design issues – light outputs

1   Under what conditions will the output be viewed? (In the range from direct sunlight to pitch dark.)
2   What will be the maximum current required by the device(s)?
3   Will a special driver circuit or decoder be needed?
4   Have you checked the range of shape, size, colour and cost of the device?
5   Will the device need a special holder or connector?
6   Will the output need a current-limiting resistor?

be activated, accompanied by an audible alarm. Every time a breath is registered a click is emitted by the unit to indicate that the unit is functioning and the infant is breathing normally.

The respiration monitor, which you can see in the photo on the right, is battery powered. To prevent it being used when the batteries are flat a warning of reduced battery power is given by a flashing battery symbol. If the batteries are not replaced a continuous audible tone is given that cannot be reset.

Simplicity, reliability and the requirement to be fail-safe means that devices such as these require considerable care in the design phase of their development.

NUMERIC DISPLAYS

Illuminated alphanumeric displays

Alphanumeric (letter or number) displays are very useful outputs when displays have to be read by a human operator. However, in order to work they have to be able to translate an electronic number in binary into a readable digit or letter. To do this a decoding IC has to be used. Decoding ICs turn on and off a pattern of seven (sometimes more) LEDs in order to display the changing digits being received in binary. For more information see Chapter 7.

LED seven-segment displays come in a variety of shapes, sizes, colours and styles but all are either supplied as common cathode or common anode. This simply means that they either have all the anodes (+) joined (or commoned) together or all the cathodes (–) joined. Each LED of the display needs its own resistor.

Figure 8.16 shows one display design. Some designs do not use a resistor for every LED segment – what other arrangement could you use?

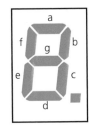

Fig. 8.16 *One LED display design*

Liquid crystal displays (LCDs)

Liquid crystal displays (LCDs) use significantly less power than LEDs and have allowed calculators and watches to run for much longer than the early LED display models. However, LCD displays still need extra illumination for night-time use. Figure 8.17 shows an LCD.

Fig. 8.17 *An LCD*

To reduce the number of components when using more than one digit see the Extension material on multiplexing (page 91).

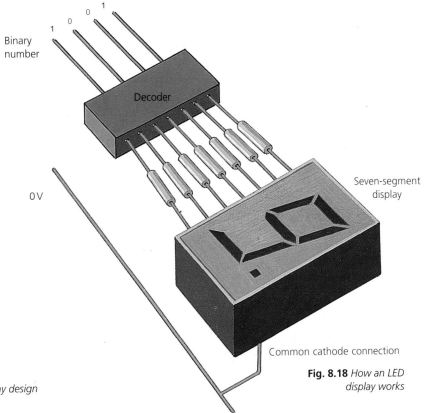

Fig. 8.18 *How an LED display works*

LATCHING OUTPUTS

It is a common problem to find that the process part of a system will only give you a short pulse to turn on an output when in fact you would like the output to latch (remain on). For example, this might be because the process element is a binary counter followed by a logic gate to detect that a certain number has been reached.

Fig. 8.20

Design problem

A car park can only accept 250 cars. A 'FULL' sign must light when the last car has entered. To do this the system counts cars in and gives a brief pulse (short on signal) after the last car has entered (Figures 8.19 and 8.20).

The sign needs to use this short signal to tell it to come on but it needs to stay alight after the signal has gone away. Some possible solutions to this problem are shown in Figures 8.21-8.23.

Fig. 8.19

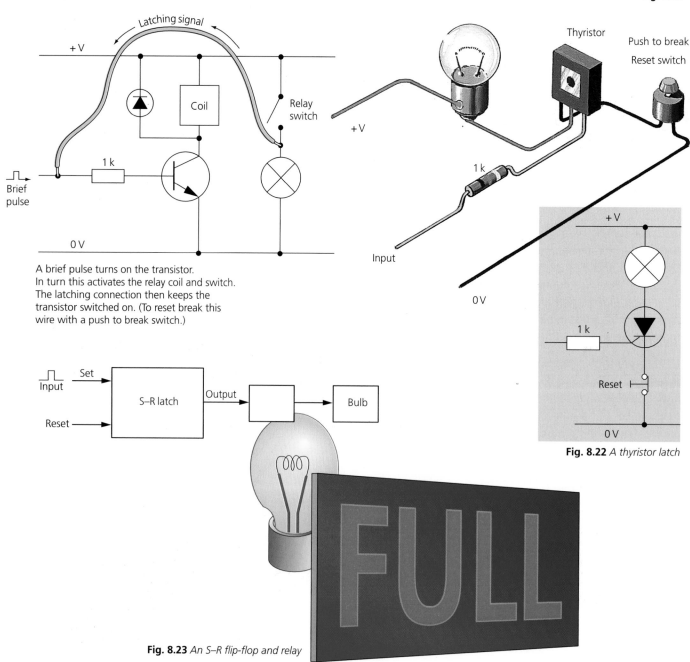

A brief pulse turns on the transistor. In turn this activates the relay coil and switch. The latching connection then keeps the transistor switched on. (To reset break this wire with a push to break switch.)

Fig. 8.22 *A thyristor latch*

Fig. 8.23 *An S–R flip-flop and relay*

ELECTRO-MECHANICAL OUTPUTS

DC motors have the advantage of reversing when the current flow is reversed and require very little in terms of control. However, they need to be used with sensors to detect how far they they have travelled if they are to be used with any precision. Used with a gear box they can be tailored to the correct torque (turning force), speed and direction. When selecting a motor check its current requirements, stall speed and that it will still turn fast enough when under load.

Stepper motors offer accuracy but reduced power when compared with normal DC motors. They need to be pulsed and told in which direction to turn. This is achieved by using a stepper motor control IC.

In return a stepper motor can be made to turn an exact number of degrees or turns. Such accuracy is needed for example to move the print head of a dot matrix printer.

To see how to control a stepper motor see the extension material on page 90.

Fig. 8.28 *DC motor with gear box and screwhead*

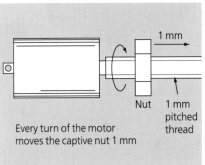

Fig. 8.29 *Producing linear movement from a DC motor*

To produce a linear (straight line) motion directly from an output device usually requires a motor and gear box that will use a rack and pinion or a screwthread. For short movements a solenoid can be used. A solenoid is an electromagnet that attracts a moving iron plunger. This plunger is often attached to a loose spring so that when the current is turned off it will spring back.

Solenoids require a large current flow and need to be driven by a relay.

Examples of DC motors, stepper motors, solenoids and simple gearing systems are shown in Figures 8.24-8.32.

Fig. 8.24 *DC motor*

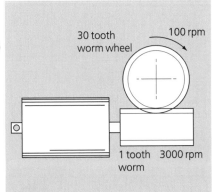

Fig. 8.25 *Typical simple gearing, driven by a DC motor*

Fig. 8.26 *Stepper motor*

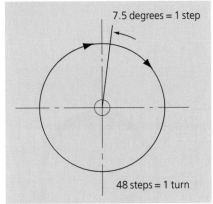

Fig. 8.27 *A stepper motor usually completes a full revolution in 48 steps*

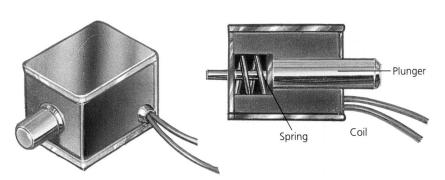

Fig. 8.30 *Solenoid*

Fig. 8.31 *Inside a solenoid*

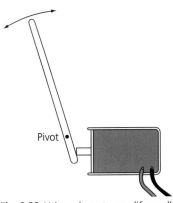

Fig. 8.32 *Using a lever to amplify small movements of a solenoid*

NAD produce a range of high-quality audio products that are designed in the UK. In common with other hi-fi manufacturers, each NAD unit is designed to look part of a co-ordinated system. This means that connections between units have to be easy to get to, match the other units and avoid too many unsightly connecting leads.

The latest challenge to manufacturers like NAD is the advent of 'home cinema' which brings the large-scale sound of the cinema into the home. This is achieved by using 'surround sound', a concept that has been made real by the use of video recordings that use DPL (Dolby Pro Logic) and decode DPL into a form that can output to five or more loudspeakers. A speaker unit is positioned on either side of the television and behind the viewers (one to the left, one to the right). The fifth speaker unit is placed by the screen to help fix the images to the sound.

NAD home-cinema
speakers and receiver

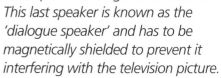

This last speaker is known as the 'dialogue speaker' and has to be magnetically shielded to prevent it interfering with the television picture.

SOUND OUTPUTS

Every day we hear sound that has been processed electronically. The choice of output available to the design engineer is quite bewildering. The main criteria for choosing an output device are listed below.

1. What quality of sound do you need? Are pure tones, speech or music required?

2. Is loudness important?

3. Is space or weight limited?

4. With increased sound the power needed to run it increases too; will the circuit provide sufficient power?

For low consumption (increased battery life), and a constant tone consider a piezo buzzer (Figure 8.33). Many piezo transducers will work without a drive circuit.

Latching circuits using a piezo buzzer may need a 100 μF capacitor in parallel to prevent it from resetting if knocked.

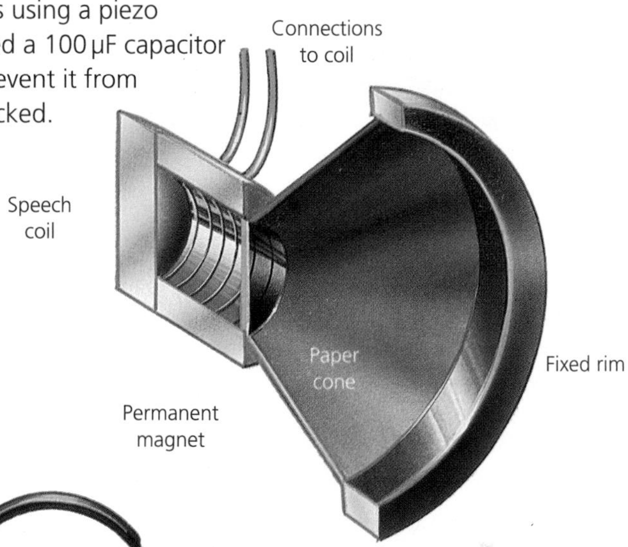

Connections to coil

Speech coil

Paper cone

Fixed rim

Permanent magnet

Fig. 8.34 *Moving coil loudspeaker*

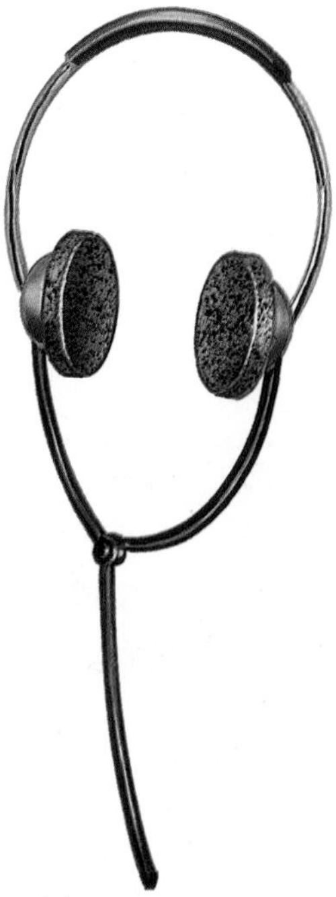

Loudspeakers need a signal that changes at an audio frequency. This signal is then converted in a fluctuating magnetic field in the speech coil of the speaker (Figure 8.34). The coil is surrounded by a permanent magnet which causes the coil to move in and out very quickly. This movement of the coil makes the loudspeaker cone vibrate and this moves the air around it.

Headphones (Figure 8.35) offer privacy and the opportunity to hear audio quality sound in situations where a loudspeaker would be too intrusive to others.

Fig. 8.33 *Piezo buzzer*

Fig. 8.35 *Headphones*

Loudspeakers are important for all audio systems, so manufacturers have to make a range of speakers that will cater for many different systems. The criteria that have to be balanced to achieve a well-matched speaker output include the ability to cope with a range of frequencies, loudspeaker impedance, sensitivity and power. To reproduce a wide range of frequencies speaker units usually incorporate two loudspeakers – a small tweeter for high frequencies and a larger woofer for low frequencies (you can see these in the photo on the right). The sound output is split between the two loudspeakers by a crossover filter network in order to achieve a balanced sound output. The speaker enclosure also has to be carefully designed to produce the best performance from the loudspeakers inside.

NAD manufacture speakers of all sizes

A loudspeaker can be driven by a 555 astable as long as the frequency is fast enough. By providing a selection of resistor values it is possible to use this arrangement to make a simple electronic organ (Figure 8.36). The resistors shown in the astable circuit (Figure 8.37) are pre-set to enable it to be tuned once it has been made.

Musical notes have an equivalent frequency (see the extension material on page 91). Practically though it is usual to tune an organ like this from another instrument.

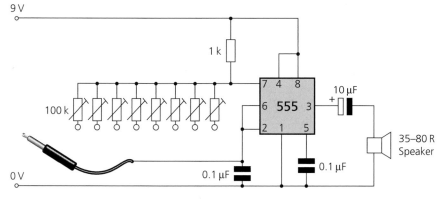

Fig. 8.36 *Student organ project using a vacuum-formed styrene case*

To produce a pulsing single note output it is quite simple to use a piezo transducer (buzzer) and a 555 astable (Figure 8.38).

Fig. 8.37 *A 555 astable with eight frequencies*

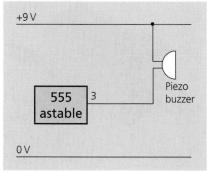

Fig. 8.38

OUTPUT DEVICES – EXTENSION MATERIAL

Speed control of DC motors

A common problem with small inexpensive motors is that they lose torque (turning power) when slowed down. One solution is to use a gear box to reduce their speed. Another way is to use a pulsing circuit that turns the motor on and off rapidly. If the period of time that the motor is on can be varied compared with when it is off the speed can be adjusted. The ratio of ONs to OFFs is called the mark to space ratio (Figures 8.39 and 8.40).

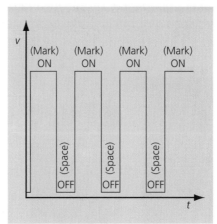

Fig. 8.39 *Mark to space ratio*

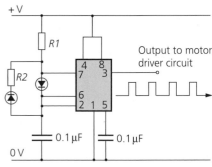

Adjust R1 and R2 to vary times

Fig. 8.40 *Variable mark to space ratio*

Stepper motor control

It is difficult to control the position of the output of a DC motor accurately without using sensors. Using a stepper motor (Figures 8.41 and 8.42) means that you can tell exactly where the output shaft is. However, to use a stepper motor a drive circuit is needed to give the correct steps. This entails pulsing the motor coils in the correct sequence. Once set up the motor can be made to 'step' forwards or backwards in steps that are usually multiples of 7.5 degrees.

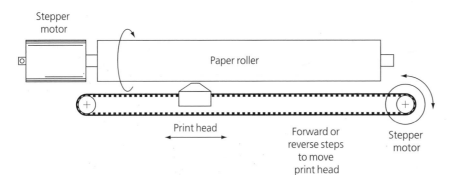

Fig. 8.41 *Dot matrix printer schematic diagram*

Fig. 8.43 *Latching solenoid*

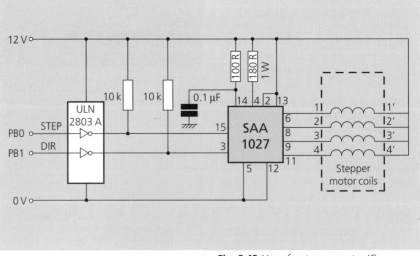

Fig. 8.42 *Use of a stepper motor IC*

Latching solenoids

A latching solenoid (Figure 8.43) stays in its extended or retracted position until another signal is received. The latching facility allows the drive circuit used to rest and so it does not consume any current whilst the solenoid is extended.

Multiplexing

If many outputs need to be used that all need the same connections you can avoid using a large number of wires that are duplicated by multiplexing the signals.

One example of multiplexing is in multi-digit displays. Here each digit would need at least seven wires to connect it to the driving circuit. However, by using multiplexing it is possible to reduce the number of wires required (Figure 8.44).

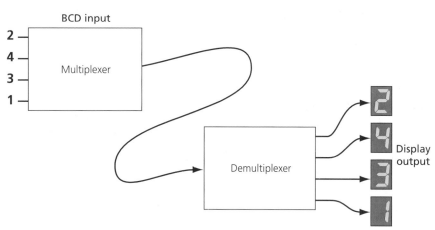

Fig. 8.44 *Multiplexing and demultiplexing*

Speech recorder ICs

Speech recording with magnetic tape is a familiar medium but even with small dictation machines the size of the motor drive and circuitry is quite bulky. To overcome this where size, space and weight are at premium a range of ICs is available that enable a very short message to be recorded directly onto the IC.

This has applications in devices that need to give short messages and an obvious use is in answering machines.

The IC works by recording the sound as a series of voltage levels in a very large bank of capacitors. When replayed the speech is amplified through a loudspeaker (Figure 8.45).

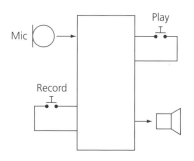

Fig. 8.45 *A speech recorder IC*

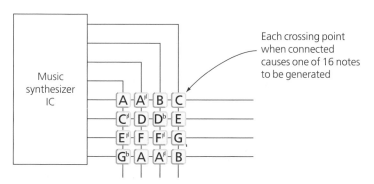

Fig. 8.48 *A matrix arrangement*

Musical note frequencies

Musical notes have an exact frequency. These frequencies and the musical notes they correspond to are shown in Figure 8.46.

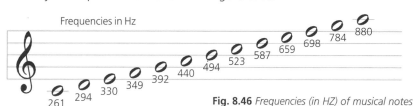

Fig. 8.46 *Frequencies (in HZ) of musical notes*

Melody ICs

A number of novelty tune devices are available that use very few components to play predetermined tunes. These are known as melody ICs (Figure 8.47). They are fine for devices aimed at children's toys.

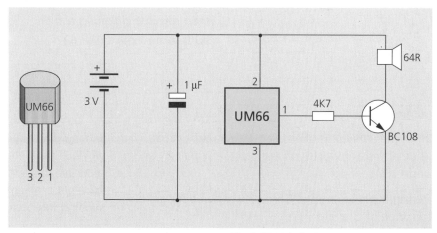

Fig. 8.47 *Melody IC*

Music synthesizer ICs

Music synthesizer ICs can include tunes and note functions that when built into an organ produce some interesting effects. They vary considerably in the number of extra components that are required in addition to the IC. Some need the keys to be matrixed (Figure 8.48) in order to produce more notes than there are pins available on the IC.

Putting it into practice

1. A student is making a fishing bite alarm which is shown in Figure 8.49 as a first design sketch. Suggest two options to place at point A in the diagram. Explain which option would probably be best.

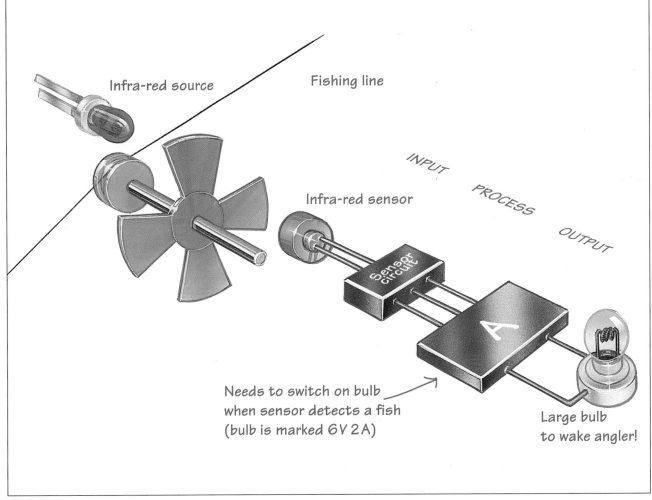

Infra-red source

Fishing line

INPUT PROCESS OUTPUT

Infra-red sensor

Sensor circuit

A

Needs to switch on bulb when sensor detects a fish (bulb is marked 6V 2A)

Large bulb to wake angler!

Fig. 8.49

2. A series resistor is often used with an LED. What value of resistor would you use with a 9 V battery and a single LED?

Explain the usefulness of Ohm's law when deciding on the value of a resistor.

3. Seven-segment displays are common output devices. Explain how the binary number 1001 is displayed as a number 9.

4. a) Sketch an LED and label both the anode and cathode connections.
b) How can the connections of an LED be identified if the legs have been cut?

5. What does latching mean? Give an example where a latching output is useful.

6. Small DC motors run at very fast speeds.
a) What problems might this cause a student designing a curtain opening system for a doll's house?
b) What problems might this present for a student wishing to operate a full size curtain opening system?

7. a) What advantages do stepper motors have?
b) Why does a stepper motor need a special drive circuit to operate it?

8. If you watch the cone of a loudspeaker you will notice that it vibrates in order to produce sound. How does the loudspeaker make the cone vibrate?

9. Why might a latching solenoid be worth considering when using a battery power supply?

10. The speed of an electric motor can be controlled by pulsing it on and off. How is this able to slow down a motor? Explain the term 'mark to space ratio'.

9·Microprocessors & computer control

CONTROL SYSTEMS

A microprocessor is a complex integrated circuit which has led to control systems appearing almost intelligent. At the heart of all the computers you see in magazines and shops is a microprocessor (Figure 9.1). This important component can be thought of as the 'brain' of the computer and some control systems. Its job is to carry out the instructions, sort out the inputs and outputs, organise the computer's memory and so on. It is its ability to be programmed that makes the microprocessor very powerful and flexible providing dedicated control systems for devices like washing machines, cars, food processors, microwave ovens, etc. as well as computers.

Fig. 9.1 *Microprocessors*

Fig. 9.2 *Robot control system in action*

A control system is a group of components connected together that will regulate itself or some other system (Figure 9.2). There are two basic types, open-loop systems and closed-loop systems. The closed-loop system is the most sophisticated and can make full use of a microprocessor's capability.

Open-loop systems

The simplest form of control system is the open-loop system (Figure 9.3). An example of this type of control system could be the heating of milk in a microwave oven. The milk is to be heated to a desired temperature. You estimate the amount of time that this would take and programme the microwave accordingly and then set it running. During the heating process no check is made to see if the milk has reached the correct temperature.

```
input  →  processing system  →  output
```

FIg. 9.3 *Open-loop system*

Closed-loop systems

A closed-loop system (Figure 9.4) will modify its output signal by comparing the input and output stages. Using the example of the microwave, a temperature probe is inserted into the milk. The microwave oven is programmed to switch off when the temperature of the milk reaches the required level. Once started the system monitors the temperature continuously until the correct temperature is reached when it will switch itself off automatically.

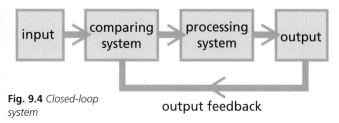

```
input  →  comparing system  →  processing system  →  output
```
output feedback

Fig. 9.4 *Closed-loop system*

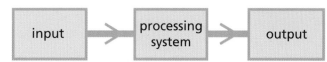

Design issues – control

1. What type of outputs will the control system need (movement, light, electrical, magnetic etc.)?
2. Will the system require the use of feedback to check events?
3. What conditions will the control system need to detect and what sensors could be used?
4. Will a desktop computer be used as part of the control system or will it need to be self-contained (on-board)?
5. What type of interface(s) will be needed?
6. What language will be used to write the control program and what are its limitations ?
7. Will the control system need to monitor several conditions at the same time and if so which will take priority?

Thomson Training & Simulation is an international company with over 2000 staff based in France, the United Kingdom and the United States. They design and integrate simulation and training systems. Although they produce simulation systems in a number of areas it is the world of aviation, both civilian and military, that accounts for much of their business. The scope of this simulation ranges from computer-based desktop packages to Full Flight Simulators for civilian and military aircraft such as the Boeing 777 (which you can see in the photo on the left), European Airbus A330/A340, Tornado and the Harrier, and helicopter trainers.

SYSTEM BOARD CONTROLLERS

When 'on-board' control is needed for a system a cost effective solution is to use a system board controller (SBC). The 'bit-by-bit controller' produced by the Technology Enhancement Programme is an example of this type of device (Figure 9.5).

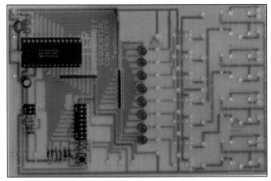

Fig. 9.5 *Bit-by-bit controller*

It makes use of a microcontroller IC which is used to store numbers in its memory addresses of which there are 64. Each number is entered as an 8 bit binary number with a maximum value of 255. Figure 9.6 shows how the bit-by-bit controller is programmed to run a simple traffic light sequence. When the sequence is run a clock pulse determines the length of time each value is held at the outputs. For example, if the clock pulse is running at 1 pulse per second (1 Hz) and the green light of the traffic sequence was to be on for

Step by Step Controller
Simple Traffic Light Sequence

Set *run* and *program* switches to 'PROG OFF' and 'STOP' positions.
Connect Battery
Set *program* switch to 'PROG ON' (note: all dip switches off unless stated)
Set *dip* switch 1 to 'ON'
Press *memory* button 5 times
Set dip switch 1 and 2 to 'ON'
Press *memory* button 5 times
Set dip switch 3 to 'ON'
Press *memory* button once
Set *program* switch to 'PROG OFF'
Set dip switch 4 to 'ON' (sets clock speed to 1 pulse per second)
To run program set *run* switch to 'RUN'

Fig 9.6 *Programming the bit-by-bit controller for a simple light sequence*

5 seconds, then the binary value that would enable the green light to be turned on would have to be stored in 5 consecutive memory addresses.

This SBC provides an open-loop control system but it does provide an option in which the sequence can be set, paused or reset automatically. Transistors and relays can be used to enable devices such as bulbs and motors to be driven.

Fig 9.7
PIC programmer and 'Schools BASIC Stamp'

Other SBCs provide more sophisticated control. The microcontroller IC (PIC16C57) used by the bit-by-bit controller has its own programming language. Both 'low level' and 'high level' languages (see page 98) are available. Using this IC with appropriate hardware (Figure 9.7), it can be programmed and then placed into a dedicated control system providing a very powerful 'on board' control system.

Unilab's '3 Chip Plus' is a system which uses an older style microprocessor called the 6502. The 6502 is programmed using a low level language called 'machine code'. Programming devices like this means that you can alter and change the sequence from the simple step by step. Both of these devices provide a more powerful control system but do require a language to be learnt.

Although these flight simulators are very sophisticated computer control devices the principles upon which they work are the same as those described in this chapter. The illustration on the right shows the various components of the control system. The instrument panel consists of input controls in the form of switches and sensors, some of which will not be too dissimilar from the joysticks used by some computer games. The outputs will be in response to any inputs made (e.g. changes in the visual display, movement of the cockpit, signals to the various cockpit instruments).

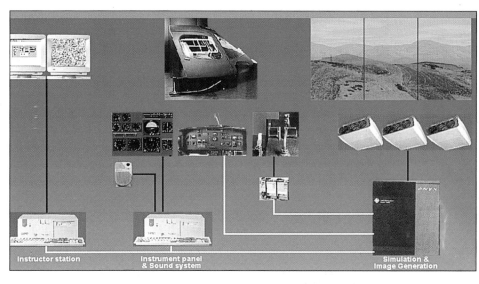

COMPUTER CONTROL

The use of desktop computers (Figure 9.8) for control provides a powerful and flexible option. The computer can be used to write programmes for some SBCs such as the '3 Chip Plus' so that checks and changes can be easily made. A program is typed into the computer. When finished it is downloaded onto the memory chip. The cable is then disconnected, so providing an on-board control system.

Fig 9.8 *Computer control*

A second option is to write and run the programme direct from the computer. An interface, like that shown in Figure 9.9, will be needed and is connected between the computer and the devices that are to be controlled. This is necessary

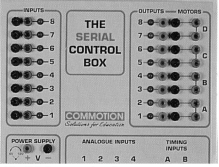

Fig. 9.9 *Computer interface*

because the computer can only provide a very small amount of current and will be damaged if you try to connect devices like motors to it directly.

FLOWCHARTS

Before writing a control program it is worth planning how the sequence is to work. A useful method is the use of flowcharts. These are similar to the block diagrams used when designing electronic circuits. The most common symbols used are shown in Figure 9.10.

used to indicate start, halt, interrupt or finish

used to indicate a process or operation

used to indicate a decision which should only result in a yes or no answer

Fig. 9.10 *Flowchart symbols*

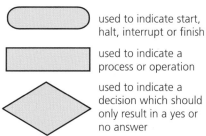

Fig. 9.11 *Pelican crossing flowchart*

When designing and writing computer programs it is important to structure the program in a logical manner. Flowcharts will help and provide a visual check that often provides solutions to difficult problems before actually writing the program.

A flowchart for a simple pelican crossing sequence is shown in Figure 9.11. Where a decision is made a loop (part of the program which repeats itself) is written so that the commands do not simply run one after the other. This will depend on the input conditions. Notice also how the program is made to continuously run and will not, under its normal operation, come to an end.

95

INPUTS AND OUTPUTS

At its simplest level computer control can be used to switch on outputs such as lights or motors. Robots and other control systems in industry will often be used to move components (pick and place) or perform operations such as drilling, spraying a car or welding metal. If the computer control system is only programmed to switch on outputs it will be unaware if the operations are being carried out correctly. Is there a component to pick up? Is there a part into which to drill a hole? If these operations are to be controlled accurately then the computer must be able to sense the outside world by the use of inputs. On these two pages some examples of input and output devices that can be used in computer control are shown. There are other devices that can be used but this will help you to choose devices that are suitable for your projects.

Input devices

Switches

Each of the digital switches shown will have wires from them which are plugged into the digital input terminals of the interface. Some interfaces have LED indicators at the inputs so you will be able to see visually if an input from the switch is being made. For more information on switches see Chapter 4, Sensors and Switching.

The Light Dependent Resistor (LDR)

If the control situation requires different levels of light to be recognised then this is likely to be the device used. The LDR is an analogue device and so its output is variable. However, it can be connected directly into the digital input connections of the interface. If different light levels need to be detected it must be connected to the analogue inputs of the interface.

Temperature sensing

Temperature sensors are connected to the analogue inputs of the interface. The computer will be programmed to read the different input values caused by changes in temperature.

Proximity and Reed Switches

Proximity sensors can be used to detect if an object moves into or away from a specified position. Examples of their use could be to detect if a door or window has been opened, if a model train is approaching a level crossing or if a safety guard is in position.

Sound sensors

It is possible to detect levels of sound by connecting a suitable sensor to an analogue input. Some interfaces have specific sockets for sound inputs so you will need to read the interface instructions.

Infra-red detectors

Two useful types of infra-red detectors are the reflective opto switch and the slotted opto switch. These are particularly useful for positional work and detecting shaft rotation. Because of their extra complexity both devices require some additional circuitry. A suitable circuit is shown on page 100. The output from this circuit is simply connected into a digital input on the computer interface.

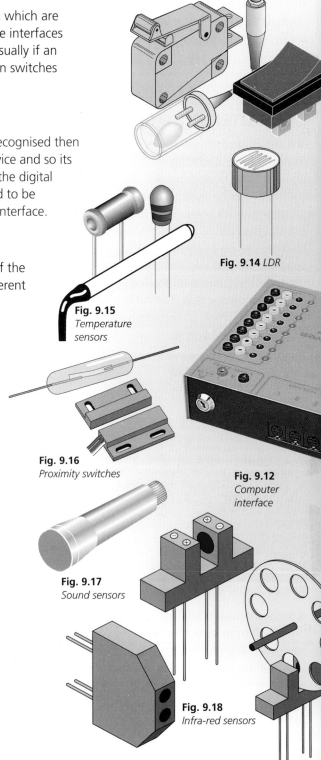

Fig. 9.13 *Switches*

Fig. 9.14 *LDR*

Fig. 9.15 *Temperature sensors*

Fig. 9.16 *Proximity switches*

Fig. 9.12 *Computer interface*

Fig. 9.17 *Sound sensors*

Fig. 9.18 *Infra-red sensors*

Output devices

DC motors

DC motors provide a rotary movement but by using them as part of a mechanical system other types of movement can be made (Fig. 9.19). The computer can be programmed to turn the motor on and off, alter the direction of rotation, adjust the speed and control the amount of time the motor is to be turned on or off. The main disadvantage of the DC motor is the difficulty in controlling precise movements and often need a gear box to slow down the rotation.

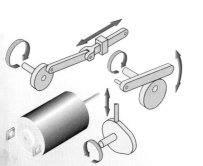

Fig. 9.19 *DC motor and motion changes*

Fig. 9.20
Stepper motor

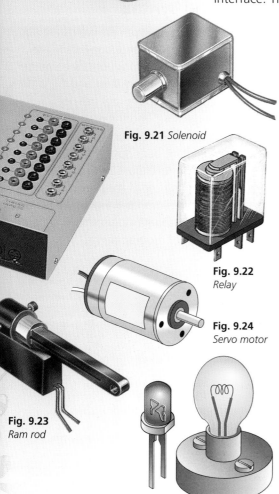

Fig. 9.21 *Solenoid*

Fig. 9.22
Relay

Fig. 9.24
Servo motor

Fig. 9.23
Ram rod

Fig. 9.25 *Indicators*

Stepper motors

The rotary motion by the stepper motor (Figure 9.20) is produced in precise angular steps, typically 7.5° or 1.8°. The rotation is not as fast as the DC motor but they have the advantage of no reduction in torque when running at slow speeds. Although a stepper motor can be controlled by connecting all of its five leads directly to a computer interface a better solution is to use a special interface (see page 100). This only needs two connections to the digital outputs of the computer interface. The computer is programmed so that the output to the 'step' connection is turned on then off (pulsed). To turn the spindle 360° with a 7.5° stepper motor it must be pulsed 48 times (360 ÷ 7.5). The other connection controls which direction the stepper motor spindle turns.

Solenoid

When a current is applied to the solenoid a soft iron bar (plunger) moves in a linear direction. This action can be used to operate mechanical devices such as switches, door bolts, valves and mechanisms requiring a linear input. To control the solenoid its two connections should be connected to the motor outputs of the computer interface. This will provide the current needed.

Electromagnetic relays

The electromagnetic relay is used as a switch and will often be found when large currents or voltages are needed.

Ram rod

The ram rod will provide a powered linear movement in both directions (forward and backward). This device uses a motor with a mechanism to create the linear movement. The movement is fairly slow and although the plunger moves a small amount after the motor has been turned off fairly accurate movements can be made. The ram rod is connected to the motor outputs and controlled in the same way as a DC motor.

Servo motors

Many of the industrial robots that you see use servo motors (Fig. 9.24). These are DC motors in which the spindle movement provides resistance feedback. The computer can measure this resistance and position the spindle with great accuracy.

Lights and indicators

It is best to use bulbs that match the voltage rating of the interface being used. This will normally be between 4.5 V and 12 V. The interface may already use LEDs as indicators for the inputs and outputs. These can be used to try out programs without having to worry about connecting up components to the interface. The LED must be connected the right way round and operate at the correct voltage, typically 2 V. To get the right voltage, a resistor must be added. If the interface is switched to 4.5 V then a 330 ohm resistor should be adequate.

The Entertainment Unit of Thomson Training & Simulation is the largest entertainment simulator manufacturer in the world. It pioneered the application of flight simulation motion technology to entertainment in the early 1980s, to recreate the g-forces and sensations of various rides, in both fantasy and real-life settings. The systems work on a principle of illusion.

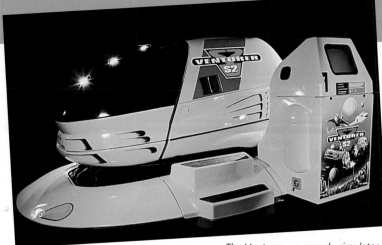

The Venturer – a capsule simulator ride that can hold up to 14 people

Large screens will show a point-of-view film, such as a racing car. Motion is added to correlate exactly with the vision, and so fools the brain and body about their environment – many people actually lean with the g-forces or brace themselves for braking or acceleration.

Inputs			Outputs		Motors	
I/P	Labels	Count	O/P	Labels	Power	Motor
8		0	8	waitlight		D
7		0	7	buzzer		
6		0	6	greenman		C
5		0	5	redman		
4		0	4			B
3		0	3	red		
2		0	2	amber		A
1	Walk	0	1	green		

Fig. 9.26 *On screen animation of control program*

CONTROL PROGRAMMING

All of the control systems described in this chapter are digital devices. This means that they operate by using a series of binary instructions (see Chapter 7).

To communicate with these devices it is necessary to 'talk' to them using a series of 'ons' and 'offs'. The first computers had to be programmed in this way and consequently it took many hours of programming to get the computer to carry out even relatively simple tasks. This led to the development of computer languages.

Low level languages

At the heart of all computer systems is the microprocessor. As the manufacturers want these to operate as fast as possible but still be programmed without having to resort to a series of numbers they make use of mnemonics (a small group of letters).

Below is an example of the mnemonics used by the PIC16Cxx control IC:

Mnemonic	Meaning
CALL	call subroutine
JMP	jump to address
INC	increment

This sort of language is a 'low level' language and although very fast is unlikely to be needed for your control programs.

High level languages

You may have heard of some computer languages like BASIC, C++, VISUAL BASIC and COBOL. These are known as 'high level' languages and use some words that are familiar to us such as REPEAT, WHILE, END, UNTIL. The number of words used by these languages is relatively small. For example, BBC BASIC has about 180 key words.

Control languages and syntax

The way in which the words are put together in a language is called its syntax. The syntax used by computer languages is very strict and if it is not correct the computer will not understand and the program will 'crash'. There are computer programs that have been specially developed for control (Figure 9.26) and these make full use of the power of the modern computer. Figure 9.27 shows a language which uses flowcharts as a way of programming.

```
REPEAT FOREVER
led =1
REPEAT 8
SWITCH ON led
SWITCH OFF led
led = led+1
END REPEAT
led = 7
REPEAT 6
SWITCH ON led
SWITCH OFF led
led = led –1
END REPEAT
END REPEAT
END PROCEDURE
```

Fig. 9.28 *'Light' program in CoCo+*

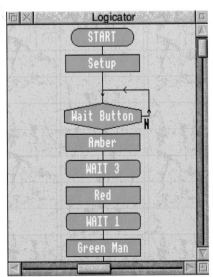

Fig. 9.27 *Flowchart programming*

The computer control system for these entertainment stations correlate the motion with the video display. The motion is provided by hydraulic rams which are controlled by the computer using servo valves. These servo valves control the amount of hydraulic fluid pushed into or out of the rams. Feedback informs the computer the extent to which the valve is open or closed. You can see the rams under the Venturer simulator in the photo on the left.

These systems also use computer control as part their failsafe monitoring. A variety of sensors are used, and if activated will initiate procedures and ensure the safety of those using the system.

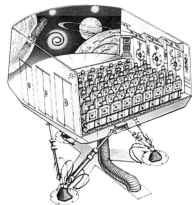

Inside the Venturer

Choosing a language

Figures 9.28 and 9.29 show two control programs. Each program performs the same task of turning eight LEDs on and off in sequence. Both are written for an ACORN computer. The program in Figure 9.28 is written in Commotion's CoCo+, the program in figure 9.29 is in BBC BASIC.

Clearly the CoCo+ program is much smaller and easier to understand. Specialist control programs do make 'control' programming much easier but some do have limited commands and are only meant for relatively simple control systems. It is important to choose a control language suitable for the complexity of the task.

Program structure

It can be seen from Figure 9.29 that the program is structured into a series of distinct sections. The 'main program' is the part which controls the sequence of events. It does this by calling the other elements called procedures or subroutines. Structuring programs is good practice and makes testing and 'debugging' much easier.

Programming inputs and outputs

Programming outputs involves turning something on, like a motor or bulb, in a set sequence. Each output will have a number, often 1 to 8. If a bulb is connected to output 1 then the command used could be something like:

SWITCH ON 1 or SWITCHON 1

The output will stay on until turned off by a command such as:

SWITCH OFF 1 or SWITCHOFF 1

Commands such as WAIT and REPEAT will enable the program sequence to be delayed or repeated in some way. For example:

SWITCH ON 1
WAIT 2
SWITCH OFF 1

Outputs will often be programmed to depend on the input. It may be necessary to see if the input meets a given condition or to wait until a condition is met, using commands like:

IF INPUT 1 ON THEN SWITCH ON 1 or
WAIT UNTIL INPUT 1 ON

The first of these program lines will look to see if INPUT 1 is on; if this is not the case it will immediately move onto the next line of the program. The WAIT command will

hold the program on that line until the INPUT at 1 is turned on.

It is suggested that when programming you plan what you want your control program to do and structure it very carefully using procedures or subroutines. This will help you to avoid mistakes and enable you to find 'bugs' easily.

```
REM Light Sequence
PROCsetoutput(&FF)
REPEAT
FOR power%= 0 TO 7
PROCbitvalue(power%)
NEXT power%
FOR power%= 6 TO 1 STEP –1
PROCbitvalue(power%)
NEXT power%
UNTIL FALSE
END
```
main program

```
DEFPROCsetoutput(outputs%)
REM Set printer port to outputs
SYS"Parallel_Op",2,&00,ouputs%
ENDPROC
```

```
DEFPROCouput(byte%)
REM Send printer outputs
SYS"Parallel_Op",1,byte%
PRINT byte%
ENDPROC
```
procedures

```
DEFPROCdelay
TIME=0
REPEAT UNTIL TIME=10
ENDPROC
```

```
DEFPROCbitvalue(power%)
bitvalue% = 2^power%
PROCoutput(bitvalue%)
PROCdelay
ENDPROC
```

Fig. 9.29 *'Light' program in BASIC*

CIRCUIT INTERFACES

Computer interfaces for digital and analogue inputs and digital outputs, like that shown in Figure 9.9, will be sufficient for many control applications. However, some devices need additional interfacing. There are two important things to remember when building these interfaces:

1 Computer outputs provide very little current capacity and therefore will require an interface for anything larger than say an LED.

2 Inputs must have a clean signal. If external power sources are used the inputs must be protected against excessive voltages and current and have a common ground to the computer or control board.

Figures 9.30 and 9.31 show the circuits of two useful interfaces. The stepper motor interface saves the need for the more difficult programming of the four individual stepper motor coils. Only two of the outputs from a computer or driver board are required. The input to pin 15 must be pulsed in order for the spindle of the stepper motor to turn. Pin 3 will determine the direction of rotation. The second interface is for use with the reflective opto switch or slotted opto switch. It is possible to purchase a slotted opto switch 'with logic'. If this device is used this circuit will not be needed.

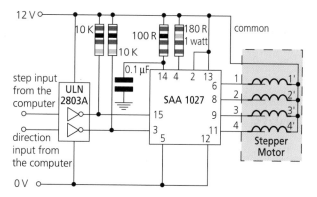

Fig. 9.30 *Stepper motor interface*

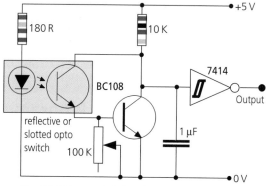

Fig. 9.31 *Opto switch interface*

Putting it into practice

1. List as many processes as you can think of where robots could be used in manufacturing and say why they would be used rather than people.

2. Draw a flow diagram that shows all the steps involved in formatting a floppy disc for a personal computer.

3. Explain the term 'on-board computer control' and state some of its advantages compared to other control systems.

4. The use of interfaces is an important consideration in computer control. Why do we need to use these interfaces?

5. What is meant by a 'structured program' and why it is important to write your control programs in this way?

6. Explain the terms 'high level language' and 'low level language'.

7. Control systems can be either 'open loop' or 'closed loop'. What is meant by these terms?

8. Microprocessors are important components in computers. Briefly explain what the microprocessor does and why it can be used in control systems.

9. Copy the table below and fill in the sensors you think could be used to test for each of the conditions listed.

Test condition	Sensor
temperature in a greenhouse	
a window is open	
a shaft has rotated two times	
a barrier in a car park is raised	
a model train is approaching a level crossing	

10. Draw a flowchart of the sequence of events for an automatic railway level crossing from the time a train approaches to the time the barriers are raised and the lights go out.

11. List the components, including all sensors, that you would need to model the automatic railway level crossing described above.

12. Write a control program for the automatic railway level crossing described above using a computer language available at your school.

10 · Circuit board production

It is important to make the distinction between modelling, using techniques such as breadboarding or wire wrapping, and the more permanent solution of a printed circuit board (PCB). For modelling techniques you should refer to Chapter 2.

DESIGNING CIRCUIT BOARDS

The design and production of circuit boards is the process used to physically connect the components shown in a circuit diagram. This is obviously done in the later stages of the designing and making of the electronic product but this does not make it any less important. The choices of what type of circuit board is to be used (Figure 10.1) and how it is to be made have important implications in the design process.

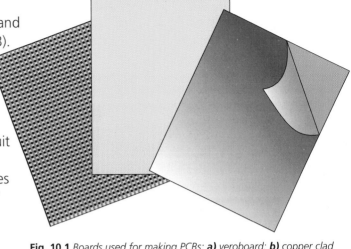
Fig. 10.1 *Boards used for making PCBs:* ***a)*** *veroboard;* ***b)*** *copper clad board;* ***c)*** *photo resist board with covering film*

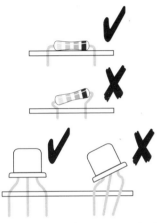
Fig. 10.2 *Correct and incorrect methods of mounting components*

Component sizes

Whichever method of circuit board production is chosen it is worthwhile planning carefully the component layout. The physical size of each component needs to be considered as well as the number of connections and its best position on the circuit board. The distance between the connections on some components cannot be altered, e.g. DIL (dual in line) integrated circuits have a spacing between the legs of 0.1 inches. Figure 10.2 shows some correct and incorrect methods of mounting components.

Stripboard

Stripboard is the simplest form of printed circuit board (PCB) manufacture and is only really suitable for simple and one-off products. It is made from a board of insulating material with copper strips bonded to its surface. Holes are pre-drilled in lines at a distance of 0.1 inches apart. The copper strips are used as the interconnections between components. The copper tracks are cut as necessary to ensure that the connections between components match those of the circuit design. The tracks can either be cut with a specialist stripboard cutter or a small twist drill (3 mm). Components will have to be arranged to suit the copper strips and not as originally drawn in a circuit diagram.

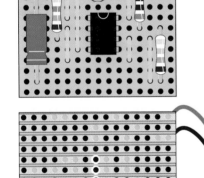
Fig. 10.3 *Component layout and copper strip side of a 555 astable circuit*

Figure 10.3 shows the component layout and the copper strip side of a 555 astable circuit. The track has had to be cut between the rows of connections of the IC. It is very important when using stripboard to ensure that tracks are cut where necessary to avoid a short circuit situation. Notice also how the components are placed parallel to the edges of the board. Always avoid placing components and wires at angles other than 90° to each other.

▷ Design issues – circuit boards

1. What type of circuit board is best suited to the electronic product?
2. What method of manufacture will be used?
3. Does the circuit board have to fit into a given space and therefore have a maximum size?
4. What are the physical sizes of the components to be used?
5. How many connections will have to be made to each component?

Artetch is based in Littlehampton, Sussex. The company was founded in 1967, and it is a major manufacturer of quality printed circuit boards. Using the latest technology, the majority of the pcbs that Artetch produce are designed and manufactured for surface mounting. However, many of the processes are similar to those described in this chapter.

The first part of the process is concerned with quality assurance. With the aid of computer technology rigorous checks are made to make sure that there are no errors within the pcb design. You can see this in the photo on the right. The software system that checks this also enables Artetch to automate much of the manufacturing of the pcbs, such as the photographic work and the drilling.

In the photo on the left you can see the photographic department.

PCB MANUFACTURE

Basic principles

Whichever method you choose there are some important things to remember. These are:

- model the circuit first to ensure that it works (see Chapter 2);
- collect data regarding the size and distance between the pins or leads of the components to be used;
- unlike the circuit diagram, tracks cannot cross;
- place components and tracks in line or at right angle to each other, parallel with the edge of the board.

Direct artwork method

This method is used to produce fairly simple PCBs often for one-off circuits.

Planning

Plan the circuit by drawing the components in their likely positions. Draw them to their approximate size on to graph paper with a 0.1 inch grid and as if looking down on the components, not from underneath.

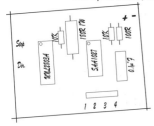

Mark the positions of all pins/leads of components. These will be the pads on the PCB (Fig. 10.4).

Fig. 10.4

Drawing the pads and tracks

Turn the paper over, and using a light source such as a light box, draw the pads.

Draw the routes between the pads checking carefully against the circuit diagram. Remember that tracks cannot cross but can pass component connections. It is worth spending time and effort at this stage to get the layout just right. This is the layout for the PCB (Fig. 10.5).

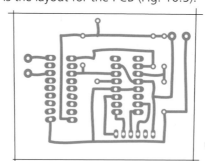

Fig. 10.5 *PCB from component side*

Cleaning

Thoroughly clean a piece of copper clad- board, cut to size, using fine wire wool (Fig. 10.6) or abrasive block. Wash and dry it (do not touch the copper surface once cleaned).

Fig. 10.6

Transferring the design

Place a piece of carbon paper between the copper surface and the paper with the PCB layout (Fig. 10.7). Mark carefully the positions of all the pads and tracks.

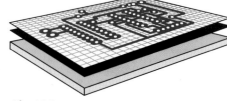

Fig. 10.7

Apply etch-resist transfer pads to the positions marked. Using either etch-resist transfer lines or an etch-resist pen, draw in all the required tracks (Fig. 10.8).

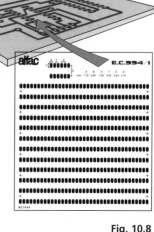

Fig. 10.8

The photographic process is carried out in a controlled environment to produce a film, which is used in the photomechanical process of printing of the circuit on to the copper surface (this is shown in the photo on the top right). The drilling of the holes is fully automated and linked to the computer system used in the first part of the process. Once the unwanted copper has been removed, multi-layered boards are bonded together. The tracks on the outer sides are coated, leaving exposed the pads to which components and wires are to be soldered. These pads are then plated with a tin and lead mix, often using a process called hot air levelling (HAL). Artetch are also using a more advanced process called alpha level, which, among its advantages over HAL, is more environmentally friendly.

Once this plating has been done, final quality checks are made to the pcbs before being dispatched to the customer. In the photo on the right you can see one of Artetch's pcbs.

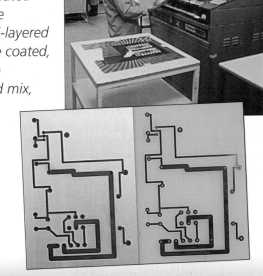

Photographic method
Hand drawn on acetate sheet

Plan the circuit in the same way as the direct artwork method (Fig. 10.5). Place a 0.1 inch layout grid underneath a clear sheet of acetate (Fig. 10.9). Accurately and neatly produce the designed layout using dry transfers for the pads and either dry transfers or a suitable pen for the tracks (Fig. 10.10).

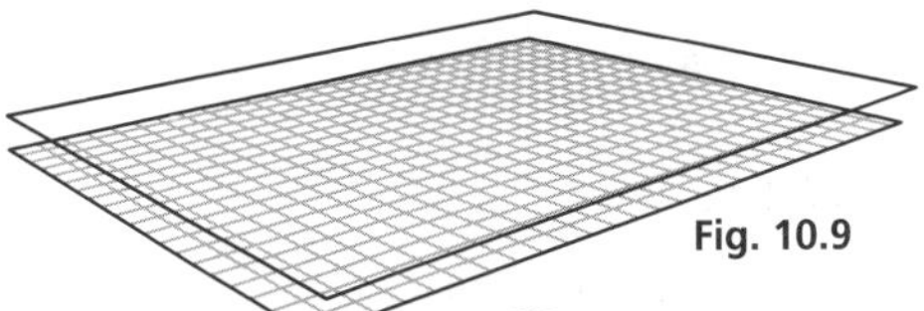

Fig. 10.9

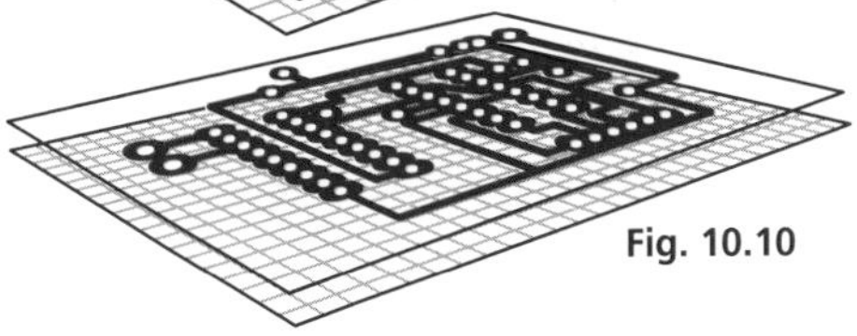

Fig. 10.10

Computer Aided Drawing – print onto acetate sheet

Computer aided design techniques (Fig. 10.11) have many advantages and emulate (imitate) industrial techniques:

- changes are easily made;
- direct plotting onto boards is possible;
- easy production of photo masks;
- component layout drawings can be produced;
- double-sided boards are possible.

Place the components first using the program library and then route the tracks on screen. When satisfied with the solution print it out on paper and photocopy it onto an acetate sheet, or for best results use a laser printer and print it directly onto the acetate sheet.

Using a light box

Place the acetate sheet onto the glass surface of an ultraviolet light box with the pad and track artwork on top. Place the photo-resist side face down on top of the artwork (Fig. 10.12).

Carefully close the lid of the ultraviolet box making sure the board or artwork does not move. Turn on the light box. The exposure time will depend on the type of ultraviolet box, the photo-resist boards used, their age and the density of the tracks and pads. Normal exposure time will be between $1\frac{1}{2}$ and 4 minutes.

Developing

Place the exposed board into the developer solution using PCB tongs and wearing suitable protective clothing including gloves and goggles (Fig. 10.13). Gently agitate the solution until a clear definition of the circuit and the exposed copper can be seen. Remove the PCB with the tongs and wash it thoroughly.

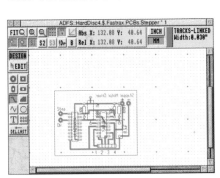

Fig. 10.11

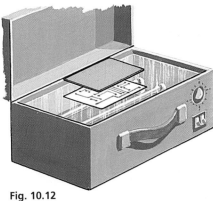

Fig. 10.12

Fig. 10.13

Etching – all methods

Bubble etch touch

Using tongs, place the board into the basket of a bubble etch tank (Fig. 10.14) and immerse it in a heated solution of ferric chloride (goggles and protective gloves should be worn). Turn on the agitator. The time taken will depend on the quality of the solution but will normally be between 8 and 15 minutes. Once etched, remove the board with tongs and wash it thoroughly.

Component placement

First of all, leads for components such as resistors and capacitors should be bent carefully by using pliers (Fig. 10.17). Position low profile components first (i.e. those that do not stick up very far) such as resistors and IC holders (use holders for any ICs).

On single-sided boards the components are placed on the opposite side to the copper tracks and pushed as close as possible to the board.

Soldering

Place the soldering iron against the pad and wire of the component. Hold it there for a few seconds then touch the solder against the pad and leg letting just enough solder encircle both (Fig. 10.19). You should always solder in a well ventilated area.

Check to make sure you do not have a dry joint – this can often be recognised by the solder being a dull grey colour and sometimes forming a ball which does not adhere to the track.

To complete the process remove any excess wire (Fig. 10.20).

Fig. 10.14

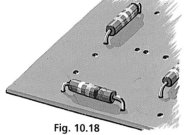

Fig. 10.17

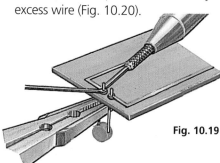

Fig. 10.19

Cleaning

Clean the board of any dry transfer or inks with an abrasive block. There is no need to remove the photo-resist from the copper tracks – it will provide a useful protective film and prevent the copper from oxidising (Fig. 10.15).

Fig. 10.18

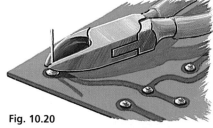

Fig. 10.20

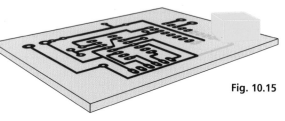

Fig. 10.15

Drilling

Drill all the holes using a suitable drill (Fig. 10.16). This will normally be about 1 mm but smaller or larger sizes may be needed depending on the components used.

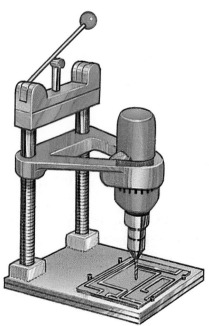

Fig. 10.16

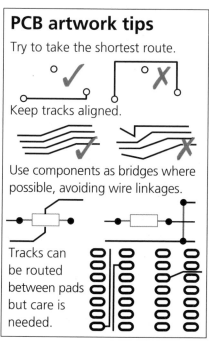

PCB artwork tips

Try to take the shortest route.

Keep tracks aligned.

Use components as bridges where possible, avoiding wire linkages.

Tracks can be routed between pads but care is needed.

11· Testing and fault finding

TESTING

In managing any project it is important to allow time for testing of your work. Testing is important at the early experimental stages of a project when mistakes are easier to put right. Complicated project work can be broken down into smaller modules which can then be tested separately as work progresses.

Before any testing can take place you need to know precisely what should happen. These expectations will normally be in your specification.

To be even clearer about how you will test your design you should list your tests in a testing schedule (Figure 11.2).

Fig. 11.1 *Electronic engineers use a range of test equipment*

Date	Test	Result	Action
11/5	Current Consumption <40 mA	30 mA	OK
13/5	Test in situ Test for water tightness	Leaks!	Seal w compo
14/5	Re test for water tightness (to 1 metre deep).	OK	

Testing Schedule –

Fig. 11.2 *A testing schedule for a finished project or module*

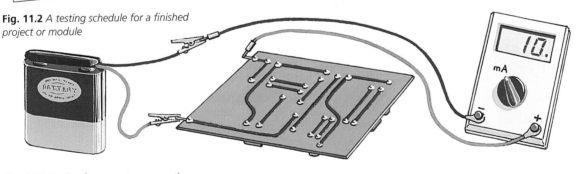

Fig. 11.3 *Testing for current consumption using a meter set to measure mA*

Design issues – testing

1. Use a testing schedule and update it as work proceeds.
2. Faults cannot be found if the design specifications are too vague – what exactly must the product do?
3. Testing may reveal faults that are mechanical as well as electronic. Is the circuit board held securely? Can the battery be changed easily?
4. Don't be put off if the circuit doesn't work first time; record all results carefully. Try to work logically.
5. If your fault finding fails, get help.

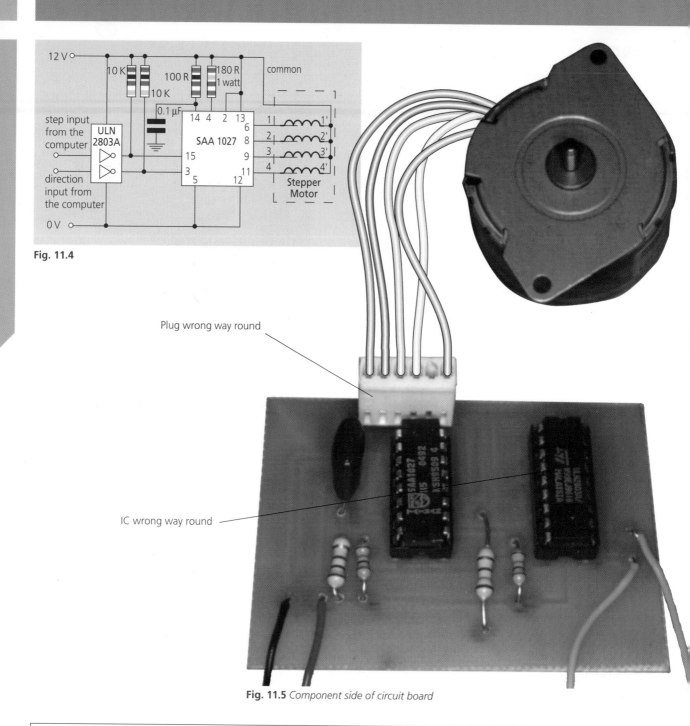

Fig. 11.4

Plug wrong way round

IC wrong way round

Fig. 11.5 *Component side of circuit board*

A logical approach to fault finding

1 Check that your circuit matches your design.

2 Check that all the components are in the correct place and are the right value. Have you double checked any colour coded components?

3 Many components can easily be the wrong way round. Check the polarity of the battery, electrolytic capacitors, diodes and the orientation of ICs.

4 Errors can be made with the pins of transistors. Recheck that they are the correct way round.

5 Check the connections of switches and relays. Do not mix up normally open and normally closed pins.

6 If an output fails to work, check that there is enough current to operate it.

7 Use a meter set to measure resistance to check for continuity of connections in the circuit.

8 Use a meter set to measure voltage to check that the appropriate parts of the circuit are at the correct potential. Are all ICs powered up?

9 Work through the circuit with a voltmeter tracing the signal. If voltage levels are changing, check that the change is enough to operate the next stage of the circuit.

10 Check individual components.

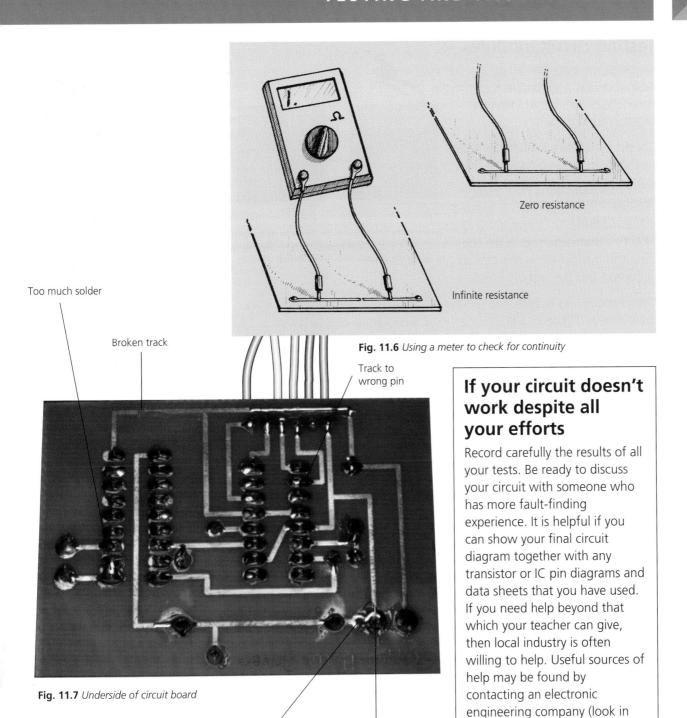

Fig. 11.6 *Using a meter to check for continuity*

Too much solder

Broken track

Track to wrong pin

Zero resistance

Infinite resistance

Fig. 11.7 *Underside of circuit board*

Dry joint

Frayed wire

If your circuit doesn't work despite all your efforts

Record carefully the results of all your tests. Be ready to discuss your circuit with someone who has more fault-finding experience. It is helpful if you can show your final circuit diagram together with any transistor or IC pin diagrams and data sheets that you have used. If you need help beyond that which your teacher can give, then local industry is often willing to help. Useful sources of help may be found by contacting an electronic engineering company (look in the Yellow Pages) or by asking your school's Neighbourhood Engineer for help.

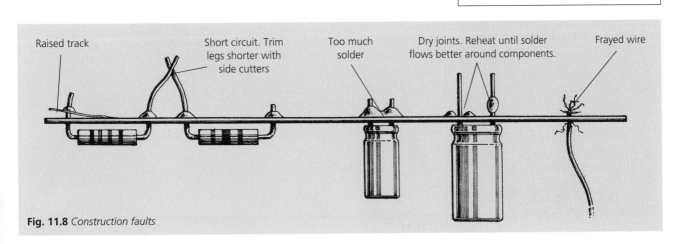

Raised track

Short circuit. Trim legs shorter with side cutters

Too much solder

Dry joints. Reheat until solder flows better around components.

Frayed wire

Fig. 11.8 *Construction faults*

Testing circuit modules

It is often more convenient to design, model, build and test circuits as building blocks that link together (Figure 11.10).

Check … that each module has both a positive and zero volt power supply. If using an operation amplifier (op amp) then three wires may be required to power up the IC.

Check … that each module has the correct number of signal connections between it and the next module(s).

Colour code wires help to identify them quickly (Figure 11.11).

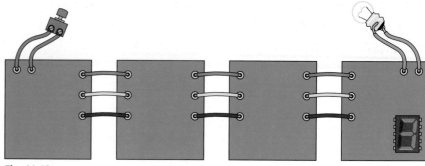

Fig. 11.10

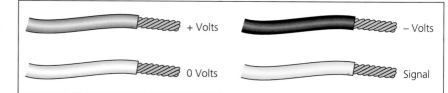

Fig. 11.11

Fig. 11.12

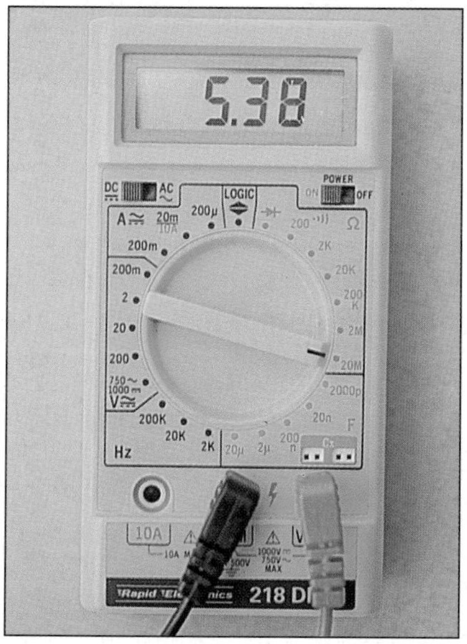

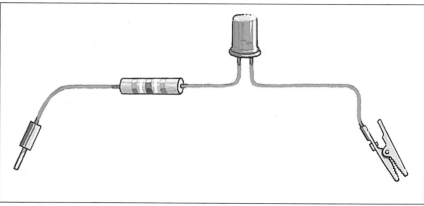

Fig. 11.13

MULTIMETERS

There are many types of multimeter but they fall into two categories, analogue (Figure 11.12) and digital (Figure 11.13). Digital meters have the advantage of making it easier to read a precise value, but analogue meters are quicker to use when looking for approximate values or degrees of change.

Multimeters are so called because they replace the functions of separate meters that measure voltage, current and resistance.

Most multimeters require you to select the range of values that you expect to examine and the function that you want to use (voltage AC or DC, resistance, current).

Some meters can also measure capacitance, indicate continuity with a buzzer, include diode and transistor testing facilities and sample and hold options. The provision of 'auto ranging' means that the user can leave the range setting to the meter but must be aware that subsequent readings may use different ranges.

When using a multimeter be sure to observe the polarity of the leads especially with an analogue meter. Most voltage readings need to be taken with the negative lead connected to the zero volt rail of the circuit.

A simple logic probe to indicate high or low voltage levels can be made up by using an LED with an appropriate current limiting resistor (Figure 11.14).

Fig. 11.14

Reference section

Use these pages to look up detailed information on formulae, codes and components.

The index will help you to cross-reference back to the appropriate pages in the main text of the book.

SIGNS, SYMBOLS AND SCHEMATICS

Component name	Symbol
conductor (wire)	
crossing conductors (no connection)	
joined conductors	
terminal	
cell	
battery	
transformer	
earth	
fuse	
push to make switch	
push to break switch	
single pole single throw switch	
single pole double throw switch	
double pole double throw switch	
rotary switch	
reed switch	
relay	

Component name	Symbol
fixed resistor	
potentiometer	
preset potentiometer	
thermistor	
light dependent resistor	
capacitor	
electrolytic capacitor	
variable capacitor	
signal lamp	
lamp	
motor	
buzzer	
bell	
loudspeaker	
microphone	
piezo transducer	
voltmeter	
ammeter	
ohm-meter	
oscilloscope	

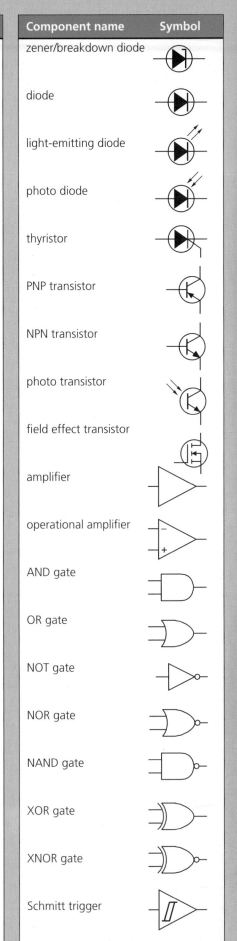

Component name	Symbol
zener/breakdown diode	
diode	
light-emitting diode	
photo diode	
thyristor	
PNP transistor	
NPN transistor	
photo transistor	
field effect transistor	
amplifier	
operational amplifier	
AND gate	
OR gate	
NOT gate	
NOR gate	
NAND gate	
XOR gate	
XNOR gate	
Schmitt trigger	

Integrated circuits and symbols

The circuit symbol for an IC will often be shown with the connections in a sequence which helps to simplify the circuit diagram. The symbol in Figure 2 shows an IC with the connections in the correct sequence labelled to help identify the connections. ICs in electronic catalogues will usually be drawn in this way.

An IC may be drawn to show the arrangement of components within its structure as shown in Figure 1.

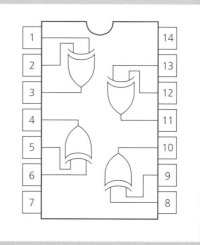

Fig. 1 *Symbol for an integrated circuit*

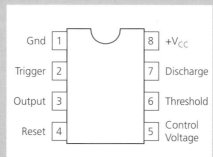

Fig. 2 *IC with connections labelled*

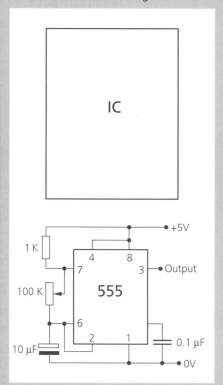

Fig. 3 *IC showing the arrangement of connecting components*

Printed circuit board pads and connections

When making printed circuit boards for school projects use the round pads, where possible, for components such as capacitors and resistors where the connections are relatively far apart. These should be as large as is practicable on the circuit board to be used. Components like transistors will often have to use small round pads in order to ensure the connections do not touch each other. Elongated pads are useful when legs are in line and close together, such as an LED. Dual-in-line pads are available on all printed circuit board computer aided design programs but if using hand methods it is important to make sure that each line of pads is the correct distance apart as shown in Figure 4.

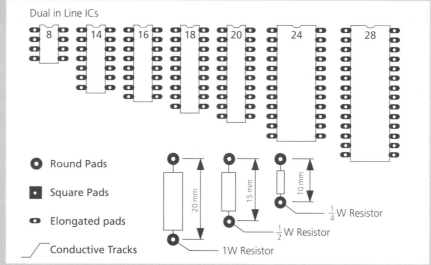

Fig. 4 *Dual-in-line Ics*

Flow charting

Flow charts will help you in planning systems. By using the graphic symbols shown in Figures 5 and 6 you will be able to produce a picture which shows how a system will operate.

Notice that when a decision is made that the link line is connected to another line. You should not make a connection to the side of a process or stop/start symbol.

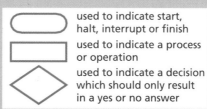

⬭	used to indicate start, halt, interrupt or finish
▭	used to indicate a process or operation
◇	used to indicate a decision which should only result in a yes or no answer

Fig. 5 *Flow chart symbols*

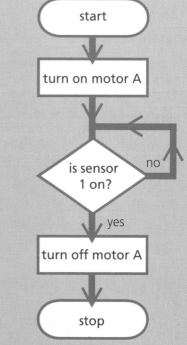

Fig. 6 *Example of a flow chart*

111

RESISTORS

Resistors are used to resist the flow of electricity in a circuit. Resistance is measured in Ohms. To try to appreciate what resistance is like try drawing pencil lines with a soft pencil and measuring their resistance with a meter.

Units of resistance

Resistance is measured in Ohms. A single Ohm is a very small unit. Resistors are often given the multipliers of Kilo and Mega to signify thousands and millions of Ohms.

Resistances can be written with or without decimal points. However, it is now best practice to substitute the letter R (for multipliers of one), K (for multipliers of one thousand) or M (for multipliers of one million) for the decimal point, as shown in these examples.

4R7 = 4.7 Ohms
1K0 = 1000 Ohms
1K2 = 1200 Ohms
5M6 = 5 600 000 Ohms

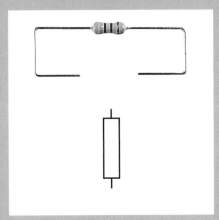

Fig. 9 *Carbon film resistor*

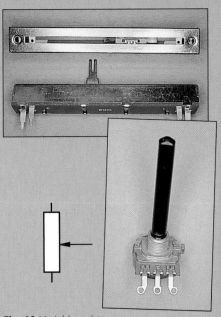

Fig. 10 *Variable resistors*

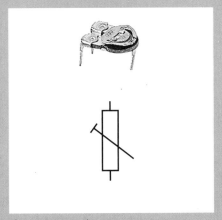

Fig. 11 *Preset resistor*

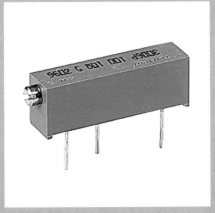

Fig. 12 *Multi-turn cermet resistor for precision adjustment*

Ohm's law

Ohm's law allows you to relate voltage (V), current (I) and resistance (R). It can be written as a formula $V = I \times R$. This can be rearranged to make $I = V/R$ and $R = V/I$.

To help you to remember this important formula use this triangle.

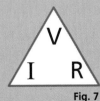

Fig. 7

Power calculations

To calculate the amount of power being used by a component you need to multiply the current flowing (I) by the voltage across the component (V). This will give the power in units of Watts.

The formula Power (P) = $V \times I$ can also be remembered using a triangle.

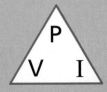

Fig. 8

Preferred values

Resistors are available in decade multiples or sub-multiples in the two following ranges (BS 2488).

E12 range: 10 12 15 18 22 27
33 39 47 56 68 82

E24 range: 10 11 12 13 15 16
18 20 22 24 27 30
33 36 39 43 47 51
56 62 68 75 82 91

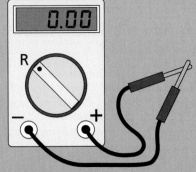

Fig. 13 *Continuity testing*

Testing for continuity

A perfect connection will have 'zero resistance'. The opposite of this is when there is no connection at all. Then the resistance will be infinite (an immeasurably large amount). Try this out using a meter set to measure resistance. Using this technique when checking a piece of work is called continuity testing.

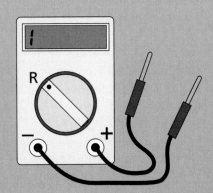

Joining resistors

Fig. 14 *Two or more resistors in series*

Fig. 15 *Two resistors in parallel*

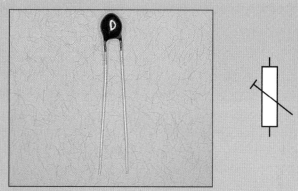

Fig. 16 *More than two resistors in parallel*

$$\frac{1}{R_{TOT}} = \frac{1}{R1} + \frac{1}{R2} + \frac{1}{R3}$$

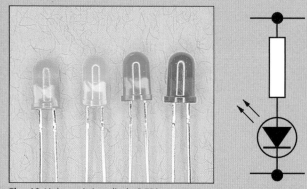

Fig. 17 *Light dependent resistor*

Fig. 18 *Thermistor*

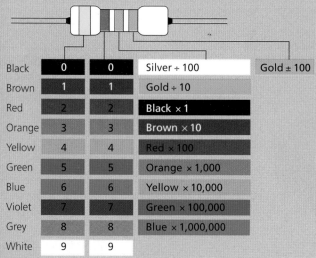

Fig. 19 *Light emitting diode (LED)*

Calculating the value of a series resistor for a light emitting diode (LED)

Check first the voltage to be used, and the maximum current the LED will take (usually about 20 mA). Then use Ohm's law to find the theoretical value of the resistor.

Example
Voltage = 9 Volts, Maximum LED current = 20mA (0.02 A)

$R = V/I$
$= 9\,V \div 0.02\,A$
$= 450R$ (The nearest preferred value is 470R)

Resistor colour codes

The resistor colour codes for four band carbon film resistors are shown in Figure 20.

Black	0	0	Silver ÷ 100	Gold ± 100
Brown	1	1	Gold ÷ 10	
Red	2	2	Black × 1	
Orange	3	3	Brown × 10	
Yellow	4	4	Red × 100	
Green	5	5	Orange × 1,000	
Blue	6	6	Yellow × 10,000	
Violet	7	7	Green × 100,000	
Grey	8	8	Blue × 1,000,000	
White	9	9		

Fig. 20 *Resistor colour codes for four band carbon film resistors*

Voltage dividers

Figure 21 shows how to find a voltage at the join of two or more resistances.

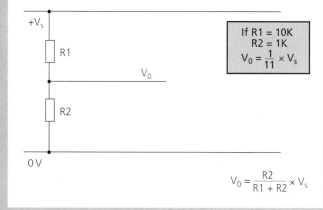

If R1 = 10K
R2 = 1K
$V_0 = \frac{1}{11} \times V_s$

$$V_0 = \frac{R2}{R1 + R2} \times V_s$$

Fig. 21 *To find a voltage at the join of two or more resistances*

CAPACITORS

Capacitors are used to store electrical charge. They are sometimes described as short-term batteries. They are frequently used in circuits to create time delays and also as part of oscillators (circuits that produce an oscillating output).

Units of capacitance

The original unit of capacitance is the Farad (F). It is a very large unit named after Faraday, who is sometimes called the father of electricity. This is the unit from which the other more useful units are derived.

What is a Farad? A capacitor = 1 Farad when it holds 1 coulomb (1 ampere = 1 coulomb per second) of charge and has a voltage of 1 volt across its terminals.

More useful units are:

μF (Microfarad), 1 μF = 1 millionth of a Farad (10^{-6})
nF (Nanofarad), 1 nF = 1 thousand millionth of a Farad (10^{-9})
pF (Picofarad), 1 pF = 1 million millionth of a Farad (10^{-12})

Common comparative values for capacitors and their codes

Fig. 22 *Ceramic disc capacitor for low values*

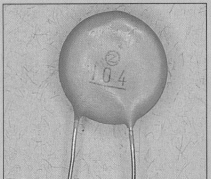

Fig. 23 *Polyester capacitor*

pF	nF	μF	code
10	0.01	–	100
15	0.015	–	150
47	0.047	–	470
82	0.082	–	820
100	0.1	–	101
330	0.33	–	331
470	0.47	0.00047	471
1000	1.0	0.001	102
1500	1.5	0.0015	152
2200	2.2	0.0022	222
4700	4.7	0.0047	472
6800	6.8	0.0068	682
10000	10	0.01	103
22000	22	0.022	223
47000	47	0.047	473
100000	100	0.1	104
220000	220	0.22	224
470000	470	0.47	474

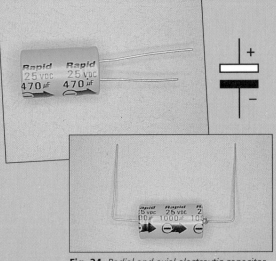

Variable capacitors are used mainly for radio-based circuit designs where a circuit needs to be tuned to different frequencies (see Figure 25).

Fig. 24 *Radial and axial electroytic capacitor*

Fig. 25 *Tuning capacitor*

Working voltages

Many capacitors, especially electrolytics, have a maximum working value marked on them. Do not exceed this value or the capacitor will be destroyed. For economy when purchasing look for the lowest voltage that is consistent with the demands of your circuit.

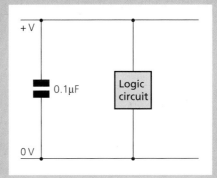

To remove 'spikes'

To remove 'spikes' place a 0.1 (μF capacitor between the power supply connections of a circuit (see Figure 26). Better still place a capacitor as close as possible across the supply connections of ICs on a circuit board.

Fig. 26 *Removing 'spikes'*

Joining capacitors

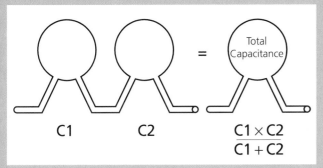

Fig. 27 *Two capacitors in series*

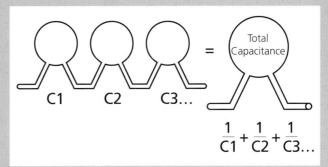

Fig. 28 *Three or more capacitors in series*

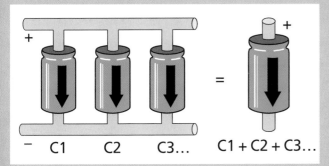

Fig. 29 *Two or more capacitors in parallel*

Charging and discharging

The charging and discharging times of a capacitor are calculated on a time constant. This is the time it takes for a capacitor to charge or discharge 2/3 of its charge. To calculate this time (in seconds) multiply the value of the resistance in Mega Ohms by the value of the capacitor in μF.

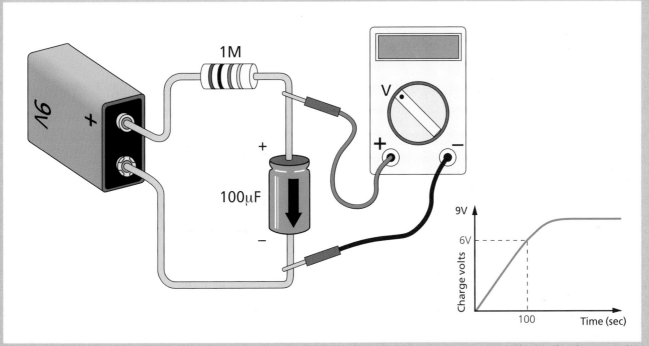

Fig. 30 *Charging a capacitor*

115

SWITCHES AND INPUT DEVICES

Switch symbols

Push to make

Push to break

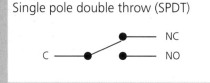

Single pole single throw (SPST)

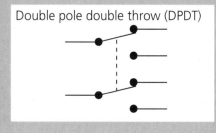

Single pole double throw (SPDT)

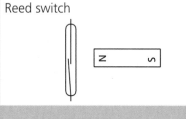
C — NC
NO

Double pole double throw (DPDT)

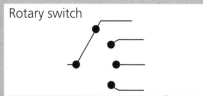

Reed switch

N   S

Rotary switch

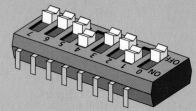

Switch types

Toggle

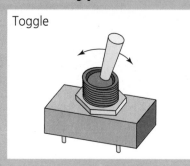

Slide

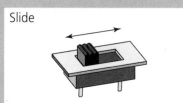

Key

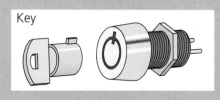

Tilt

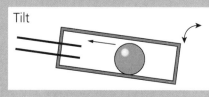

Rocker

Push button

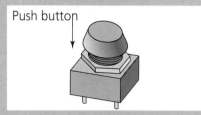

Micro switches

These are useful for applications where a switch is needed to detect movement (see Figures 31–33).

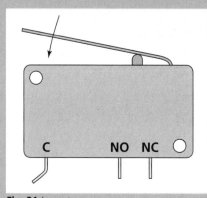
C   NO   NC

Fig. 31 *Lever type*

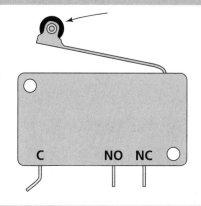
C   NO   NC

Fig. 32 *Roller type*

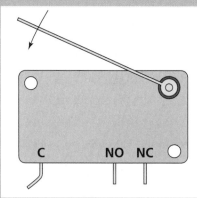
C   NO   NC

Fig. 33 *Sensitive wire lever type*

DIL switches

These are useful when setting input bits to a digital device that needs to be provided with a code or configuration. They are designed to be compact and therefore are quite fiddly if used frequently (Figure 34).

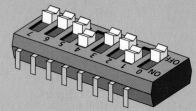

Fig. 34 *DIL switch*

Binary coded switches

These can provide a quick method of entering a pattern of bits to a device (Figure 35).

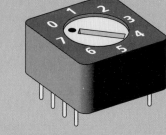

Fig. 35 *Binary coded switch*

Sensor inputs

Light dependent resistor (LDR)

This has a maximum resistance in the dark of approximately 10 Mega Ohms, decreasing according to the amount of light shining on the circular window of cadmium sulphide (Figure 36).

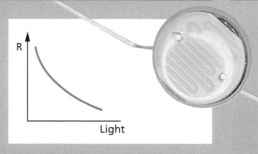

Fig. 36 *Light dependent resistor*

Thermistor

Thermistors are heat dependent resistors, the resistance of which decreases with heat (negative temperature coefficient types) (Figure 37). They are available in different resistance ranges.

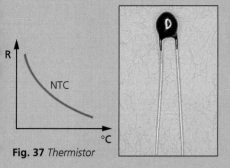

Fig. 37 *Thermistor*

Photo transistors

These react quicker than LDRs and have the amplification and switching properties of a transistor (Figure 38).

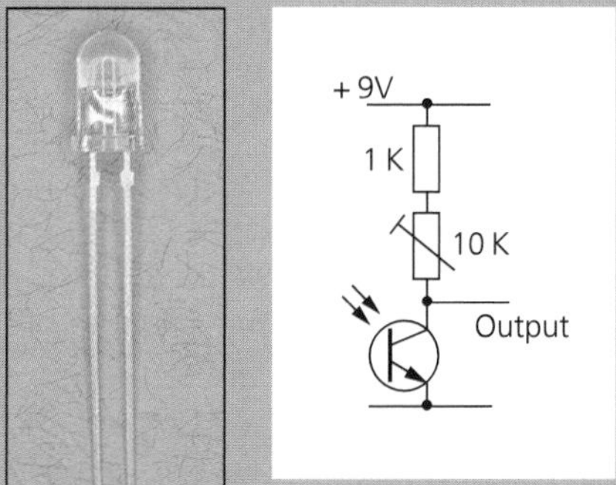

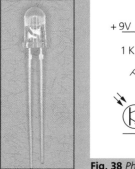

Fig. 38 *Photo transistor*

Photo diodes

These have the advantage of working faster than LDRs and are used mainly to detect infra red light. They are used in reverse bias mode (pointing upwards). When in the dark the diode will conduct a negligible current but when illuminated this increases enough to trigger a transistor (Figure 39).

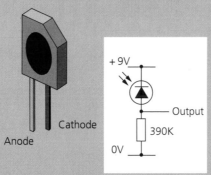

Fig. 39 *Photo diode*

Slotted opto and reflective opto sensors

These ready made packages include aligned infra red photo diodes and LEDs (sources and sensors). More expensive versions also include a logic compatible output (Figure 40).

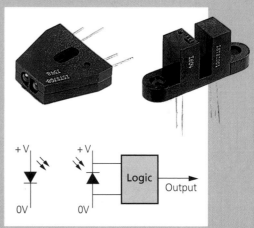

Fig. 40 *Reflective opto and slotted opto sensors*

Useful switching circuits

Digital systems require signals to be definitely on or off. With single transistor switching this is often not 'crisp' enough. The solution is to use a Schmitt trigger gate (usually a NOT gate) (Figure 41).

A DPDT switch can be used to reverse a motor (Figure 42).

SPDT switches can be used for two-way lighting (Figure 43). Either switch can turn the bulb ON and OFF.

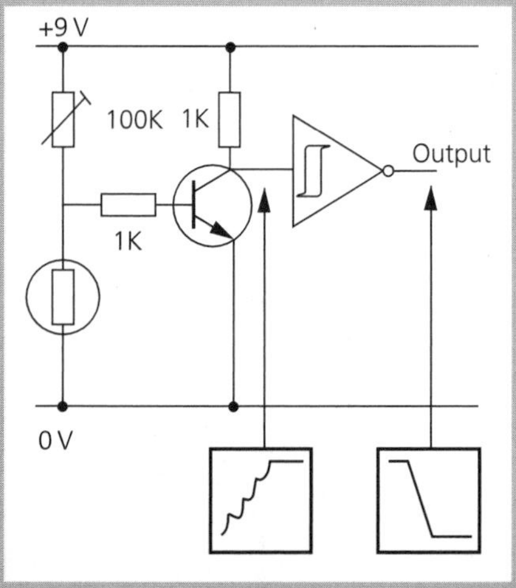

Fig. 41 *Using a Schmitt trigger gate*

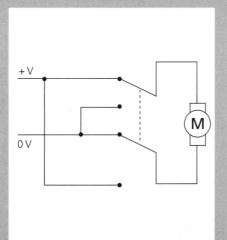

Fig. 42 *Using a DPDT switch to reverse a motor*

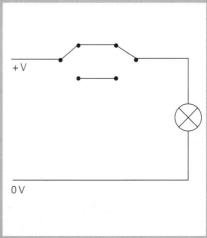

Fig. 43 *Two-way lighting using SPDT switches*

INTEGRATED CIRCUITS

Finding pin 1

On the top surface of a DIL package is a notch or dot. Pin 1 is always to the left of this notch or dot (Figure 44). The pin numbering is always anticlockwise.

Linear integrated circuits

IC timers

The single 555 timer (Figure 46) can be used as a monostable or an astable timer and is suitable for time delays of up to about 20 minutes.

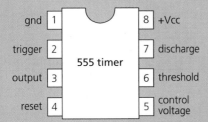

Fig. 46 *Single 555 timer*

The 556 timer (Figure 47) is a dual version of the 555 timer. Each timer can be controlled independently so it is possible to use one timer as an astable and the other timer for a monostable operation.

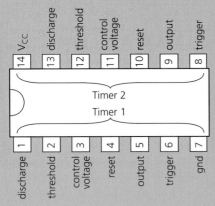

Fig. 47 *Dual timer 556*

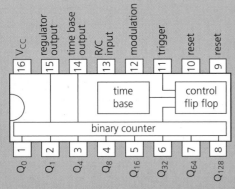

Fig. 49 *UA2240 timer*

Power supply connections and voltage regulators

When designing and building circuits it is important that the correct power supply connections are made. A voltage level (e.g. +12 V) may be shown as: +V which will often indicate that the IC is linear (analogue); V_{CC} indicates the IC is TTL (transistor transistor logic); V_{DD} shows the IC is CMOS (complementary metal oxide semiconductor). The 0 volt will be shown as Gnd (ground) or Vss on a CMOS IC (Figure 44).

The 78L/79L and 78/79 series voltage regulator ICs are used to provide accurate voltages (Figure 45).

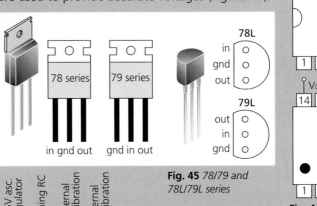

Fig. 45 *78/79 and 78L/79L series*

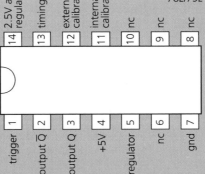

Fig. 48 *ZN1034E precision timer*

The ZN1034E is a precision timer (Figure 48). The UA2240 timer (Figure 49) is a programmable timer. Each is capable of delays from microseconds to days.

Darlington drivers

The ULN2003/4 (Figure 50) and ULN2803 Darlington arrays provide a current of up to 550 mA per output. The ULN2003/2803 can be used with TTL or CMOS. The ULN2004 can be used with CMOS when using a supply voltage of between 6 V and 15 V.

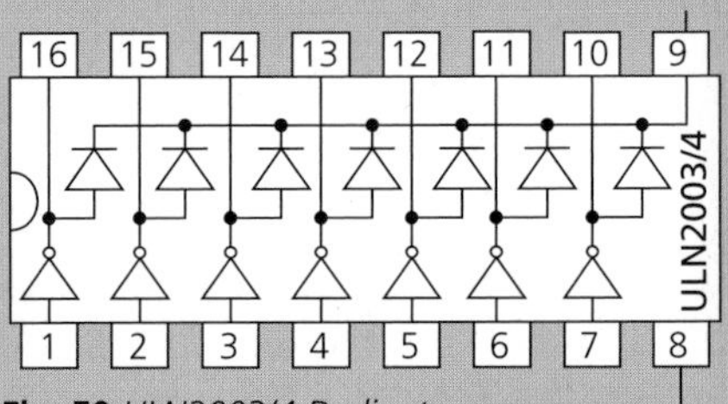

Fig. 52 *LM3909 LED flasher*

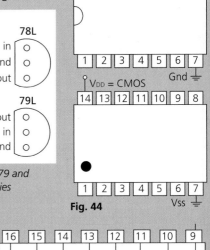

Fig. 44

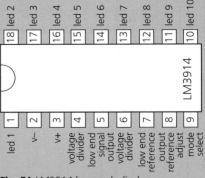

Fig. 50 *ULN2003/4 Darlington array*

LED display drivers

The LM3914 (Figure 51) converts an analogue input voltage into an LED bargraph display. The input voltage will determine the number of LEDs that are illuminated.

Fig. 51 *LM3914 bargraph display*

Using a 1.5 V battery and a capacitor the LM3909 (Figure 52) provides a voltage boost that will flash an LED. This IC can also be used with an 8 Ohm speaker as a tone generator.

Digital integrated circuits

CMOS and TTL ICs operating voltages and compatibility

The 4000 CMOS series has an operating voltage (V_{DD}) of between 3 V and 15 V. The 74HC CMOS series has an operating voltage of between 2 V and 6 V and the 74HCT between 4.5 V and 5.5 V. The 74HCT series can provide direct replacement for TTL ICs (74xx series) and has the advantage of CMOS technology. The 74xx series must have a power supply of exactly 5 V (V_{cc}).

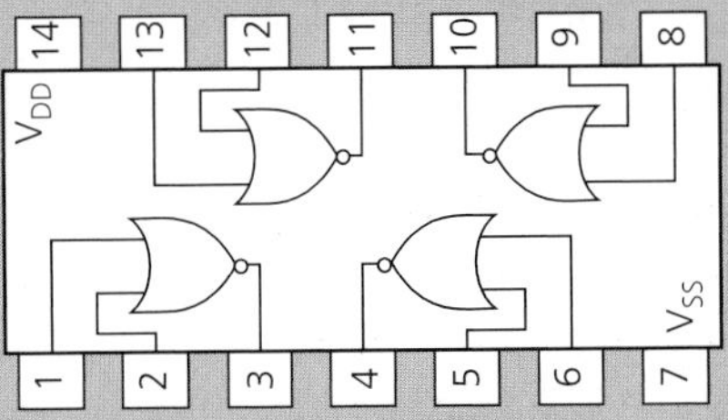

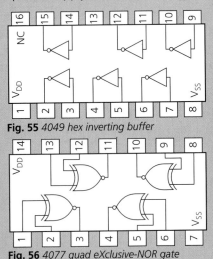

Fig. 57 *4001 quad 2-input NOR gate*

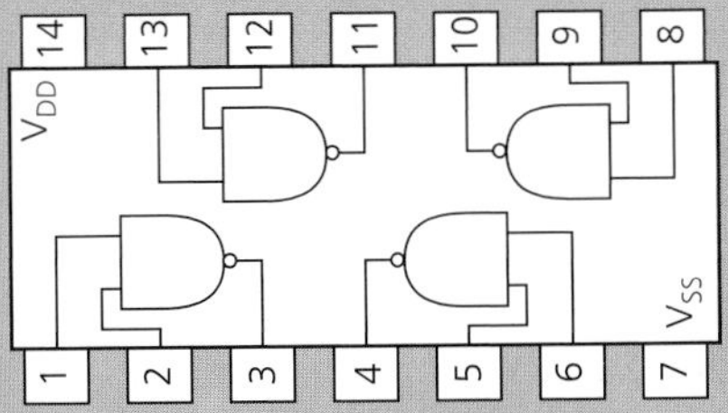

Fig. 53 *4011 quad 2-input NAND gate*

Fig. 55 *4049 hex inverting buffer*

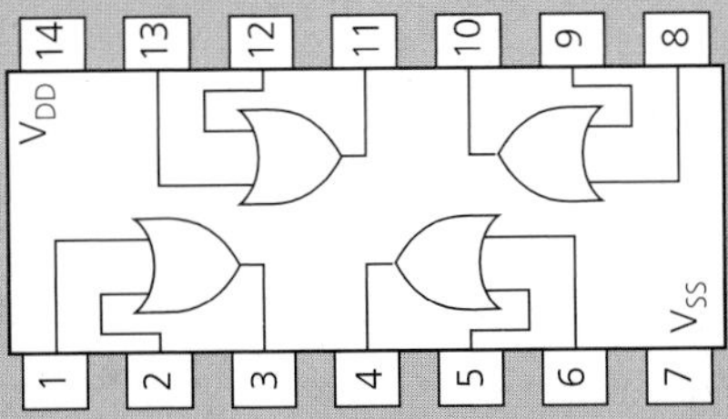

Fig. 58 *4071 quad 2-input OR gate*

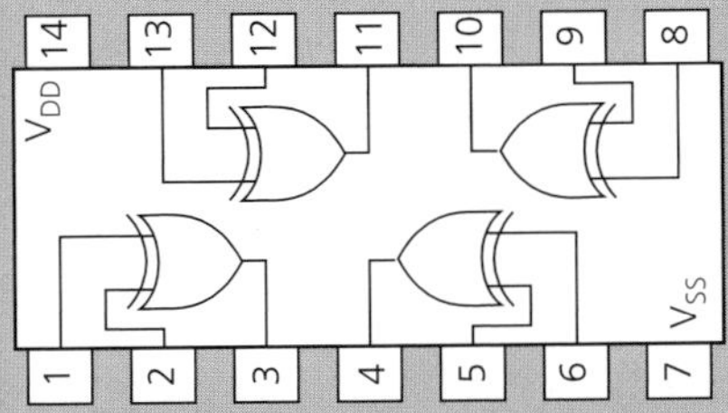

Fig. 54 *4070 quad eXclusive-OR gate*

Fig. 56 *4077 quad eXclusive-NOR gate*

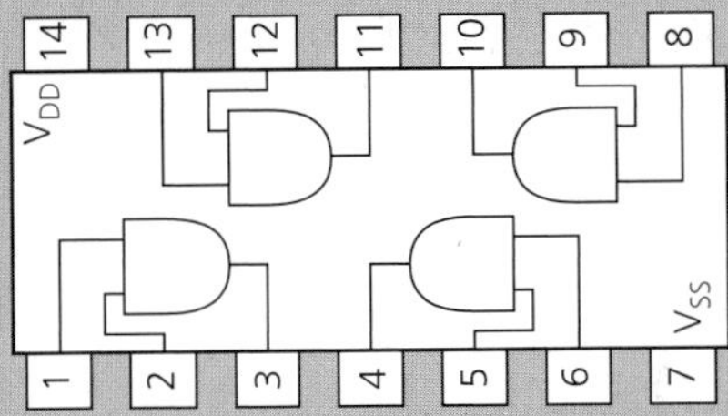

Fig. 59 *4081 quad 2-input AND gate*

CMOS counters

There are a number of counters available in both the CMOS and TTL series of ICs. The counters shown here are used in various sections within this book. Chapter 7 provides more detailed information about these ICs with some example circuits.

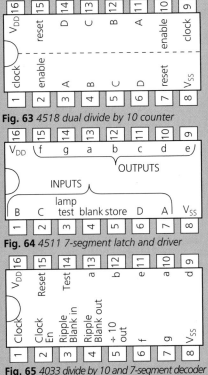

Fig. 63 *4518 dual divide by 10 counter*

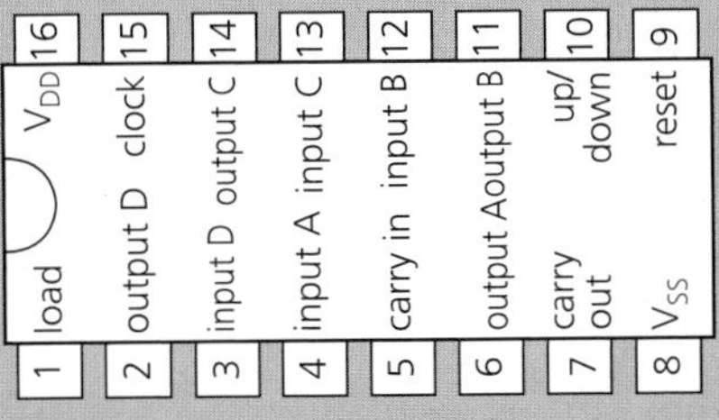

Fig. 66 *4510 divide by 10 up-down counter*

Fig. 64 *4511 7-segment latch and driver*

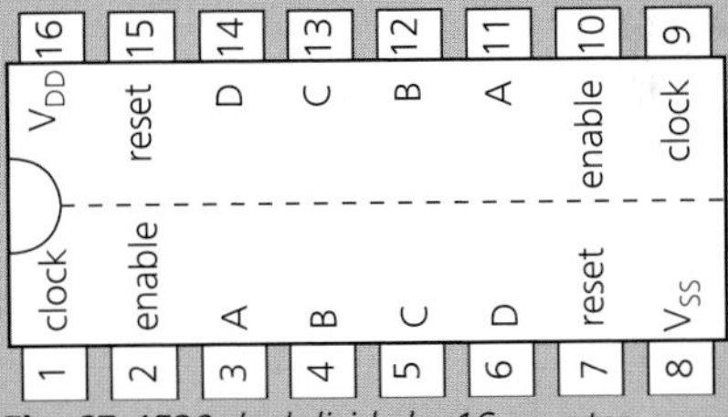

Fig. 67 *4520 dual divide by 16 counter*

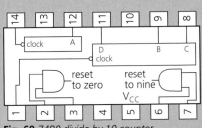

Fig. 60 *7490 divide by 10 counter*

Fig. 65 *4033 divide by 10 and 7-segment decoder*

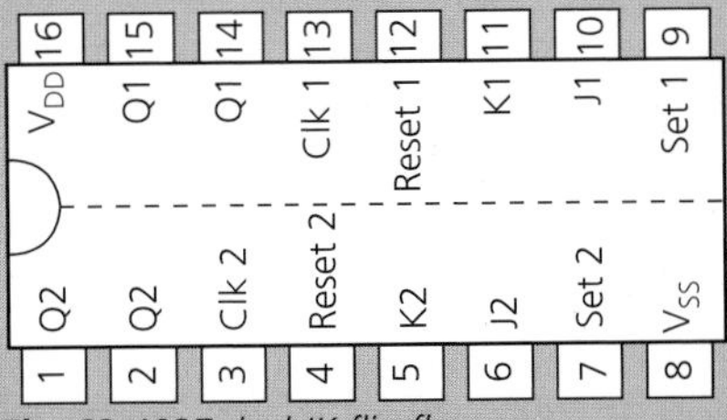

Fig. 68 *4027 dual JK flip-flop*

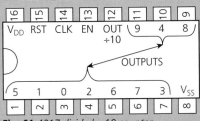

Fig. 61 *4017 divide by 10 counter*

PIC16C54 8-bit CMOS microcontroller

The PIC16C54 (Figure 69) is one of a series of microcontroller ICs that can be programmed through the use of a computer using available programming hardware and software. Programming can be carried out in BASIC or RISCOS machine code. These ICs can provide a very cost effective method of producing on board control systems.

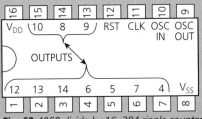

Fig. 62 *4060 divide by 16, 384 ripple counter*

Fig. 69 *PIC16C54 microcontroller IC*

TRANSISTORS

Types of transistor

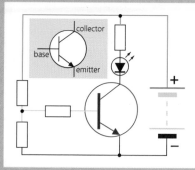

Fig. 70 *N-P-N bipolar transistor*

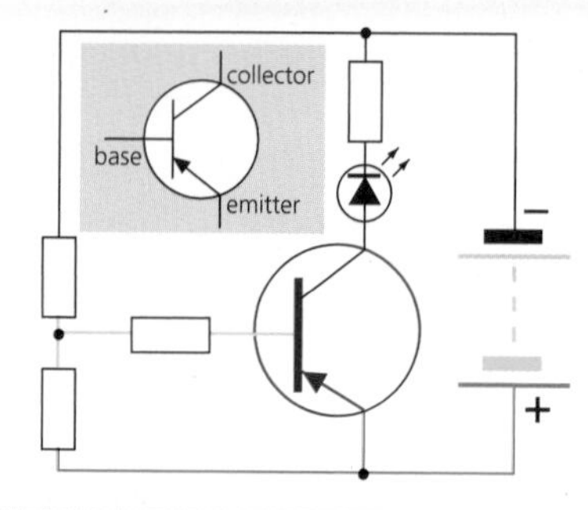

Fig. 71 *P-N-P bipolar transistor*

Fig. 72 *MOSFET (field effect transistor)*

Transistor tables and pinout data

NPN transistor data

Code	Case	I_C (Max)	V_{CE}	h_{FE}	Power	Application
		mA	(max) V	min/max	mW	
BC107	TO18	100	45	110–450	300	Audio Driver
BC108	TO18	100	20	110–800	300	General Purpose
BC109	TO18	100	20	200–800	300	Low Noise Audio
2N3904	TO92	200	40	100–300	350	Switching
ZTX300	E-Line	500	25	50–300	300	General Purpose
2N3053	TO39	700	40	50–250	5000	General Purpose
BFY51	TO39	1000	30	40 min	800	General Purpose
BFY52	TO39	1000	20	60 min	800	General Purpose
BC441	TO39	2000	60	40–250	1000	General Purpose
2N3055	TO3	15000	60	20 min	115000	High Power Amp

PNP transistor data

BC178	TO18	100	25	125–500	300	General Purpose
BC478	TO18	150	40	110–450	360	General Purpose
ZTX500	E-Line	500	25	50–300	300	General Purpose
2N2907A	TO18	600	60	100–300	400	General Purpose

Darlington pairs

TIP120	TO220	5000	60	1000	65000	General Purpose
TIP121	TO220	5000	80	1000	65000	General Purpose

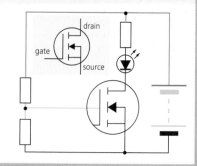

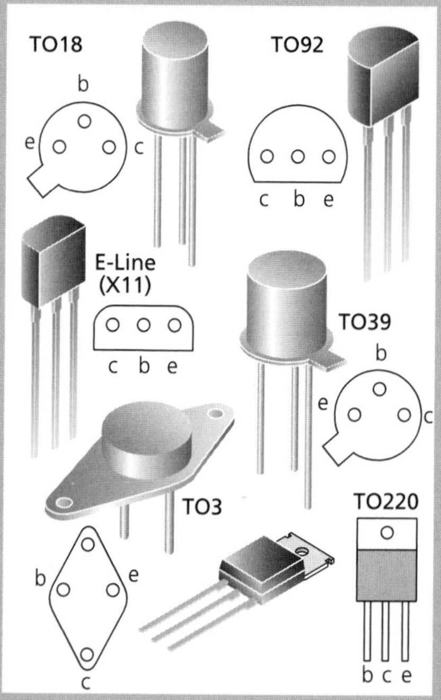

Fig. 73

Note: the pinout data shown only refers to the transistors listed on this page. Other transistors may have different pinout configurations even if using the same case. For example, the TO92 has several pinout configurations but the 2N3904 will always have the pinout arrangement as shown above.

Transistor data glossary

Code: the means of identifying the transistor; consists of a series of letters and numbers.

Case: the shape, physical size of the transistor and the pinout information. The layout of the pins can be different even though two different transistors may have the same type of case.

IC (max): the maximum amount of current (I) that the transistor is able to pass through its collector (C).

VCE (max): the maximum voltage (V) that the transistor is able to carry across its collector (C) and emitter (E) connections.

hFE: the gain of the transistor. Often a minimum and maximum value is given as the gain may vary for a transistor with the same code.

Power (mW): the maximum amount of power that the transistor can sustain. This is given in milliwatts and is calculated by the product of V_{CE} and I_C (Power $= V_{CE} \times I_C$). Where the power is constantly high excessive heat may be generated. This should be dissipated by means of a heatsink or damage to the transistor may occur.

Application: indicates the principle use for which the transistor is designed.

Transistor calculations and formulae

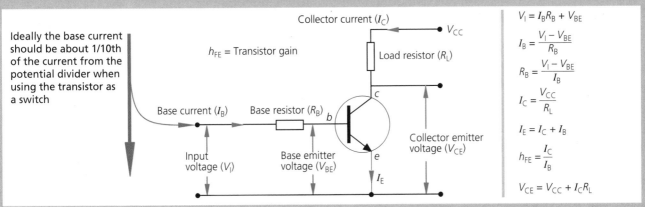

Ideally the base current should be about 1/10th of the current from the potential divider when using the transistor as a switch

h_{FE} = Transistor gain

Collector current (I_C)

V_{CC}

Load resistor (R_L)

Base current (I_B) Base resistor (R_B)

Input voltage (V_I)

Base emitter voltage (V_{BE})

Collector emitter voltage (V_{CE})

$$V_I = I_B R_B + V_{BE}$$

$$I_B = \frac{V_I - V_{BE}}{R_B}$$

$$R_B = \frac{V_I - V_{BE}}{I_B}$$

$$I_C = \frac{V_{CC}}{R_L}$$

$$I_E = I_C + I_B$$

$$h_{FE} = \frac{I_C}{I_B}$$

$$V_{CE} = V_{CC} + I_C R_L$$

Fig. 74

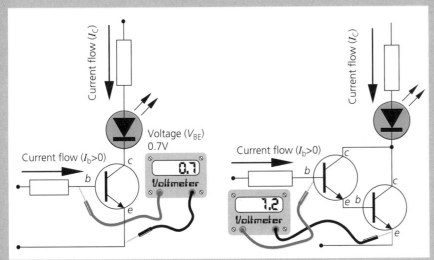

Current flow (I_C)

Current flow (I_C)

Voltage (V_{BE}) 0.7V

Current flow ($I_b > 0$)

0.7
Voltmeter

Current flow ($I_b > 0$)

1.2
Voltmeter

Fig. 75

Fig. 76

Biasing voltages

Bipolar

To forward bias a single bipolar transistor the voltage between the base and the emitter must be greater than 0.6 volts.

For a darlington pair the voltage must be at least 1.2 volts.

MOSFET

To switch on a field effect transistor the voltage at the gate should be between 0.8 and 2.0 volts.

Common transistor circuits

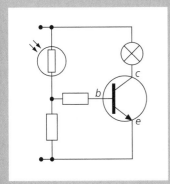

Fig. 77 *Single transistor amplifier*

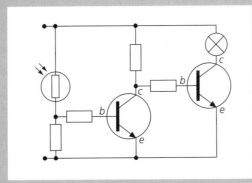

Fig. 78 *Inverting amplifier*

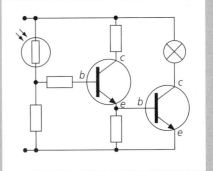

Fig. 79 *Non-inverting amplifier*

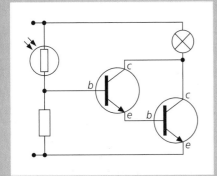

Fig. 80 *Darlington pair*

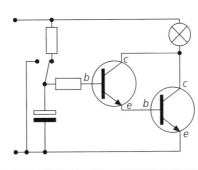

Fig. 81 *Simple timer circuit*

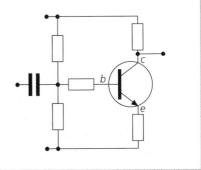

Fig. 82 *Single transistor a.c. amplifier*

OPERATIONAL AMPLIFIERS

The op amp and open loop gain

Figure 83 shows the 741 op amp, an industry standard general purpose operational amplifier. As with all op amps there are five main connections: the supply connections (+V and –V), the inputs (V_N non-inverting and V_I inverting) and the output (V_O).

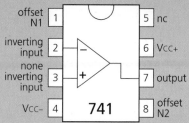

Fig. 83 *The 741 and CA1340E op amp connections*

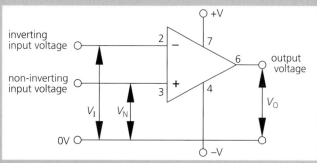

Fig. 84 *Open loop gain*

The gain of the op amp in an open loop circuit is given by:

$$V_O = A_O(V_N - V_I)$$

where A_O is the open loop voltage gain.

The output V_O is dependent on the difference between the two input voltages V_I and V_N :

$V_I > V_N$ then V_O is negative
$V_I < V_N$ then V_O is positive
$V_I = V_N$ then V_O is zero.

Characteristics and properties

Gain: the open loop voltage gain is typically 10^5

High input impedance: typically 10^6 to 10^{12}. This means that very little current is drawn from the circuit or device connected to the inputs of the op amp.

Output current: the output sink or source current of the 741 op amp is about 10 mA. Sufficient to drive an LED. A transistor will be needed for greater current loads.

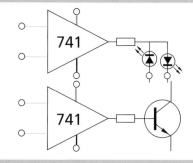

Fig. 85

Negative feedback

Using negative feedback enables greater amplification control. The gain for the non-inverting amplifier is calculated using the formula:

$$A = -R_f \div R_i$$

The gain for the inverting amplifier is calculated using the formula:

$$1 + (R_f \div R_i)$$

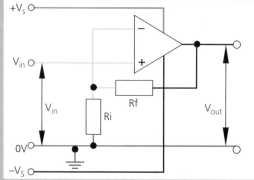

Fig. 86 *Non-inverting amplifier*

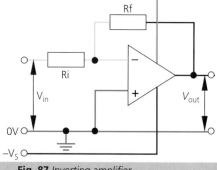

Fig. 87 *Inverting amplifier*

Types of op amps

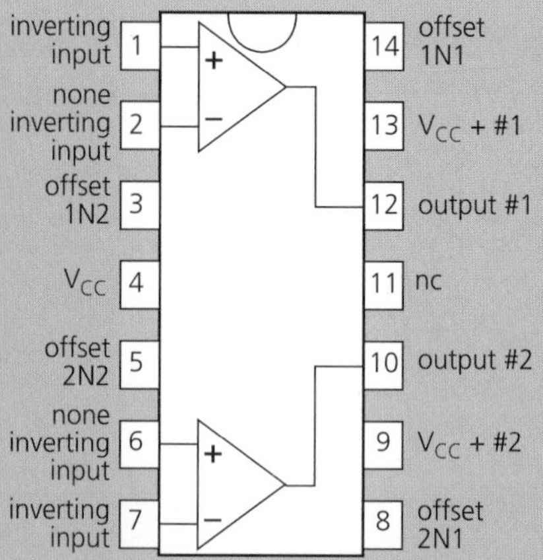

The 747 dual op amp (Figure 88) consists of two 741 op amps with identical pinouts but with a common –V_{cc}.

The RC 4558 (Figure 89) has two op amps which are electrically similar to the 741 op amp but, unlike the 747, has no offset null adjustments.

The LM324N is ideally suited for single supply applications and can operate with voltages as low as 3 V (± 1.5

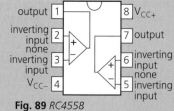

Fig. 89 *RC4558*

V). The LM348 has four 741 op amps using common supply connections.

The CA3140E (Figure 83) is a more efficient op amp than the 741 but the voltage across the inputs must not exceed 8 volts.

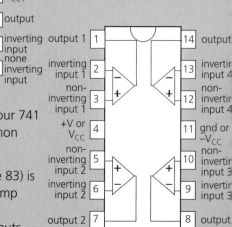

Fig. 88 *747 dual op amp*

Fig. 90 *LM324N and LM348N*

Acknowledgements

The publishers would like to thank the following:

For their help in providing case study material:

David Carter and David Parsons at Electronic Temperature Instruments; Sharron Gibbs at Robinson Marshall; Duracell; Opus Technology; Vickers Medical; Neil Lloyd at Deltronics; Susan Boobyer at Seiko Europe; Junghans; National Physical Laboratory; BBC; Graseby Medical; NAD; Thomson Training and Simulation; Chris Buckland at Artetch; Les James and Charles Segar at Servomex plc.

For their help with supplying materials to photograph:

Students at Heathfield Community College (Fig. 8.36)

For their invaluable help with photography:

Les Cross

For permission to reproduce photographs and illustrations:

Ace Photo Agency (p. 61 top, 8.20)
Aerotech Ltd (1.17)
Besam Ltd (7.1)
Casio (4.13)
Commotion (2.9, 9.9, 9.26)
Les Cross (1.2, 1.3, 1.6, 2.1, 3.2, 3.5, 3.6, 3.23, 4.16,
    4.17, 4.28 photo, 4.33, 4.43, 4.44, 4.45, 4.53, 5.1,
    5.28, 11.5, 11.7, 11.13, p. 112 Fig. 10, p. 113 Figs 17,
    18 & 19, p. 114 Figs 22 & 24, p. 117 Figs 36, 37 & 38)
Data Harvest (4.1, 8.6)
Deltronics (9.12)
Duracell (3.3)
Economatics (9.8, 9.27)
ETI (1.25, 1.26, 1.27, 1.31, 1.32, 1.33, 1.36, 1.39)
Ever Ready (3.1)
Honeywell (4.2)
Intel (9.1)
Michael Manni Photographic (9.5)
Milford Electronics (9.7)
Opus Technology (6.2)
Panasonic (1.4 bottom left, 4.30 photo)
David Rampley (1.29, 1.30, 1.35, 2.8, 8.36)
Rapid Electronics (1.13 left, 3.11, 3.14, 3.29, 3.30, 4.5,
    8.10, 8.11, 8.43, 11.12, p. 114 Figs 23 & 25, p. 117
    Fig. 40)
Robinson Marshall (2.3, 2.13)
Rohde & Schwarz (11.1)
RS Components (1.13 middle, 1.14, 4.54 left)
Science Museum/Science & Society Picture Library (1.1,
    1.4 top right and top left)
Science Photo Library (1.7, 1.16, 9.2)
Sony (1.4 bottom right, 1.9, 8.3)
Stäubli Unimation (1.11)
Unilab (2.4, 2.7)
Zanussi (6.1)

Published in 1997 by Collins Educational

An imprint of HarperCollins*Publishers* Ltd

77–85 Fulham Palace Road
Hammersmith
London
W6 8JB

© 1997 HarperCollins*Publishers*
Reprinted 1997

Barry Payne and David Rampley assert the moral right to be identified as the authors of this work.

ISBN 0 00 320012 4

British Library Cataloguing in Publication Data
A catalogue record for this book is available from the British Library.

Designed by Ken Vail Graphic Design (production management Chris Williams)
Cover Design by Ken Vail Graphic Design
Cover photographs: Tony Stone Images, Nokia and Economatics

Illustrated by Simon Girling & Associates (Mike Taylor, Alex Pang), Ken Vail Graphic Design, Barry Payne

Printed and bound by Scotprint Ltd

Series planned by: Graham Bradbury and Alison Walters
Commissioning Editor: Alison Walters
Editorial Assistant: Tamsin Miller
Copyeditor: Helen Roberts
Production: Sue Cashin

Index

Index